Selma's Peacemaker

RALPH SMELTZER AND
CIVIL RIGHTS MEDIATION

Selma's Peacemaker

RALPH SMELTZER AND CIVIL RIGHTS MEDIATION

Stephen L. Longenecker

TEMPLE UNIVERSITY PRESS

Philadelphia

Temple University Press, Philadelphia 19122
Copyright © 1987 by Temple University. All rights reserved.
Published 1987
Printed in the United States of America

The paper used in this publication meets the minimum
requirements of American National Standard for Information
Sciences—Permanence of Paper for Printed Library Materials,
ANSI Z39.48-1984

Library of Congress Cataloging-in-Publication Data

Longenecker, Stephen L., 1951–
   Selma's peacemaker.
   Bibliography: p.
   Includes index.
   1. Afro-Americans—Civil rights—Alabama—Selma.
2. Smeltzer, Ralph E., 1916–1976. 3. Selma
(Ala.)—Race relations. I. Title.
F334.S4L66   1987   305.8'96073'076145   86-30128
ISBN 0-87722-489-7 (alk. paper)

To Lew and Carol

Contents

Preface

This is the story of a peacemaker and his efforts to help a small city in Alabama avoid tearing itself apart as it struggled to cope with the civil rights revolution. This is the account of Selma, Alabama, straining to preserve peace, and Ralph Smeltzer, a northern preacher with a self-appointed ministry to help Selma remain peaceful. Selma is generally remembered for the "Battle of the Bridge," where state troopers and the sheriff's posse brutally assaulted a column of peaceful marchers, and for the murder of Viola Liuzzo by a carload of Ku Klux Klansmen. But Smeltzer's role of reconciliation is also a critical, if little known, chapter in Selma's civil rights conflict.

When the tide of integration rolled across the South in the 1950s and 1960s, Selma remained a center of hard-core opposition to even minimal civil rights progress. As frustrated blacks became increasingly vocal and militant, the city teetered on the brink of social explosion, and when the Reverend Martin Luther King, Jr., made Selma the focal point of a national voting rights campaign, he added to the pressures boiling in Selma. Ralph Smeltzer came to Selma more than a year before King, and he established unique and extensive contacts with both the black and white communities. He made it his goal to know Selma better than even its natives did. He moved quietly through Selma, exchanging information between the various groups, making suggestions, and urging direct communication. He contributed to the unification and emergence of Selma's black leadership, and he prophetically warned Selma's white establishment that unless changes were made, King would come to Selma and significantly increase the city's crisis in human relations, which all agreed would be bad for Selma. Nevertheless, Smeltzer failed to move the whites, and the tragedy he predicted for Selma became a reality.

After the march to Montgomery and the departure of national figures and the press, Selma's problems remained. During this crucial period Smeltzer's mediation averted a student walkout at Selma's black high school and a march on the public playgrounds. In May 1965, Smeltzer began to phase out his activities in Selma, but for several months after his last visit, he maintained close contact by telephone.

Although Smeltzer successfully preserved his anonymity, he left a trail in the form of a massive notebook, which fills over two reels of microfilm. These files or notes are the major source of documentation for this book, and without them this work would not have been possible. Because Smeltzer thought publicity would be counterproductive, many people in Selma were unaware of his presence; others, who remembered him very favorably in general terms, were unable to provide a significant amount of detail. Several remembered Smeltzer best as a "gentle" man. Because he was careful to listen and let others do most of the talking, he learned much about Selmians, but they learned little about him.

Many Selmians think of the civil rights days as a nightmare they want to forget, and several admit attempting to blot out those events. People tend to remember best, not what Smeltzer or others did twenty years ago, but what they did. Participants in the Selma drama are especially adept at recalling the good things they did and are more eager to tell their stories than to answer penetrating questions. In deciding whose versions to accept, I have relied on the most detailed accounts, which are usually the Smeltzer notes, and I have usually tilted in favor of written records as opposed to events recalled after twenty years. The notes, which Smeltzer kept on all his professional and professionally related activities, not just those in Selma, are considered by his intimates to be an honest attempt to record what he heard. Occasionally, at staff meetings, Smeltzer's colleagues were puzzled about the nuance of a past decision or discussion as recorded in his notes; certainly that was how Smeltzer heard the discussion, but others remembered it differently. What could they say? Smeltzer was usually the only one with a written record. Yet differences in memory occurred infrequently, and Smeltzer's associates agree that his Selma notes are accurate. After conducting interviews in preparation for this project, I gained new respect for the integrity of Smeltzer's notes.

I knew Smeltzer personally and admired him. I spent twelve months as an intern staff assistant in 1974–1975 in the Church of the Brethren Washington Office when Smeltzer directed it. Our friendship continued until his death in 1976, and although I knew him for only a few years, the experience was valuable and educational. While my relationship with Smeltzer raises the possibility that this book will lose its objectivity, my friendship with him is also an advantage because it gives me a special understanding of his personality. If I thought that my friendship with Smeltzer detracted from the book, I would not have attempted this project, but the verdict regarding my objectivity is the reader's responsibility.

Many contributed to the production of this book. Interviews were granted by L. L. Anderson, Jim Clark, Roswell Falkenberry, Marie Foster, Bernard Lafayette, Muriel Lewis, Frederick D. Reese, Mary Blocher Smeltzer, Joe T. Smitherman, Edgar Stewart, Sol Tepper, Frank Wilson, Leland Wilson, and Kathryn Windham. Telephone interviews were conducted with Richard Ault, Art Capell, Louise Clark, Robert Frye, Rosa Miller Hobbs, Charles Mauldin, John Newton, Hazel Peters, J. A. Pickard, Carol Sommers, and Lee Whipple. Mary Blocher Smeltzer was always cooperative and lent me a number of old photographs. Also, thanks to Patricia Blalock of the Selma–Dallas County Public Library for providing information on the library's integration and for going way beyond the call of duty to lend to a stranger in Pennsylvania her personal copy of Amelia Boynton's book. David J. Garrow and Charles Fager were invaluable to me in sharing their expertise and encouragement. They deserve much of the credit for the best parts of this effort. Garrow deserves special thanks for making available his copies of the FBI files on Selma, and he has been just as generous to me in many other ways. The staffs of the following libraries were always helpful: Millersville University, Franklin and Marshall College, the Selma–Dallas County Public Library, the Martin Luther King, Jr., Center for Nonviolent Social Change, Howard University, Princeton University, the Brethren Historical Library and Archives, and the Library of Congress. Joan Carey of the John F. Kennedy Presidential Library sent a valuable document. Elinor Sinnette of the Moorland–Spingarn Research Center at Howard University was gracious with their oral history collection, and Louise Cook at the Martin Luther King Research Center in Atlanta answered all sorts of questions. Jim Lynch of the Church of the Brethren Archives in Elgin, Illinois, provided many services and is amazingly skillful in mining the bottomless pit known as Ralph Smeltzer's files. The Quarryville, Pennsylvania, Community Library performed amazing feats of interlibrary loan. Others who contributed are Louise Bowman, John Buschman, Diane Rutledge, Fred Swartz, and Tammy Wade.

My production editor at Temple University Press, Mary Capouya, was extremely helpful, and I especially appreciate her patience and cheerfulness. Her expertise and professionalism greatly strengthened this effort.

Special gratitude goes to my family for tolerating the long hours I spent away from them and with the keyboard.

To all who helped, thanks. Any errors belong to me.

Selma's Peacemaker

RALPH SMELTZER AND
CIVIL RIGHTS MEDIATION

1

A City on a Bluff

There are only two kinds of people in politics: niggers and Democrats.

Turn-of-the-century saying in Selma

There hasn't been a lynching around here for fifty years.

A white resident of Selma

Our big problem was the Negro himself, who wouldn't risk the possible loss of his job and other kinds of hardships just to vote.

Bernard Lafayette, SNCC

We killed two-year-old Indian babes to get this country and you want to give it to the niggers.

An anonymous Alabaman

Sheriff Jim Clark was disturbed. He scratched his head, rubbed his belly and shuffled his feet. He never thought we could get that many people to the courthouse to register. Well, the white man has had us shuffling for three hundred years. We're going to catch up with him and he knows it.

James Foreman, SNCC

The issue of desegregation is now upon us, and we are confronted by both its great promise for a just and morally strong America and by many practical difficulties. This is the testing ground of democracy and the measure of faith and commitment to the ideal of human brotherhood under God.

Ralph E. Smeltzer

Ralph Smeltzer and Selma, Alabama, have little in common. Smeltzer devoted his life to peace and service; social tension, racial violence, and an incredibly bad press mar contemporary Selma's history. Selma does not have a single congregation associated with a historic peace church; Smeltzer spent his career as an employee of the Church of the Brethren, whose major distinguishing feature is biblical pacifism.[1] The Brethren, with their roots in Pennsylvania–German Anabaptism and emphasis on simple living and nonviolence, seem especially alien in the Black Belt cotton lands of central Alabama. Nevertheless, during Selma's struggles in the 1960s, the city's gravest crisis in modern times, Smeltzer became an important behind-the-scenes figure.

Smeltzer Before Selma

Smeltzer's concern about nonviolence and oppression in Selma was philosophically consistent with the pattern of his life. Ralph Emerson Smeltzer was born May 26, 1916, in Chicago, but he grew up in southern California. As a high school student he worked in the local orange groves and ran a paper route, and at La Verne College he was a cheerleader, debater, and campus newspaper editor. He earned a bachelor's degree in biology from La Verne, and in 1941 received a master's degree in biology and education from Claremont College's Graduate School. In June 1942, the Calvary Church of the Brethren ordained him as a preacher.

When the Japanese struck Pearl Harbor, Smeltzer was a long-term substitute social studies teacher at the Jacob Riis High School in Los Angeles. For most men of Smeltzer's age, the global conflict brought a uniform and boot camp; for Smeltzer, the war meant challenges to his religious faith. When the Los Angeles school district required all teachers to sell defense stamps to students, Smeltzer refused because the practice conflicted with his Christian pacifism, and the district demoted him to a short-term substitute. Smeltzer offered to produce a victory garden, but the district concluded that his compromise proposal was insufficient. In March 1942, Smeltzer and his wife, Mary, protested the war by attaching to their income tax return the following statement:

> WE PROTEST the use of this for war purposes. We feel it a privilege to contribute to the support of our democracy, the U.S.A. We do not believe in the method of War in solving its problems. Consequently—we strongly *disapprove* and *protest* the use of any of this money for war purposes.

Their dissent caught the attention of the Federal Bureau of Investigation, which contemplated placing the Smeltzers in "custodial detention." Agents of the FBI questioned the Smeltzers' neighbors, former employers, and landlords, but they learned little about Ralph and Mary except that they were religious people interested in church work. One respondent told the FBI that the Smeltzers' "American loyalty was unquestioned" but that both were so sincere in their religious beliefs that they were "radical in respect to war." The agents noted that Smeltzer was a conscientious objector to both combatant and noncombatant military service.[2]

Selma's blacks were not the first oppressed racial minority to attract Smeltzer's sympathy; both he and his wife were concerned over the discrimination against Japanese Americans that erupted with the outbreak of the war. Through the winter of 1941–1942, the Smeltzers attended monthly meetings of the Southern California American Friends Service Committee, which also sympathized with the situation of Japanese Americans, and they made several late-night drives to the downtown Los Angeles post office to mail reports to Church of the Brethren national staff.

As the government's policy toward Japanese Americans evolved, it became clear that civil liberties would become an early wartime casualty. Evacuees received only a few days' notice to sell their property or make emergency arrangements for its storage. Some locked their possessions in garages, made arrangements with trustworthy whites, or stored property in local Japanese temples and churches. These schemes were to prove luckless because 80 percent of privately stored goods were broken into or stolen during the war. Bargain hunters and junk dealers appeared like vultures. For many Japanese Americans, the material rewards of a lifetime of hard work were gone in a week or two.[3]

Smeltzer took a day off from school to help the first Japanese Americans forced to move, fishing families on Terminal Island in San Pedro Harbor, who received 48 hours' notice to depart. Smeltzer was shocked to see U.S. Army jeeps, with mounted machine guns, patrolling the streets, while looters sacked the former residents' houses from alleys. In the next few weeks, all Japanese Americans in the Los Angeles area were evacuated, usually in the early morning hours. The Smeltzers arose at 5:00 A.M., helped serve the evacuees breakfast, and then hustled off to school.

In the summer of 1942, the Smeltzers directed a summer work camp for migrants in the San Joaquin Valley. A number of Japanese Americans from the coast had relocated there in the expectation that the government would require no further moves. The anti-Japanese mania did not stop, however, and in the summer of 1942 these Japanese Americans, mostly farmers, were also evacuated. In spite of threats from local police and veterans groups, the Smeltzers organized efforts to provide transportation to the train station and food for the evacuees. The Smeltzers and others went to the station on evacuation day and endured angry words and waving fists from bystanders but were otherwise unharmed.

After temporarily housing Japanese Americans at racetracks, stadiums, and fairgrounds, the authorities moved them into hastily constructed permanent centers. Each family was allotted a bare room, 20 feet by 24 feet; small families were given even smaller rooms or shared a room. The camps were like military barracks, and according to Milton Eisenhower, national director of the War Relocation Agency, the construction was "so very cheap, that frankly, if it stands up for the duration we are going to be lucky."[4]

After all the West Coast Japanese Americans had been removed to detention camps, the Smeltzers applied to teach school at one camp, Manzanar Relocation Center, northeast of Mount Whitney, near Lone Pine, California. The Smeltzers lived with barbed wire, guard towers, sentries, searchlights, and ten thousand Japanese Americans at Manzanar for seven months. Guards at the camp, who were instructed to shoot anyone leaving without a permit and anyone refusing to halt when ordered, were considered trigger-happy; "shooting a Jap" might provide relief from the tedium of guard duty. (At least one shooting incident did occur at Manzanar, apparently without reason: A Japanese American was shot while gathering scrap wood.) Although the camp's classrooms had limited numbers of books and, on the first day, no chairs—the students sat on newspapers—student motivation and self-discipline were excellent, and the Smeltzers found the teaching situation to be easy.[5]

Caucasians at Manzanar lived segregated from Asians and in superior facilities, so the Smeltzers got themselves assigned as houseparents for a group of twenty young *Kibei* boys (i.e., boys born in the United States but educated in Japan and thus less Americanized than the average Japanese American). The *Kibei* had suffered a double rejection. They were not welcome in Japan because they were too Westernized; but on returning to the United States, they found that whites suspected them of being disloyal because they had retained much of their Japanese heritage, and other Japanese Americans saw them as too "Japanesey." On their part, the *Kibei* disdained what they considered to be a surrender by other Japanese to American culture and were often thrust into the camps before they had a chance to adjust to American society. Thus the *Kibei* were an especially angry group of Japanese Americans from whose ranks often emerged camp dissidents and troublemakers. Authorities required the Smeltzers to take all meals except Saturday night supper with the Caucasians.[6]

Smeltzer's most unforgettable experience at Manzanar came in December 1942 when misunderstandings between evacuees and camp authorities split camp residents into pro-Japanese and pro-American factions. Anti-American youth gangs seriously beat a supposed collaborator with the camp administration and threatened to attack him again as he lay in the hospital. Authorities jailed a *Kibei* leader of the Kitchen Workers Union as a suspect. When a rally protested treatment of Japanese Americans, guards attempted to disperse the crowd with tear gas, and several guards shot into the crowd, killing two, including a high school boy who was shot in the back.[7]

That evening the anti-American group threatened to kill the pro-American leaders. A friend of the Smeltzers came to their room and frantically asked Ralph to rescue her husband, who was hiding, and take him to the guardhouse for safety. Smeltzer found the man, insisted that he leave behind a knife he carried for protection, hid him on the floor of the Smeltzer Model-A Ford, and drove without lights around the camp's edge. As Smeltzer neared the gate, he raced the car across an open field to the guardhouse and safety. Fortunately, the guards were not alert, or they would have fired on the car.

From the beginning, the Smeltzers searched for ways to free the evacuees from the camps, and they soon concluded that the best solution for the Japanese Americans was relocation in the east. Accordingly, the Smeltzers made arrangements through the Brethren Service Commission to establish a resettlement hostel at Bethany Seminary, a Brethren institution in Chicago. At Bethany the Smeltzers counseled Japanese Americans about jobs and helped them with the transition from detention camp to a potentially hostile, unknown city. The hostel provided temporary living conditions and, more important, provided a sense of security for the Japanese Americans, many of whom were nervous about the reception they would receive from the local community.[8]

The FBI continued to monitor Smeltzer's activities. After he visited a relocation center in Arizona in the spring of 1943, the Phoenix FBI office investigated to determine whether he had participated in any subversive activity; the bureau also examined the Smeltzers' project in Chicago, where two informants cleared the Smeltzers of subversive activity. The FBI agents finally concluded, in September 1943, that although the Smeltzers were "extremely religious and friendly to the Japanese," there was no evidence that they were weakening the war effort.[9]

By April 1944, Ralph and Mary Smeltzer had assisted more than a thousand Japanese Americans and decided to close the Chicago hostel to avoid creating a "Little Tokyo" there and to establish a new hostel in Brooklyn. But the Brooklyn community and local politicians, including New York Mayor Fiorello La Guardia, publicly opposed resettlement projects, and local newspapers ran articles for a month about the proposed hostel and its problems. Nevertheless, and in spite of threats against the Smeltzers' lives and property, the project continued. The arrival of the first Japanese Americans at the Brooklyn hostel produced a squad of reporters, a front-page photo in the *Brooklyn Eagle,* and a front-door police guard who was to become both spy and protector. Gradually the community accepted the hostel, and the operation functioned normally.[10]

Smeltzer's concern for the downtrodden and his relationship with the church continued after World War II. Before the war ended, Smeltzer joined the Brethren Service Commission in Elgin, Illinois, as an administrative assistant; and in November 1945, the church appointed him to go to Japan to supervise relief work. Smeltzer waited eight months on the West Coast, but when he still had not received military clearance to proceed to Japan, he turned his attention to Austria.

Gaining admittance to Austria proved to be much simpler than going to Japan. In Washington, D.C., Smeltzer discovered that General Mark Clark, U.S. High Commissioner in Austria

Because Smeltzer was successful in working behind the scenes in Selma and "becoming invisible," there are no pictures available. Here Smeltzer presents testimony before the Senate Foreign Relations Committee in support of the proposed Arms Control and Disarmament Agency, August 16, 1961.

The Smeltzers were reunited at the Vienna airport in May 1948. Smeltzer worked with the *Volksdeutsche* refugees in Austria from 1946 to 1949.

In 1942–1943 Mary Blocher Smeltzer and Ralph Smeltzer were houseparents and teachers at the "Y," a barracks housing about twenty *Kibei* boys at the Manzanar Relocation Center, where Japanese Americans were interned during World War II.

and commander of American troops there, not only approved of the Brethren plan for Austria but also encouraged the group. Smeltzer obtained a passport and military permit in an unprecedented ten days, and by November 2 he was in Vienna. He was forced to leave behind his wife and two children, ages two years and six months.

In Austria, Smeltzer found another oppressed minority group—the *Volksdeutsche,* refugees of German ancestry from Eastern Europe. The *Volksdeutsche* were the largest, neediest, and most neglected refugee group in Austria. Relief agencies ignored them because of their ethnic link to the despised Third Reich, and neither the U.S. Army nor the United Nations Relief and Rehabilitation Agency (UNRRA) recognized them (although privately many officials admitted that the *Volksdeutsche* were the most appreciative and deserving refugee group).

Smeltzer soon assembled a small team of relief workers, who began scrounging materials and aid from various points in Europe. For more than a year, however, Brethren officials in the States failed to send any of the promised supplies, and morale among Smeltzer's colleagues plummeted. He later complained that "counseling staff members in this situation, trying to find constructive outlets, and developing satisfying alternative 'side projects' was one of the most stressful periods I have had during my lifetime." Finally, one of Smeltzer's aides, Helena Kruger, got her home congregation in Pennsylvania to send 1,440 hatching eggs and 65 sacks of feed to rejuvenate Austria's poultry industry. The eggs arrived by air on March 12, 1947.

By September 1, 1947, supplies from stateside began to flow; they included a carload of cereal, a carload of dried fruits, and 3,500 pairs of shoes, in what was to be a total of 160,240 pounds of supplies. To provide fresh milk for Vienna, Smeltzer devised a plan to purchase a hundred milk goats in Switzerland and distribute them among indigent families in Viennese suburbs. Each recipient of a goat promised to pass along the first offspring to another needy family. With the assistance of a Swiss government official, Smeltzer purchased the goats in Gstaad, loaded them aboard a freight train, and personally rode with and tended them until they arrived in Vienna.

Twenty-one months after Smeltzer had left his family in California, conditions in Austria finally permitted Mary and the children to join him. They were the first civilian relief agency family to receive the necessary military clearance. The Smeltzer children were now two and three-and-a-half years old, and as he waited by the airplane for his family, a stewardess took the children past him. Neither the children nor the father recognized each other!

For his service, the Austrian government awarded Smeltzer a medallion with the inscription *Das Wiener Kind dankt seinen Helfern* ("The Viennese child thanks you for your help").[11] The Smeltzers remained in Austria until June 1949, when they returned to Illinois for Smeltzer to attend Bethany Seminary.

On completion of his seminary education, Smeltzer resumed his career with the Brethren by becoming Director of Peace and Social Education for the Brethren Service Commission. After denominational reorganization, his employer was the General Brotherhood Board, still headquartered in Elgin, Illinois.[12]

On the job Smeltzer developed a working style characterized by organization and attention to detail. Typical was his habit of taking notes. He recorded in a looseleaf notebook every conversation, meeting, and phone call. (In Selma, he even made notes of chance conversations in airports or restaurants.) He never took notes in front of people, unless he knew them extremely well, but he spent his many spare moments on buses and in airport terminals making notes. His notes were a legend among his colleagues on the Brethren staff; to some, the really amazing thing was that Smeltzer could actually retrieve the information he wanted from his voluminous files. Over the years, the notes filled more and more files, and the cabinets themselves became a topic of conversation. "He cherished his notes," remembers one colleague on the Brethren staff.[13]

Smeltzer meticulously planned every part of his working day. He had timed his morning routine to the minute so that he would know how long it took him to dress, shave, and do his running in place and exercises.[14]

Smeltzer's theology included strong concern for political and social reform. He believed that Christians express through the political system their love for people who are not part of their immediate society. According to Smeltzer, God is as concerned about political, economic, and social systems as about personal relationships because these systemic relationships affect "millions of God's children." Smeltzer noted that Brethren were extremely effective at mixing religious and personal ethics and applying the teachings of the church as they interacted with the world. When Brethren encountered political and economic structures, however, they ineffectively applied the church's social ethics. Brethren broke down the wall of strict separation between religious and personal ethics but not between religious and social ethics. While some claimed that Christianity is concerned only with inner spiritual development, Smeltzer believed that "God is especially concerned about *politics* because political decisions have the greatest influence on the greatest number of his children around the world." (The emphasis is Smeltzer's.) An example of his concern for institutional and social justice is his memo to the nominating committee of his local congregation in Elgin in March 1963, requesting greater opportunity for women to serve in the "top posts." Years before a popular women's movement, he suggested a structured ballot in which two women would be nominated for an office, "not a man and a woman because in most such elections the man wins out over the woman."[15]

In his position on the denominational staff, Smeltzer's portfolio contained a number of issues, including racial relations, and during the 1950s he became interested in the civil rights movement. Smeltzer encouraged the church to support the movement, but he also hoped that the tension and violence associated with this social upheaval would be minimal.[16] He praised the movement's nonviolent tactics, but worried about "violence, riots, and hate" in the future. Smeltzer encouraged

Brethren to write to both black and white southern leaders to express support for nonviolent integration. He believed that desegregation was not only just but also would benefit national security. In 1958, he wrote: "The activities of the segregationists have been said to be worth more to the Communists in Asia and Africa than whole armies would be." He urged President Dwight D. Eisenhower to travel to the South on a "mission of peace and goodwill" that would enhance America's stature in world opinion and recommended that Brethren write to the White House with this suggestion. Smeltzer encouraged integration even if a majority opposed it; he said that if Branch Rickey had polled the Brooklyn Dodgers before putting Jackie Robinson on the roster, they undoubtedly would have rejected Robinson, but that after they knew the talented second baseman personally, they accepted him as a teammate.[17]

Smeltzer believed that the racial revolution was a major event in the life of the church, and in the 1960s civil rights became a predominant part of Smeltzer's job. As Director of Peace and Social Education, Smeltzer encouraged Brethren leaders to take action and provided them with information, suggestions, and other resources. At Easter, 1960, he attended the organizing conference of the Student Non-Violent Coordinating Committee (SNCC) in Raleigh, North Carolina.[18] In 1962, when the Brethren adopted a statement, "The Time Is Now," Smeltzer encouraged them to follow its words with deeds by ending segregation within the church and providing the patient and sustained efforts the racial crisis required. Race dominated Smeltzer's work during 1963–1964, which he called "the year for racial justice."[19]

Selma Before the Civil Rights Movement

Selma, Alabama, is proud of its history. The city sits on a scenic bluff in a bend of the Alabama River, a location first noted by the French on a 1732 map. Selma was organized in 1817, incorporated in 1820, and named by William Rufus King after the walled Highland city of a legendary Scottish prince. King became one of Alabama's first two U.S. senators and in 1852 was elected Vice-President as Franklin Pierce's running mate.

No sooner was the surrounding Dallas County created in 1818 than it was designated as the site for the state capital, and the Governor laid out a town where the Cahaba River enters the Alabama, about eight miles from Selma. Cahaba, the new town, became a social and business center, but flooding soon forced the movement of the capital. Further inundations cost Cahaba the county seat, which moved to Selma. During the 1870s, most Cahaba families migrated to Selma; Cahaba, which the area's Chamber of Commerce calls "a seat of civilization famed throughout the South," was a ghost town by 1900.[20]

Selma has been heavily influenced by its heritage, especially its race relations. The storm that Smeltzer tried to contain and the revolution he encouraged were legacies of the South's long history of race relations. The crises of the 1960s did not suddenly appear like summer thunderclouds but were created by generations of racial interactions.

Nineteenth-century Selma lay in the heart of the slave and cotton economy of the antebellum South. Large plantations with columned mansions abounded, and the Alabama River provided an important transportation artery for daily shipments of cotton downriver to Mobile. Although white masters and black slaves generally lived in a paternalistic peace, in the 1830s rumors circulated in rural Dallas County of a slave rebellion in Selma. Whites had what amounted to paranoia regarding slave rebellions, and a Dallas County commander of a militia battalion rose to defend the white race. He called his men to arms, harangued them with a "patriotic" speech, and led them toward Selma. As night fell, the unit camped, but flashes of light and rumbling noises in the direction of Selma awakened the soldiers. The commander, Major Benjamin "Old Snort" Grumbles, told his assembled troops, "Boys, niggers are now killing the white people of Selma;

you must go and help kill the niggers." Then, explaining that he
was too old to fight and had a wife and ten children at home to
protect, he bade the troops farewell and left. Fearing the worst in
Selma, the militia broke camp and marched immediately, but a
fierce rainstorm turned the roads to mud. It was noon before
the unit reached the city, to discover that the slave revolt was
only a rumor and that the noise and lights had been from a thun-
derstorm.[21]

Antebellum Selma was not a secessionist hotbed—each of the
Democratic candidates in the 1860 presidential election enjoyed
support in Selma[22]—but the city did its duty for the Confederacy
during the war nonetheless. Selma became a manufacturing
center with a foundry and rolling mill that was of strategic importance to the Confederate war machine, and the city produced
a number of ironclads, including the ram *Tennessee,* for the Confederate Navy. Cotton sheds were converted to factories, and the
authorities requested the ladies of Selma to save their urine,
which was used to make niter, a critically scarce and strategic
material in the Confederacy.[23] In 1863 Jefferson Davis visited
Selma to inspect the cannon foundry and spoke to a large crowd
from a hotel balcony. Davis appealed for volunteers for garrison
duty so that the current garrison troops could take to the field.
This move, he forecast, would enable the South to destroy General William S. Rosecrans and bring ultimate victory to the Confederacy.

In the last days of the war, Selma became part of Union
Commander Ulysses S. Grant's continental strategy for simulta-
neous action on all fronts to knock out the tottering Confederacy.
While General William T. Sherman marched through Geor-
gia and South Carolina and Grant battered General Robert E.
Lee in Virginia, Union General J. H. Wilson struck from Tennessee through central Alabama with Selma and its military treasure
as his target. Strategy called for Wilson's 12,500 mounted troops,
armed with repeaters, to join forces at Selma with General Edward Canby's column driving north from Mobile. Canby never

made it to Selma, but Wilson did. All able-bodied men in Selma, regardless of position, were placed in the line of defense. Twenty Confederates were killed in the battle, including a Presbyterian preacher and five other civilians who had taken up arms to defend their city. After a 50-mile running skirmish with Confederate General Nathan Bedford Forrest's defenders, Wilson captured Selma on April 2, 1865, the same day Richmond was abandoned. Following the battle, Selma was at the mercy of a drunken mob of soldiers, who sacked the city and then left for Montgomery. The Yankees destroyed the manufacturing facilities and military stores of Selma, except for the large barrels of whiskey, which they drained cup by cup.[24]

The Civil War and subsequent emancipation offered only limited advancement for southern blacks, who lost progress steadily in the Reconstruction years. In 1869 and 1870, the Ku Klux Klan, organized by General Forrest, rode in nearby counties, but the Klan never amounted to much in Dallas County because Selma's ruling establishment, a group of former Confederate officers led by General Edmund Pettus, looked down on the lowly class origins of many Ku Kluxers and because they considered the Klan to be ineffective.[25]

Although significant social changes swept the South following the Civil War, Selma's hierarchical socioeconomic structure continued well into the twentieth century. By 1930, Selma contained only one public school for blacks, which went only to ninth grade, although there were a number of black private schools. Streets in the black section of Selma were unpaved, and in rural Dallas County a paved roadway always led to a white-owned house. The pavement ended at the white property, and those wishing to visit black families had to park their cars and travel along wagon paths and open fields. Whites at the end of the road could stop unwanted pedestrians from walking over their land and thereby further isolate black families.

Black sharecroppers were perpetually indebted to their landlords, and when necessary, whites used a combination of intimidation, coercion, and violence to maintain power over the sharecroppers. Particularly moving is the story of John Henry—a real person, not the John Henry of the folk song—a quiet, intelligent sharecropper who consistently produced good crops. When John Henry held back two cotton bales from his annual crop to buy clothes and shoes for his ten children (instead of turning over his entire crop), his boss demanded the remaining bales. An argument developed, and John Henry, a black who talked back to whites, was beaten almost to death in front of his screaming family. Two other blacks were ordered to throw the unconscious John Henry into a truckbed, and after riding into the country, the attackers allegedly forced blacks to bury the still-alive man.[26]

By the 1960s, Selma contained a few people who were very rich and many who were very poor—and usually black. A group of well-to-do, well-bred patricians with long genealogies in the community dominated; in Dallas County in 1965, 753 families, of whom all but 28 were white, earned over $10,000 a year. In contrast, 6,480 families, more than 5,000 of them black, earned less than $3,000 per year, including 2,400 black families who earned less than $1,000 yearly. The median family income was $1,393 for blacks and $5,150 for whites, a figure inflated by the wealthy at the top end. Blacks also suffered in education. Median school years completed by people in Dallas County were 9.0 for all citizens but only 5.8 for blacks.[27]

Voter registration in Selma remained a difficult process, even for qualified whites. For example, J. A. Pickard, the superintendent of schools, was not registered until a year and a half after he moved to Selma. For blacks, the situation was all but impossible; it took Marie Foster, a dental hygienist, eight years to be a registered voter. Applicants were required to complete a questionnaire with twenty-one questions and to submit to oral questioning by the registrars. Officials quizzed applicants on such information as the number of words in the Constitution, the duties of the Vice-President, or the function of the Supreme Court.

If the applicant did not provide an answer that was correct in the registrar's opinion, the applicant failed. Also, applicants needed to have a registered voter vouch for their character. About three weeks after application, prospective voters received a postcard informing them whether they had passed.[28]

For decades in Dallas County black votes remained a tiny fraction of the electorate—but their numbers were large enough to be important in very close elections. In 1960, only 13.7 percent of voting-age blacks were registered in Alabama, and in 1961, blacks who made up half of the voting-age population of Dallas County, had only 156 of 15,000 registered. (The number of black voters had increased by only 14 since 1954.[29]) Yet, in a 1958 election for sheriff, Dallas County's tiny black vote may have made the difference. Governor James "Big Jim" Folsom had filled an unexpired term with the appointment of Jim Clark, who managed Folsom's campaigns in Dallas County and now reaped his reward. A Selma police captain, Wilson Baker, was one of two men who challenged Clark in the Democratic primary, and he forced a runoff election. Just before the runoff with Clark, Baker appeared before a Ku Klux Klan rally, which Selma's blacks insisted cost him the black vote and the support of some whites. Baker lost the election. Nevertheless, in Dallas County the sheriff's department counts the votes, and Baker believed the election was stolen. He soon left Selma to teach at the University of Alabama.[30]

In 1961, the Justice Department filed a suit against the Dallas County voting registrar, J. P. Majors, alleging racial discrimination. Majors soon resigned, and nine months later, Judge Daniel H. Thomas ordered Majors's three successors, led by Victor B. Atkins, to turn over the registration records to the Justice Department. Almost two years later, Thomas found that although the previous registrar had practiced discrimination, the current board did not. Since it had taken office, the new board had approved 71 of 114 black applicants, although Dallas County's black voters still totaled only 242. Thomas devoted a

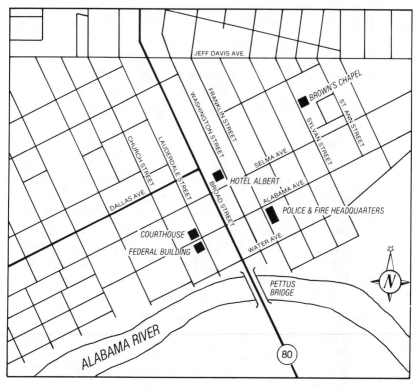

Downtown Selma, 1965. Map by Erika Wingenroth.

substantial portion of his opinion to stating that the Justice Department could use its time better on other kinds of cases.[31]

Early Civil Rights Activities in Selma

The first organization to assign civil rights organizers to Selma was SNCC, which sent Bernard and Colia Lafayette, Fisk University students, in February 1963, to begin a voter education project. Because Selma's overpowering repression produced in blacks a pervasive fear of whites and an assumption that any association with the civil rights movement would result in reprisals, SNCC had "scratched [Selma] off the map as a place" for a project. An earlier group of SNCC staff had concluded that the city had little to contribute to the movement. When Bernard Lafayette visited Selma in November 1962 to get a second opinion on Selma, he discovered otherwise.

The Lafayettes' task was formidable not only because the "patron saint" of many whites was Jim Crow but also because of the widespread black pessimism. The Lafayettes even had trouble finding a place to stay because landlords feared their presence might encourage bombings. Eventually they found lodgings with a local teacher, Mamie Moore, whose home became a center of student activity. Residents told Bernard Lafayette that the Dallas County Voters League (DCVL), a moderate organization promoting black voter registration, was ineffective and that "you've come to the worst place in the world." Lafayette, who discovered that he could work effectively at the grass roots by approaching people as they sat on their front porches, realized that people always told him they were registered to vote, even if it was untrue, because they were embarrassed not to be registered. Many blacks agonized over conditions in Selma, and Lafayette considered the reluctance to admit that they were not voters to be a sign of pride. Although in some communities blacks showed no interest in registering, Lafayette encountered only a positive attitude about voting in Selma. Blacks felt competent to choose candidates, but the voting registration test and the slow-paced, inconvenient process intimidated them. Also, many felt they had passed the test but were told that they had failed.

A local black attorney, J. L. Chestnut, brought Bernard Lafayette to the black Elks Lodge. The Elks listened to Lafayette explain that he was there to help them and then concluded that "he's barkin' in the dark." Many Elks thought there was "no way" that Lafayette could do what he proposed, but the Lafayettes were encouraged by the Elks' willingness to discuss voting rights and because the Elks' leader, Edwin Moss, was extremely supportive.[32]

In spite of the despondency that surfaced frequently among Selma's blacks, the Lafayettes found signs that the city would support a civil rights movement. Although blacks generally considered their city to be hopeless, the self-esteem of some individuals was encouraging, and the young people provided another reason for optimism. A group of teenagers, mostly from the high school, distributed leaflets and formed a choir. When Selma's youth began to create new words to old freedom songs, organizers recognized this as a sign that the kids had internalized the goals of the movement and that their commitment would support a movement. Here is one of the first songs from Selma:

> Freedom is a-coming,
> And it won't be long.
> Freedom is a-coming;
> Help me sing a song.
> Freedom is a-coming,
> And it won't be long.
> If you want to be free,
> Come and go with me.
>
>
> O-O-Oh, we are fighting for our equal rights
> So come on, let's stand up and fight.
> Fighting on and singing a song.
> I hope it won't be long.[33]

In spite of the potential discerned by organizers in Selma, the obstacles were very real and difficult; activists faced a long, hard road. Lafayette's strategy for the voter registration drive was to recruit people to come to Marie Foster's citizenship class, which aimed to circumvent one obstacle to registration by teaching people how to fill out the registration application beforehand. Foster's class met first in January 1963. After mailings to and announcements in local black churches, one lonely soul showed up for the first meeting; Foster taught him to write his name. Two people came to the next meeting, then four; a few weeks later, fourteen showed up to meet Bernard Lafayette.[34] Ignorance was another barrier; some thought that when they went to register, they were actually voting.[35]

Organizers struggled to find churches that would allow their buildings to be used as meeting sites. Deacons of the Tabernacle Baptist Church summoned the pastor, the Reverend L. L. Anderson, a vocal civil rights advocate, to the campus of Selma University to tell him that they disapproved of his activism. The deacons were well-educated, sophisticated men, including a Phi Beta Kappa from Brown University, but they were reluctant to be identified with the movement. These middle-class blacks were treated marginally better than most blacks by Selma's whites, who expressed the feeling that the situation might be different if all blacks could be like the small band of professional blacks in Selma. The deacons accused Anderson of leaving his friends and ignoring the reasons for which he had been called to fill Tabernacle Baptist's pulpit. The deacons also knew that black churches in the South had been bombed, and so many of their fears of reprisals were legitimate. Anderson replied that he was called to set free the captives and referred the deacons to Scripture. He then threatened that if he were not allowed to hold civil rights meetings in the church, he would put a pulpit and loudspeakers out in the street beside the church and would tell people that the deacons were afraid. According to Anderson, the deacons, some of them in tears, relented and assured their pastor that if the church was destroyed, they would try to build another.[36]

Monthly meetings of the Dallas County Voters League attracted an average of forty people, but in May, James Foreman and Lafayette addressed the first mass meeting, which was attended by three hundred and fifty. The local paper, the *Selma Times-Journal*, quickly pointed out that this number did not fill the hall to capacity. (Black leaders believed that more people were turned back by police blocking sidewalks and streets.) This first mass meeting became a memorial for Bill Boynton, Amelia Boynton's husband and long-time activist and president of the Voters League, who died within hours of the meeting. A riot nearly developed when a group of young whites appeared at the meeting, armed with table legs from a local furniture company. The sheriff's department placed a man with a walkie-talkie inside the meeting hall, and after the meeting adjourned, anxious blacks asked him if they would be safe outside. The officer called outside, and soon the answer returned: Their security would be assured if they left quickly. They did so, and no incidents occurred. Attendance at mass meetings declined after that, but in mid-June several hundred attended a mass meeting featuring James Bevel of the Southern Christian Leadership Conference (SCLC).[37]

Selma's whites noticed these activities. One evening, several white men called to Lafayette to come out of his home and help them push their stalled car. Lafayette went outside, and when he bent over the car bumpers, he was clubbed over the head with a gun butt. He was knocked to the pavement, then returned to his feet, only to be struck a second time. He got up, and facing his assailant, he noticed the nervousness of the man with the gun. With blood washing down his face and dripping on his shirt, both Lafayette and his attacker retreated. Lafayette was attacked the same night that Medgar Evers was killed, and FBI agents told him that the attack was part of a three-state conspiracy against Evers, himself, and a preacher in Louisiana. Lafayette's wound required six stitches, but he was back on the job the next day.[38]

A week later, Bossie Reese, who was counting blacks in the

voter registration line, was pulled into Sheriff Clark's office, punched, and arrested. A high school student who witnessed the affair frantically ran the few blocks to the SNCC office to tell Lafayette, who immediately went to Clark and demanded to visit Reese. Lafayette was concerned about Reese's safety and wanted to know the charges. Although Lafayette believed that he got a runaround, he considered it very important to let Clark know that he did not intimidate blacks.

In April, someone fired two shotgun blasts into voting rights worker Lonnie Brown's home. Clark sent deputies to monitor Voters League meetings, and blacks began to fear increased economic retaliation from whites. Lafayette was arrested by Clark for vagrancy as he left a mass meeting, but by the time he appeared in court the next day, the Justice Department had flown in a court stenographer and two attorneys.[39]

Selma's First Civil Rights Demonstrations

In spite of setbacks, SNCC's efforts bore fruit. The fall of 1963 produced a spurt of civil rights activities, including demonstrations and numerous arrests, hitherto unknown in Selma.

The Lafayettes left Selma, as scheduled, in mid-1963. In their wake was a cadre of local workers consisting of young people and Amelia Boynton, Marie Foster, James Lawson, and L. L. Anderson. Boynton's office, a room 15 feet by 40 feet in the heart of the black business district, served as headquarters for her insurance agency, real estate business, and employment agency, plus the office of the attorney James Chestnut and SNCC. In August, a group of blacks petitioned local political and commercial leaders for better pay, jobs with higher status (e.g., salesclerk), equal access to public buildings, and the removal of segregation signs. Both the mayor and the business leaders refused to see them.[40]

In September, a new SNCC organizer, Worth Long, came to Selma, and with the later arrival of James Foreman and John

Lewis, SNCC committed much of its top leadership to Selma. Worth Long initially wanted to delay demonstrations because he thought the town was not yet ready for them. But when he arrived in Selma, the town's young black activists were restless because of the rebuffs from the mayor and business leaders and because their self-imposed deadline for the appointment of a biracial committee had expired. The students insisted on marching. News of the bombing of the Sixteenth Street Baptist Church in Birmingham further motivated the demonstrators.[41]

A sit-in at the Carter-Walgreen drugstore sparked Selma's unrest. The drugstore incident resulted in five arrests and two beatings; fifteen-year-old Lulu Brown was knocked off the lunch counter stool, and Willie Robinson needed seven stitches after being struck on the head from behind. Black youths reacted to the arrests and beatings by marching in the streets, and Sheriff Clark retaliated with large-scale arrests. Mass meetings at Brown's Chapel and the First Baptist Church attracted eight hundred adults and five hundred students plus a ring of fifty state patrolmen surrounding the meetings.[42]

Demonstrations continued, and Clark arrested close to three hundred people during a one-week period near the end of September. One march got only about a block away after leaving a church before being stopped by Clark's men. After kneeling on the sidewalk to pray, demonstrators quietly boarded the buses the police had waiting. Club-wielding state troopers chased the approximately four hundred black spectators lining the sidewalks back into their homes. Also, about forty students were picked up and given a choice of jail or returning to school; they chose school! Worth Long, who had been in town for only forty-eight hours, and the Reverend Benny Tucker were arrested and sentenced to 180 days in jail and fines of $300. John Lewis also was jailed.

Most of the demonstrators were high school students who had boycotted classes to protest mistreatment of the black students at the Carter-Walgreen drugstore. Of an estimated two hundred fifty demonstrators during this period, one hundred fifty were high school students, and many others attended Selma University, an unaccredited black junior college. Several parents who knew their children intended to participate were charged and fined for contributing to the delinquency of a minor.

Because of a shortage of bail money, arrested students were not freed immediately, and those who remained in jail complained that officials mistreated them. Girls as young as twelve reported that they became ill because they were kept in a "sweatbox" with no air circulating. According to one local black leader, although adults were not ready to go into the streets, they supported the youngsters and would demonstrate themselves soon, especially if a national figure, someone like Dick Gregory, urged them on.[43]

Gregory came to Selma on October 5. His wife, Lillian, had been jailed in Selma while demonstrating, and he spoke to a crowded mass meeting. While deputies menaced from outside and white officials took notes inside, Gregory verbally lashed the white establishment for two hours with a viciousness foreign to Selma. Gregory claimed that southern whites had no real identity except "segregated drinking fountains, segregated toilets, and the right to call me nigger. And when the white man is threatened with losing his *toilet,* he's ready to kill!" Gregory said that if blacks disappeared, the whites would "go crazy looking for us!" He called southern police "peons" and "idiots."[44]

The 1963 demonstrations climaxed with Freedom Day on October 7. As national press, FBI agents, Justice Department observers, and famed black author James Baldwin watched, more than three hundred fifty blacks stood in line outside the Dallas County Court House waiting to be processed for voter registration. Since the Board of Voter Registration never processed more than thirty or forty applicants in a day, most people who stood in the line knew they had no chance of getting inside the building. Clark's deputies and posse provided law enforcement and refused to allow those waiting in line to be "molested," which to Clark meant that SNCC workers could not bring food and water to those standing in line. Shortly after the office opened, Clark arrested three SNCC workers carrying signs proclaiming register-to-vote slogans. Blue-helmeted state troopers, commanded by Major Joe Smelley and armed with clubs, guns, and electric cattle prods (i.e., tubes with batteries that completed an electrical circuit on touching skin), arrived to help the posse keep order. Clark and Smelley would not permit the people standing in line to leave for lunch or to use a toilet and then return to the line; at mid-afternoon two SNCC workers attempted to deliver food to those in line, but they were arrested. Next, pushing and shoving troopers turned on the press. Several sheriff's deputies pushed a CBS photographer into the street and struck him with nightsticks; the photographer used his camera to deflect a blow to the groin. The line of applicants broke up at 4:30 P.M. when the courthouse closed. That evening, the mass meeting was filled.[45]

So great was the fear of violence and riot that the federal government made plans to send the 101st Airborne to Selma if order broke down. An army general and two lientenant colonels visited Selma on October 3 to develop a contingency plan. Although their visit was not secret, it did not become public until March 1964.[46]

Among the people waiting in line at the courthouse was a group of women employed at Dunn Rest Home in Selma. After the proprietor of the home, George Dunn, saw his employees in line, he fired them. When Dunn tried to photograph one of the women, Elnora Collins, she refused, and Dunn allegedly struck her across the back with a prod and tried to hit her in the face. When Mrs. Collins attempted to block Dunn's blow with her arm, she sustained a cut. Dunn also allegedly struck another woman, Annie Lee Cooper, with his prod, and the rest of the black staff quit in protest. The white community blacklisted the women, and they were unable to find new employment.[47]

Ralph Smeltzer learned about the plight of the Dunn Rest Home women in late October when he went on a fact-finding trip to Atlanta to meet with representatives of Martin Luther King's

Southern Christian Leadership Conference (SCLC) and SNCC leaders. Smeltzer shared with civil rights leaders a long list of the ways that the Church of the Brethren had helped the movement so far, including distribution of food and clothing to Mississippi and Tennessee, endorsement and participation in the August 28 March on Washington, and offers of Brethren Volunteer Service workers to SCLC and the bombed Birmingham church.[48]

2

A City Divided Against Itself

We tried to tell the city officials that many responsible white citizens disagreed with the position of the city government but were afraid to speak out openly. The Mayor and the two judges contended, however, that they spoke for a unanimous white community.

John M. Pratt, National Council of Churches

You shouldn't put all of the blame on the white man because we had a lot to do with it ourselves.

Reverend C. C. Hunter

I never thought [demonstrations] would happen in Selma. But I tell you this. We are not going to give in. If we let them have one inch, they would want to go all the way.

A Citizens Council spokesperson

We have no problems in Selma. . . . If [outside agitators] would all get out and stay out, we'd work things out here in our own way. . . . You can walk anyplace in Selma at any time of day or night without fear of being clubbed, which is more than you can say for Washington, D.C.

Mayor Chris B. Heinz

As a historic peace church, can our own church members serve as reconcilers and peacemakers between whites and Negro leaders?

Ralph E. Smeltzer

On Sunday, September 29, 1963, four black teenage girls attempted to enter an all-white Baptist worship service in Selma. After the girls were denied entrance by the Baptists, they crossed the street to Pastor John Newton's First Presbyterian congregation, which was thirty minutes into its service. Ushers sat the girls in the balcony, which was customary for late arrivals. As the girls entered the balcony, the clatter of their high-heeled shoes on the wooden floor caused worshippers downstairs to look up to see what had created the commotion. The disturbance caught Newton in the midst of a pastoral prayer, but he "didn't miss a comma" in praying for "the Lord to help us all." Although several worshippers walked out and never came back, a regularly scheduled Deacons' and Elders' meeting that afternoon concluded that the incident had gone well.

By Sunday evening, however, members of the church, especially the deacons and elders, received protest phone calls, and the next day the volume of calls increased. Meanwhile, civil rights activists flaunted their victory at the Monday mass meeting with a standing ovation for the four girls, heroines who had "integrated" a white church. On Tuesday the *Selma Times-Journal* ran a story on the incident, and the pressure on the Presbyterians became intense. For three nights, teens littered toilet paper and tin cans on Newton's lawn. At a special meeting called on Friday, the deacons and elders remained willing to stand by their original decision, but although Newton supported them, the membership did not. The church members, even Newton, felt as if they had been used by the blacks and temporarily rescinded their open policy.[1]

Smeltzer Discovers Selma

The opportunity to help the Dunn Rest Home women and the entire Selma community intrigued Smeltzer, and he recommended to his superior W. Harold Rowe that the Brethren investigate Selma further. Rowe agreed. Smeltzer would travel to Selma, and others on the Brethren staff who worked with relief projects would accept his recommendations. That summer, the church had sent 13 tons of food and clothing to Clarksdale and Greenwood, Mississippi, when workers for voting rights had lost jobs, and Smeltzer became interested in a similar response for Selma.[2]

On November 25, Smeltzer arrived in Selma for a three-day fact-finding visit. Although it is not clear when Smeltzer decided to pursue mediation as well as relief in Selma, he long believed that the peace churches could help the South by contributing to reconciliation. Mediation was on his Selma agenda from the start. Smeltzer was warned that he would be followed from the moment he arrived and that he must be careful about being seen or identified with controversial groups such as SNCC if he wanted to be accepted by the community. Smeltzer knew that a researcher from the American Civil Liberties Union (ACLU) complained that he had been "run out of town" on his second day in Selma, and so Smeltzer called Amelia Boynton, who had promised to arrange a ride for him at the Montgomery airport, and canceled the transportation because she was too closely identified with SNCC.[3]

On this trip and on two subsequent visits in early 1964, Smeltzer concentrated on building trust and gaining information before offering himself as a mediator. In a memo to himself he laid out his strategy: "I've got to know as much or more about the Negro community than whites and as much or more about the white community than Negroes." He wanted to make all groups "dependent upon me for information and guidance." He emphasized the need to remain low-key: "I need to stay behind the scenes, work quietly, work through others, suggesting or encouraging a little here and a little there. *But never getting impatient*" (Smeltzer's emphasis).[4] In meeting with representatives of as many of Selma's factions as possible, he asked people if an outside mediator could help, but he downplayed his intent to mediate and emphasized instead his willingness to listen and learn. Always dressed in conservative business suits, he sought a low profile and left a serious, businesslike impression.

Some of Smeltzer's colleagues on the denominational staff in Elgin wondered if he could remain in the role of a quiet bipartisan because his convictions about social justice were so strong. He frequently encouraged, even pushed, other staff members to be more active in support of the church's positions on peace and social justice. Could Smeltzer resist taking the role of the prophet or advocate in Selma? Could he remain neutral in a situation where he would surely find widespread injustice?[5]

During his first visit, Smeltzer quickly experienced the minor dislocations in life style that the civil rights revolution had brought to Selma. He needed a place to write—probably to make his famous notes—and so he went to the Carnegie Library. But he found no chairs at the tables and soon discovered that they had been removed after the library was integrated by the library board—quietly and without pressure—in May 1963. The board believed that removal of the chairs would help the community adjust to integration, for although the library was now technically integrated, removing the chairs meant that blacks and whites could not sit together at tables. The library planned to bring back the chairs as integration in the community progressed, and, later, they were quietly returned.[6]

Smeltzer, needing a place to write, at first inquired about using a back room or corner. Then he noticed footstools and asked to sit on one, but the librarians were reluctant to permit this. They suggested that Smeltzer sit at a low table in a corner where no one would see him, which he did. The librarians stole curious glances at the stranger and, when he was leaving, inquired about his home town, but they were helpful and allowed him to use the phone. They apologized for the inconveniences and seemed sympathetic to integration, which surprised him.

In September 1963, the *Selma Times-Journal* complained that almost no blacks used the library; only eight blacks had applied for cards, and only three returned for books. Yet Smeltzer noticed several blacks there during his visit in November.

Smeltzer found Selma to be sharply divided into two separate communities, one black and one white, with little meaningful communication between them.[7] Not only was interracial communication almost nonexistent, but communication between individual moderates was negligible. Moderate whites felt isolated, and no fellowship or organization existed to support collective moderate action. The Citizens Council, a segregationist organization, intimidated moderates and controlled the city's power structure, while jealousy and distrust fragmented the black leadership.

Early Contacts with Selma's Whites

Smeltzer's conversations with whites in Selma uncovered deep divisions in that sector of the population. Conservative, die-hard segregationists dominated the town and controlled municipal politics, but the fractured white community did not universally adhere to their position. And Smeltzer quickly learned that Selma's clergy showed divisions on the race question that typified the various opinions in the larger community. During his first visit, Smeltzer spoke with three members of the white mainline Protestant clergy, and each had a different view of the situation. Smeltzer also discussed race relations with several laypersons during his early visits.

One of Selma's most progressive pastors was Dr. John Newton of the First Presbyterian Church, who impressed Smeltzer with his insights and abilities. Newton thought the odds were against progressive and peaceful racial relations—in the short term as well as the more distant future—and he believed that the cessation of demonstrations and arrests was only temporary; more trouble was on the way. Black pastors did not realize how deeply rooted segregation was in white congregations. According to Newton, Selma's unyielding image in the press ironically made compromise more difficult than it might have been because the hard-line reputation, instead of disturbing Selma's leaders, became a source of pride. More optimistically, Newton reported the existence of a group of community leaders working for progress and hoping to give Mayor Chris Heinz a graceful way to back down from his die-hard position. Although Smeltzer tried twice to get the names of the group's members, Newton refused to betray their confidence. Taking an unusual stand for a Selma white, Newton suggested that black demonstrations should continue because, without pressure, the community would go on for another hundred years without concessions.

Other pastors were less sympathetic than Newton toward the civil rights movement but equally pessimistic about the movement's chances for success. Smeltzer heard that compromise was all but impossible. Although blacks complained bitterly about police brutality, a leading white pastor told Smeltzer that the police had been patient and fair, and had avoided brutality. In a slap at the civil rights movement, some whites claimed that a black boycott of downtown businesses was ineffective except for a number of whites who stayed away to avoid the anticipated commotion. Several pastors joined the chorus condemning outsiders as agitators.

Although a few white congregations took small steps toward superficial integration, Selma's churches were basically segregated, and a Lutheran minister estimated that only five of the seventy pastors in Selma were willing to associate with blacks. The Methodists and Baptists decided not to admit blacks who might test their segregation policies, but the Presbyterians and Episcopalians did admit them. After the Episcopalians saw what happened to the Presbyterians when the four teenagers visited, however, they decided to leave the seating of black worshippers to the discretion of the ushers. Traditionally, the Episcopalians had always admitted blacks, especially for weddings and funerals, but sat them in a side wing, and this was to have been their policy if tested. Only after the Presbyterian episode did the Episcopalians choose the ambiguous usher-discretion policy.

Trinity Lutheran Church admitted blacks to worship and welcomed all area Lutheran pastors, including blacks, to meetings held about four times a year. These integrated meetings received no publicity, and other pastors in Selma were unaware of them. On one occasion, when Colonel Al Lingo, head of the

Alabama state police, had state troopers at the armory, the
Lutheran pastors quietly met in an integrated setting across the
town at Trinity. Had Lingo known about it, he would have been
enraged. A representative of the Citizens Council learned about
one meeting and complained to a prominent Lutheran layperson,
who refused to discuss the matter.

Although Smeltzer's conversations with white clergy were in-
formative and a useful first step, discussions with representatives
of the die-hard viewpoint were not immediately open to him. The
Citizens Council was the prime exponent of the white suprema-
cist philosophy and the predominant force in Selma's white
community. The Citizens Council not only controlled Selma's
municipal politics but also public opinion. The Citizens Council
boasted the charter membership of influential whites in Selma
and served as a respectable alternative to the Ku Klux Klan and
the National States Rights Party, which, in the eyes of Selma's
gentry, were contaminated with the unwashed. Selma's Citizens
Council was the first of its kind in Alabama and claimed to be
the largest in the state. Although many moderates feared the
council's influence, it limited itself to legal tactics and concentrated on pressuring public opinion. The Selma chapter had no
membership roster, no regular newsletter, no procedure for electing officers, and no major activities beyond a fish fry or barbecue
from time to time; nevertheless, almost sixty-five hundred people
attended a meeting at which Governor George C. Wallace was
the featured speaker. Mayor Heinz and the City Council were
strong adherents of Citizens Council philosophy. Smeltzer had
considerable difficulty in establishing contact with this segment
of white Selma; not only did it take him longer to obtain interviews with the die-hards, but he was not accepted by them as
readily as he was by blacks and moderate whites.[8]

The Citizens Council was ready with all its power to
stonewall the tide of integration. One businessperson estimated
to Smeltzer that, because of civil rights activities, Selma's
employers would fire one thousand blacks; employers would fire
blacks whether they had participated in demonstrations or not.

Every workplace had the list of the forty-two Dunn women, and blacks who registered to vote would also be blacklisted.

More than any other individual, Sheriff Jim Clark represented the die-hard segregationists. In many ways, Clark, a heavy-set lawman with a sizable temper and paunch, fit the northern stereotype of a southern sheriff. Clark's uniform was enough to raise Yankee eyebrows. He wore a military-style outfit topped off with a gold-braided officer's cap, and he dangled a billy club and an electric cattle prod from his belt. Civil rights workers considered Clark to be irrational and capable of highly erratic behavior, although Clark's supporters viewed him as a soft-spoken, hard-working southern gentleman. A story circulated in Selma that a genteel lady, disgusted with Clark's tactics, put on her white gloves and went to his office to complain. The sheriff's courtesy so charmed her that she did not have the heart to raise the topic and left after exchanging small talk.[9]

Clark supplemented his paid deputies with a volunteer posse composed mainly of uneducated poor whites and organized into three units: a mounted posse, a water posse, and a posse on foot. Other than a *Sheriff's Posse* decal on their hats or helmets—few wore actual police helmets—the posse had no standard uniform, and Clark paid for some of the posse's equipment himself. Posse members wore khaki GI shirts and pants or work clothes. Some armed themselves with large pistols, which hung from leather holsters, and most carried unpainted, hand-turned billy clubs and cattle prods of varying length (the larger the prod, the bigger the jolt). Before the civil rights era, the posse performed flood-relief services in Dallas County, but later Clark and his posse traveled around the state to "help" when civil rights demonstrators threatened the status quo.

Clark believed that racial unrest would continue to plague Selma and that Alabama would suffer from more turmoil. The sheriff claimed that his on-site observations of civil rights actions around the state gave him valuable experience in curtailing violence, and, if outside agitators again disturbed Selma's domestic tranquillity, Clark recommended a show of force.

Clark's policies were unchallenged publicly by Selma's whites, but privately some of the influential families questioned his flashes of temper and mass arrests, and they distrusted the class of people surrounding Clark. For example, one influential business person thought Clark had a "head like a rock," and was supported by a group of "ill-advised advisers" and unquestioning hangers-on.[10]

The Citizens Council mind-set so controlled public opinion that the few who stood up for civil rights usually suffered for it. When in 1962 George T. Hrbek, pastor of a Lutheran congregation in Selma, objected to a Montgomery Baptist minister's biblical defense of segregation, the wrath of the Citizens Council descended upon him. In a low-key attempt to help Hrbek, Newton suggested to the newly formed Ministers Union (not to be confused with the Ministerial Alliance, a black organization) that it adopt a resolution supporting freedom of speech regardless of a person's position on race. Other pastors vetoed the proposal by arguing that it would create severe controversy and serve no useful purpose. Hrbek soon left Selma.

The only other time the Ministers Union discussed civil rights came when a Catholic priest, the Reverend Maurice F. Ouellet, called a meeting as the 1963 demonstrations were imminent. Ouellet hoped that the ministers would approve a strong public statement endorsing equal justice, or at least go on record in support of toleration, but his colleagues disappointed him. One Protestant described Ouellet as "far out," and another said he was not to be taken seriously. Several Baptists walked out of the meeting, and the Ministers Union voted to do nothing about the demonstrations. Because of Ouellet's outspokenness, white officials asked him to leave town and accused him of being responsible for the demonstrations. When he refused to depart, whites went to his archbishop. Ouellet was also threatened with arrest.[11]

The largest crack in Selma's wall of ecclesiastical segregation was the action of the four girls at the Presbyterian church. Selma's black activists, however, were not aware of the bad feelings, among even sympathetic whites like Newton, caused by their public celebration of the victory, and the Presbyterian event may have been counterproductive. In one of his first actions as a mediator, Smeltzer relayed to several black leaders the impact of their celebration and advised them not to publicize or publicly celebrate "victories."

Although the Citizens Council intimidated most white moderates, the centrists held the potential to alter Selma's balance of power. Moderates were the key to Smeltzer's success as a mediator, and he needed to cultivate them. White moderates supported modest integration and opposed Citizens Council intransigence and intimidation, and many moderates had little respect for the inflexibility and even the intelligence of local politicians. For example, one moderate told Smeltzer that Mayor Heinz and the City Council were fairly low-grade politicians but that they represented the thinking of Selma, similar to the situation that created Governor George Wallace's statewide popularity.

Nevertheless, white centrists demonstrated little appreciation for the black perspective. Many moderates complained to Smeltzer about being isolated on racial issues, and their support for the civil rights movement was limited. For example, one white moderate admitted that the Citizens Council served a purpose by restraining radical, uneducated, uncultured blacks; by preventing black violence; and by averting a black takeover of the city. (Nothing suggested that white extremists had been similarly restrained.) An influential Presbyterian laywoman, who enthusiastically supported John Newton and his progressive policies, told Smeltzer that in spite of the lowly state of the city's political talent, Selma's blacks were much more debased because they lacked education, culture, high moral standards, and good work habits. Her black maid frequently failed to report to work, and the maid's twelve-year-old daughter was pregnant. This Presbyterian said that Selma's blacks were not restless or unhappy unless agitated by outsiders, and she abhorred the thought of school integration.[12] Because it was obvious that moderate whites had failed to establish contacts with moderate blacks, much less the activists, Smeltzer encouraged the establishment of a bridge between moderates in the two racial groups. Misunderstandings about the black community that Smeltzer heard from white centrists proved that communication was poor and that he could make a contribution if his mediation ministry succeeded.

But Smeltzer's efforts to gain the confidence of any whites, whether moderate or hard-core segregationist, were hindered by the traditional southern distrust of outsiders, a feeling that the civil rights movement intensified. Since the days of the abolitionists, the South has always been suspicious of outsiders, especially Yankees. Many Selma whites complained bitterly to Smeltzer about outsiders, who were blamed for a variety of problems and whose greatest contribution would be to leave Selma. Outsiders allegedly agitated children and paid them to demonstrate; high school students arrested had fifty-cent pieces on them, and Selma University students got five dollars. Sympathetic whites told Smeltzer that the mayor would think of him as an outsider no matter what he said. Whites doubted that local blacks would press their cause, so if outsiders stayed away, things ought to simmer down. Even industries could not help much because, of course, they were headed by outsiders. One pastor, who supported moderate integration of his church, believed that Selma really did not have a racial problem until the outside agitators arrived; another preacher was reluctant to talk with Smeltzer because he was an outsider.[13]

Anyone associated with the federal government was suspect as an outsider. Selma voters despised the national Democratic party and voted for Richard Nixon in 1960, and Selma's arch-conservatives rejoiced when President John F. Kennedy was shot. Kennedy's death touched off a lively celebration at the Holiday Inn, and the bars sold more liquor than usual.

Smeltzer's position as an outsider was even more difficult because two delegations from the National Council of Churches (NCC) had preceded his first trip by a month. The NCC visits had angered Selmians and had enhanced normal feelings of suspicion toward outsiders. Several moderate whites felt betrayed by the NCC delegation, which claimed to be an impartial, fact-finding project. The NCC people implied neutrality, but it turned out that they were committed to the civil rights movement and, according to some white moderates, even provided bail money for SNCC members. Two sympathetic women, assuming the discussions were confidential, had confided their views to the NCC delegation, only to have the story released to the *New York Times,* which upset the women considerably, although their names did not appear in the article. The *Times* article contained a negative tone; the NCC delegation complained that they were brushed off and that one of them had been turned away from Sunday morning worship by a Methodist usher. The article implied that prospects for progress in Selma were slim.[14]

Then a second NCC delegation arrived, which also claimed to be on an impartial, fact-finding mission. Yet this group talked to civil rights leaders, including the controversial Amelia Boynton, and one of the NCC women, Polly Cowan, delivered an emotional pro–civil rights speech at the same meeting at which Dick Gregory spoke, whose strong statements certainly irritated almost every white in Selma. Again, white moderates felt betrayed. The second NCC delegation even suggested to several moderate white women that they work with Boynton, who in the minds of many whites wore a scarlet *R* for "radical" on her sleeve. If Smeltzer was another NCC type, moderate whites would have nothing to do with him. The NCC indeed had created an obstacle for Smeltzer to overcome.

Early Contacts with Selma's Blacks

Just as Selma's whites were split, so were its blacks. More than one hundred years of white oppression had not produced a united black front but had created a community that, similar to the white community, was divided between moderates, aggressive activists, egos, rivalries, and age differentials. Before Smeltzer could contribute to the communication of Selma's civil rights movement, he needed to coalesce that movement and encourage it to unify. Smeltzer wanted to contribute to interracial peace in Selma by improving communication, but before the whites could listen to the message of the civil rights movement, blacks had to unify and speak as one voice.

Organizers of demonstrations represented the most aggressive black position in Selma and painted for Smeltzer a picture of brutality and oppression. Activists such as Worth Long, Marie Foster, and Amelia Boynton complained to Smeltzer about economic discrimination and coercion, one of the most lethal weapons in the white arsenal. For example, Long, Boynton, and Foster cited the Dunn blacklist. Although some of the Dunn women had been able to find other work and had received compliments on the quality of their work, they were soon fired after Dunn and others called their new employers. Smeltzer had arranged for the Brethren to send sewing machines to Selma for the Dunn women, but Long, Foster, and Boynton suspected that Dunn and the Ku Klux Klan would prevent the machines from arriving or that any church housing them might be bombed.

Boynton's activism had so stigmatized her that blacks feared losing their jobs if they went to mass meetings or even were seen with her. In 1954, when Boynton's husband, Bill, complained about the lack of black jurors in the rape trial of a black gas station attendant, the white community retaliated with economic coercion. Blacks were pressured into canceling policies with Boynton's insurance agency, and Boynton's creditors demanded payment. When Bill Boynton died in May 1963, Amelia believed that white harassment had contributed to her husband's death. Another reason many blacks kept the Boyntons at arm's length was that Bill Boynton had left another wife and family to marry Amelia, which scandalized Selma.[15]

According to the black leadership, Selma turned down three new industries because they had to be integrated, and five industries had closed in the last six years. A new battery factory employed three hundred whites, but only two blacks. (Newton agreed; the company had a nondiscriminatory history, but the local Chamber of Commerce said that the firm was not welcome in Selma if it did not comply with local customs.) Other blacks confirmed that some people had lost jobs for registering to vote. A black city employee told Smeltzer that the city let it be known that jobs would be lost if black employees attempted to register.

Long, Foster, and Boynton described shocking examples of law enforcement brutality and harassment, usually perpetrated by the sheriff's department. For example, Clark allegedly broke a bottle over a black prisoner's head and kicked him in the groin because he had a beard; to Clark, the beard meant that the man must be either a SNCC member or a Black Muslim. Long was arrested and beaten on his second day in town, and he had not participated in any demonstrations.

Smeltzer was accepted by Selma's black community much more quickly than by the whites. He established cordial relationships with three of the leading blacks—C. C. Brown, Edwin Moss, and F. D. Reese—and eventually pressed whites to accept these three men as negotiating representatives from the black community.

The black leader who more than any other movement activist in Selma distanced himself from the demonstrations was the Reverend Claude C. ("C. C.") Brown, of the Reformed Presbyterian Church on Jeff Davis Avenue. Brown's philosophy emphasized that blacks needed to take the moral uplift, educational, and economic approach to improvement. He allowed mass meetings to use his church and spoke at several of them, but he opposed some of the demonstrations, including those that kept students out of school, especially for more than a day. He felt that emotional, inflammatory statements and purely negative criticism of whites were unproductive. Brown respected SNCC leaders, but he considered many SNCC workers—with their beards—to be uncouth misfits, although he granted that perhaps the movement required this type of person if it was to be successful. Brown thought that SNCC's office in Selma, which he called the "Franklin Street mess," was a dirty hangout where unacceptable sexual freedom and immorality were rife. Brown contended that the Dunn women wrongly walked out of the rest home and ignored the needs of helpless patients. Brown knew that Dunn also was wrong, but he believed the walkout unfortunately created civic sympathy for Dunn.

Brown's contribution to the civil rights movement was the trust of and access to the white community he enjoyed. Brown was proud of his stature among whites, but he complained of the abuse he suffered from fellow blacks because of his success. Other black leaders, especially movement organizers, were jealous of his success, he claimed, and the ostracism and envy were difficult for him to endure. Once whites invited him to a meal at Parrish Cafeteria for a committee meeting, but the black waiters called him "uppity" and made more trouble for him than the whites. In spite of the envious feelings other black leaders held for him, Brown said that because he had a reputation for getting things done, many of them approached him for financial assistance and counseling.

Although Brown was a moderate-to-conservative black, he challenged Jim Crow, and his support for the movement, while not matching the white-hot intensity of the zealots, was sincere. He maintained that there was no need to exaggerate conditions at prison camps because they were bad enough. (Civil rights leaders claimed that there was sand in the food.) Brown complained that the girls' section of the camp had an unscreened toilet, without a seat, in the middle of the room, in clear view of male guards walking by.[16]

Representing a middle position between SNCC activists and Brown was Edwin Moss. Like the rest of the black leadership, Moss was born and raised in Selma. Moss managed fund-raising efforts for the Fathers of St. Edmund mission, a job that gave him financial independence and consequent immunity from white economic coercion. Moss's office, an operation that impressed Smeltzer, had 28 automatic typewriters and equipment capable of addressing and sending thirty-five thousand mailing pieces daily throughout the United States. In 1950, Moss organized a black credit union with $3 million in assets. Moss believed that Selma's banks feared his credit union and moved to undercut it by becoming more lenient to black borrowers, which pleased him because that meant a better deal for blacks.

Moss's primary concern was employment. The only jobs available to blacks, such as janitors or errand "boys," required little skill or responsibility and were poorly paid. The only professional occupations filled by blacks were teachers, doctors, and ministers. Selma also had one black lawyer. Even a store like Barton's, which employed blacks and enjoyed much black trade, did not allow black employees to handle money. Moss was also concerned about the plight of black men stationed at Craig Air Force Base on the outskirts of Selma. Because the local U.S.O. was segregated, many of the black airmen came to the Elks Lodge, which he directed.[17]

Only one prominent black, the Reverend Frederick D. Reese, managed to earn the respect of all factions of Selma's black movement. Reese was a Baptist preacher, a public school teacher, and a friendly, earnest man with outstanding leadership abilities. A graduate of Alabama State University, Reese spent nine years teaching at the Wilcox County training school before returning to Selma to teach math and science at Hudson High School. In 1961, the Selma Teachers Association, a black organization, elected Reese as its president, and his first act was to urge black teachers to register to vote. Many black teachers were not registered; and even black educators with masters' degrees had been rejected by the voter registration board. Reese also took the lead in securing sabbaticals, maternity leaves, and year-round pay for the city's black teachers. In 1962, Reese became president of the Dallas County Voters League.[18]

Selma's black leaders leveled an amazing collection of charges at one another. Although some leaders were more critical than others of their colleagues, the lengthy list of criticisms included immorality, financial corruption, drinking too much, and having bad debts. Some of the most outspoken activists suffered criticism that they harbored racist hatred of whites, but others attacked moderates for being too inclined toward compromise.

Moss was accused of trying to infiltrate Protestant groups with the poison of Romanism, and one prominent black questioned the legality of another black's business venture, calling it a "typical nigger operation." Even Father Ouellet, the only white working openly with the civil rights movement in Selma, received a bit of the fire. Some blacks feared that Ouellet, like Moss, was interested in spreading Catholicism more than anything else; for example, Ouellet allegedly encouraged the participation of public but not parochial school students in the demonstrations. The one emotion that enjoyed support in both black and white Selma was anti-Catholicism. Most black leaders, with the notable exception of Reese, were controversial with some other group in the black community.[19]

Even at the public mass meetings, Selma's blacks could not resist undercutting one another. Claude Brown complained bitterly that after he spoke for thirty minutes on the history of the black movement and its successful methods, a speech Brown thought was well received by the audience, the Reverend L. L. Anderson stood up and contradicted everything he said. Anderson charged that Brown had ignored the current situation, including the injustices committed by whites and the wrongs of "you crackers standing around the edge of the hall."[20] At a May 1963 mass meeting, after James Foreman and Bernard Lafayette spent the evening encouraging their listeners to sacrifice to earn their rights, another local black pastor, the Reverend C. C. Hunter, convener of the meeting, closed with extemporaneous remarks stressing that blacks needed to clean up their own act before they could begin to request "some of those other things that have been mentioned here tonight." In its coverage of the event, the Selma Times-Journal prominently noted this dissension in its lead paragraph.[21]

Smeltzer devoted some of his time to mediating among the divided black leaders and trying to unify them. Together, Reese, Brown, and Moss represented a variety of groups in the black community: Reese was a Baptist, Brown was a Presbyterian, and Moss was a Methodist employed by Catholics. Reese was an educator, Moss had roots in the business community, and Brown was active in the YMCA. Reese was younger than Brown and Moss, and his views sometimes seemed radical to them.[22] On the other hand, although Brown was more conservative, he was included in the leadership because the white establishment trusted him so much, and he was thereby able to get things done. Moss occupied the moderate ground between Reese and Brown.

Efforts to Help the Dunn Women

Before departing from Selma on his first visit, Smeltzer met with two white moderates, Rosa Miller Joyce and Carol Sommers, who showed sympathy for moderate reform, and he told them about the blacklisting of the Dunn women. Joyce and Sommers were concerned and immediately made plans to use their contacts with doctors to get the women jobs at two large white hospitals in Selma. Joyce and Sommers hoped that the Dunn blacklisting would so disgust the community that the Citizens Council would suffer a backlash. Because the women were enthusiastic and eager to help—they were glad to have something specific to work on—Smeltzer decided temporarily to delay sending the sewing machines in case Joyce and Sommers might be able to solve the problem locally, which was preferable to outside intervention.

Joyce and Sommers's reaction to the news of the blacklisting illustrated that a basic problem in Selma was one of communication. They had little insight into the black community and told Smeltzer that, without him, they would have obtained little information on the blacklisting. Smeltzer assumed that this was a situation in which someone like him, with contacts in both the black and white communities, could help.

Smeltzer's optimism over Joyce's efforts to aid the Dunn women proved premature. About a week after Smeltzer's conversation with her, she reported by telephone that it would take longer than she thought to solve Selma's problems. Mayor Heinz was cordial and shocked about the blacklist, but he also sympathized with Dunn's problems created by the walkout. People with whom Joyce talked about the boycott were appalled, but the hospitals refused to hire the Dunn women by rationalizing that, if the women had walked out on Dunn, they could do it again. The doctors she contacted were scared. Although the Selma schools could not make any special efforts to employ the women, the district would hire some of the women if they applied normally, and when Dunn asked the school district to dismiss a teacher and coach who was the husband of a striking Dunn woman, the principal refused. Also, Superintendent Pickard refused to pass along the blacklist. Some of the women got jobs at a local black hospital, and Joyce would personally give one woman work. According to Joyce, now not only the Dunn women but all who registered to vote were on a blacklist. In an admission that Selma's problems would not soon be resolved, Joyce recommended sending food, clothing, and sewing machines for anyone in need, not just registrants.

By mid-January 1964, Joyce thought that all of the Dunn women had been employed. One of Joyce's friends had personally employed Annie Lee Cooper, one of the women Dunn struck, but when Cooper's car broke down, she had to give up the job. A doctor's wife gave another woman a job, but fearing that her husband might object, she did not tell him that the new employee was a Dunn woman. Smeltzer tended to generate enthusiasm among those in his presence, but sometimes the enthusiasm departed with him when he left, which may partially explain why efforts to assist the Dunn women were not so successful as hoped.[23]

Craig Air Force Base

Selma's economic bastion was the local military installation, Craig Air Force Base, which trained pilots. Craig was a major employer, and its workers and payrolls pumped life into Selma's economy. The base was also the county's largest employer of blacks.

The base commander, Colonel Richard Ault, was a cautious man whose major interest was running the base and avoiding entanglement in Selma's increasingly sticky problems. Ault's hands-off attitude regarding Selma's race relations led to a refusal to grant Smeltzer an interview, but it turned out that the colonel had once been a member of the Church of the Brethren, an entree that gave Smeltzer a productive telephone conversation with Ault.

Colonel Ault supported integration and claimed that his base was integrated, but he disagreed with unspecified tactics of the civil rights people. Ault also felt deceived by the NCC group because they represented themselves as a fact-finding group but then complained about the base to the Pentagon, the Justice Department, and the press—and got so much attention in Washington that Ault was called to the capital to account for himself. Another group in Ault's doghouse was SNCC, because after he told SNCC leaders that the base was integrated, they lied—in Ault's opinion—to the press in claiming that Craig was segregated.

Officials at the Department of Defense gave Smeltzer a different version of race relations at Craig. According to the Pentagon, the SNCC report on Craig was a legitimate interpretation, but few complaints were received about the racial situation at Craig because most of the whites and about half of the blacks on the base were southerners, who accepted segregation as normal. Recently, several incidents had occurred, and problems were beginning to surface at Craig. For example, when two black airmen refused to move to the rear of the segregated bus that ran from Selma to the base, the driver called the military police, who removed the two airmen for their own protection. After the incident, Ault told the base's black airmen that he was working on the situation and asked them to avoid creating controversy, but

Ault also admitted to them his inability to influence the bus company.

Smeltzer learned that the blacks at Craig respected their officers but that they wanted regular meetings with the base's officers in order to work more forcefully on the racial situation. Blacks felt a cool atmosphere, feared reprisals, and reported unofficial discrimination. For example, black airmen thought they were transferred often in order to prevent their promotion.

Craig's black airmen evidently felt that change was unlikely; therefore, approximately three-fourths of them signed a letter to the House and Senate Armed Services Committees complaining about base conditions. The airmen listed the following grievances:

- Segregated barracks.

- Segregated transportation to and from the base. If the bus company refused to integrate, the airmen requested that the bus be banned from the base.

- Inadequate housing. According to the letter, many black airmen left their families behind because of the poor facilities. There was a housing area next to the base, the Nathan Bedford Forrest project, but all black applicants had been rejected.

- A segregated U.S.O.

- Segregated educational opportunities for airmen in Selma.

According to the letter, the white airmen, approximately 75 per cent of them Alabamans, used the constant threat of reprisals to make it difficult for blacks to protest discrimination. Pentagon officials were upset that the men had not followed proper channels through the military command structure. They wondered why the men did not talk to Ault about their complaints and surmised that blacks must have felt that such a conversation would be unproductive.[24]

Smeltzer recognized that Ault and many of his officers were part of the Selma community and that Ault was torn between integration at Craig and cordial relations with Selma. Smeltzer suggested to Pentagon officials that if Ault received an order to desegregate, it would take him off the spot by placing the blame on the far-off Pentagon. Ault could tell the community that he had no choice but to integrate; orders are orders. But Deputy Assistant Secretary of Defense for Civil Rights Alfred B. Fitt told Smeltzer that Ault already had all the authority he needed to integrate; if he wanted more, all he had to do was ask. The Pentagon realized that Ault's assignment was difficult but felt that he was not aggressive enough on civil rights. The Department of Defense planned to correct many of the problems in the Craig airmen's letter and hoped to persuade Ault to move more assertively. Fitt urged Smeltzer to continue his work because Selma desperately needed a communicator and because Ault could use all the help he could get.[25]

Demonstrations End but Problems Remain

Although the demonstrations ceased on October 1963, chiefly because of a lack of bail money, Selma's civic atmosphere remained tense. Blacks searched for methods to further their drive for justice, and whites retaliated. As Smeltzer became more familiar with the community, he became increasingly convinced that he could help Selma as a mediator and increasingly aware of the security problems involved in his mission.

Governor Wallace, relying on Clark and Smelley as eyewitnesses, charged that the Justice Department had chauffeured the Reverend Martin Luther King, Jr., from Birmingham to Selma for a mass meeting on October 15. After an initial denial, the department admitted that one of its attorneys lent a government car to a private citizen, who used the vehicle to transport King. The attorney later resigned.[26]

In response to this mischief from Washington, Dallas County opened a grand jury investigation of Justice Department activities in Alabama. Robert D. Wilkinson, foreman of the grand jury, charged that Justice Department lawyers were responsible for polluting Dallas County with a variety of disgusting perversions, including dope addiction, insurrection, juvenile delinquency, and sexual misfits.[27]

Although movement strategy during the winter of 1963–1964 called for no demonstrations, black leaders continued to exert pressure with a Christmas boycott of downtown businesses, and on December 19 Clark arrested a group distributing "Don't Buy Segregation" leaflets in the business district. The printer of the leaflets, J. B. Pritchett, and his son, James, were also arrested. The next day, Clark and Dallas County Solicitor Blanchard McLeod raided SNCC headquarters, searched the files, and confiscated financial records, news clippings, and various papers and reports; not even three wall cartoons escaped the dragnet! There were threats and arrests, and Clark told one SNCC worker, James Austin, "We've been trying to get you for a long time."[28]

The raid on SNCC headquarters meant that Smeltzer had to be more careful about his security. If Clark found evidence that so much as hinted at Smeltzer's sympathy for the civil rights movement, Smeltzer's bipartisanship would no longer be credible, and his mediation ministry would be over. He asked Boynton not to file any correspondence she had with him because her files could be raided, and he requested that she destroy an earlier letter he wrote to her.

Although compliance with the Christmas boycott was not complete, Selma's merchants were hurt, and rumors circulated of a new blacklist of all those who had attempted to register to vote. White moderate groups not only did not have any meetings, plans, or proposals but they still were not even in contact with one another. Typical of the feelings among progressive whites was a woman who told Smeltzer that she planned to attend a biracial meeting in Birmingham but that her husband was violently opposed to it, and she was afraid to tell anyone she was going.

By January 1964, the relief supplied that Smeltzer had recommended arrived in Selma, but he was careful not to take credit in order to avoid identification with any groups, either within or outside Selma. If whites found out that Smeltzer or his church had helped the Dunn women or had sent welfare aid to blacks, his neutrality would be doubted. Smeltzer knew what had happened to the NCC visitors when white moderates discovered that the delegations supported civil rights. Smeltzer's desire to disassociate himself from the aid was not entirely successful within the black community because some activists gave him much credit and believed that his "church went all out" to send a large amount of canned goods, plus cash to pay rent and utility bills.[29]

Therefore, Smeltzer told a steering committee of the Voters League that Church World Service sent the relief at his suggestion but that he had nothing to do with the timing, quantity, or arrangements of the supplies. He also requested that W. Ray Kyle, who operated the Brethren Service Center in New Windsor, Maryland, avoid any Church of the Brethren identification with the Selma relief. Specifically, Smeltzer urged Kyle to use his title, Manager of the Church World Service Material Aid Center, to avoid any Brethren reference. Smeltzer told Kyle that it might not seem important but that there were "strong reasons, in fact compelling reasons" for keeping separate identities. Smeltzer was disappointed when, after he had specifically asked Boynton to use the Church World Service title for Kyle, she identified Kyle with the Brethren Service Center in a letter to New Windsor.[30]

Security was tight regarding the supplies, which were kept in a church in Birmingham and then transported to the basement of a Selma pastor's, Ernest Doyle's, home. Boynton did not tell the steering committee in Smeltzer's presence where the materials were, but Doyle called him the next day with the information. The committee was also concerned that a white cemetery worker at the Birmingham church, who showed suspicious curiosity about the truck, would be a major security leak. The decision to give the Dunn women first crack at the materials provoked criticism that they and Doyle kept too much for themselves and provided another example of black disunity.

Security in Selma was a major concern for Smeltzer. Because he knew that telephones in other parts of the South had been tapped, he used pay phones almost exclusively and encouraged others engaged in sensitive conversations to do the same. On Smeltzer's first trip, he also contacted the Justice Department in Washington to let them know he was in Selma for a few days, and later he received more detailed advice on security from the department's John Doar. Doar suggested that Smeltzer mail his notes each day rather than leave them in a hotel room. Doar cautioned Smeltzer to avoid being identified with the federal government, not to discuss confidential information over the phone, and that most damaging would be a leak of names or notes on moderates. Doar believed that as long as Smeltzer did not break a law and did not receive publicity, he should be safe, but Smeltzer could not expect protection. Doar added that he considered the Selma police and the local FBI to be fair.

Further contributing to Smeltzer's security fears was a late February speech by Sheriff Clark to a meeting of the Selma Exchange Club in which Clark claimed that the National Council of Churches had a representative working in Selma, and Claude Brown told Smeltzer that Clark thought that the NCC man was a spy. Clark did not name the NCC worker; did he have Smeltzer in mind? Since the NCC had no one in Selma, Clark's alleged spook must either be John Fry, who was doing an article for *Presbyterian Life,* or Smeltzer. Brown offered assistance, including bail, if Clark arrested Smeltzer.[31]

Although pessimism predominated in Selma, several rays of sunlight poked through the gloom. Moss reported that the city had plans for playgrounds and a swimming pool in black neighborhoods. Blacks could get their streets paved if they paid for the paving, and the city promised to put up street signs. A laundry had been integrated, although pressure from whites had forced it to resume segregation within only two months.

Smeltzer's goals aimed at increasing his role as a mediator and encouraging black-white cooperation, and crucial to his mediating role would be getting all groups dependent on him for information. He hoped to get Brown to introduce him to Heinz, which would not only acquaint him with the mayor but also enable him to show Heinz that he had contacts with Selma's blacks. Smeltzer planned to ask Heinz to name blacks with whom he would consult on the pool and playground projects and then to offer to ask civil rights leaders if the mayor's names were acceptable. Also, Smeltzer decided to deal with city and county leaders separately because city whites were more experienced with educated blacks and seemed more willing to compromise.

On Smeltzer's second visit, he tried to encourage direct communication between key people in Selma rather than relaying to them what various leaders thought. He prepared to suggest others in Selma with whom people should confer and hoped to have blacks and whites with common ground, especially the moderates, establish communication. He also wanted to make a special effort to work with Selma's pastors.

Smeltzer believed that the key to the civil rights movement was voting rights because that issue attracted the most support from whites and because of the long-range effects the black ballot possessed. He told segregationists that, sooner or later, blacks would vote, and he suggested that blacks would become an important voting block; politicians who wanted to win would eventually need black support. If blacks were denied suffrage in the South, however, they would move to the North where they could vote and help enact even stronger federal civil rights legislation. Smeltzer maintained that the South could achieve political, social, and economic progress, but only on the basis of justice and equal opportunity for blacks.

Smeltzer impressed those he met with his concern and sincerity. People noted his deeply held convictions and ability to listen, and they liked him because, unlike other northerners, he made no accusations and was nonjudgmental. He developed a reputation for being genuinely interested in helping and making peace, and black leaders were especially appreciative.[32]

Although Smeltzer collected a gloomy analysis in Selma, his first contact encouraged his hopes that he could help. During future visits he planned to work with the white moderates: to listen, to gain trust, and to offer information and suggestions. Perhaps he could influence Selma's decision makers through the moderates and avoid a confrontation with the white establishment. He knew he would have to be patient; results would be slow. In a memo to himself he wrote, *"Interesting how this visit worked itself out step by step"* (Smeltzer's emphasis). Smeltzer believed that it was "God's leading" that made his ministry effective.

3

A Darkening Horizon

When I was a boy and the circus would come to town, we'd all get out of school because they'd have elephants and tigers and the rest of it. And one interesting thing that I never forgot: I saw that elephant one evening. The keeper had a small chain around the foot there, and the other end dropped over a small stake, a stake that I honestly believe I could have pulled up, but the elephant had been trained that he couldn't pull up this stake because he was trained at a time he couldn't pull it up. When he was young, a baby, he was trained, "You stay here until somebody moves you." Now here's the great big nine-feet-tall elephant with a little chain over his foot and the other end over that stake and he stood there. And every once in a while he'd pick that heavy foot up and drop it down and wag his tail a little.

But later on I saw that same elephant that couldn't pull up that stake, with his head lodged against a train boxcar loaded with the things they carried. And a man who weighed possibly a little more than a hundred pounds, with a pointy piece of metal in his hand, the man knew that the elephant couldn't pull up the stake but could push a whole train. Every once in a while the man would encourage him that he could push the whole train. He didn't holler at him—he'd just encourage him to push this train. And that elephant was walking along pushing a whole train of boxcars.

When I stood there and saw that, as a little boy, I cried because I had seen them dehumanize my daddy and disrespecting mamma and I thought that was so typical of my folks. Look at that elephant—can't pull up a stake, pushing that whole train.

Reverend L. L. Anderson,
Tabernacle Baptist Church

Many of Smeltzer's initial mediation endeavors occurred early in 1964 at the federal government's major presence in Selma, Craig Air Force Base, where he worked to improve communication between black enlisted men and base authorities. While the pace at Craig toward equal rights was too leisurely to satisfy black activists, the base commander, Colonel Richard L. Ault, harbored sympathy for the goals of the civil rights movement.

Craig was a federal institution, but Black Belt bigotry spilled onto the base in a variety of ways. For example, Selma athletic teams often came to Craig to compete, but even church teams insisted on the rigid laws of Jim Crow. Local athletes refused to compete against Air Force teams with black team members, and one squad refused to play if Craig insisted on using the assigned umpire, a black enlisted man. The umpire was paid, he departed, and the game proceeded.[1] In contrast, Selma's Roman Catholics, who worshipped in segregated churches in Selma, readily attended integrated Mass at Craig.

Black airmen at Craig repeated to Smeltzer the complaints they had voiced in their letter to the Pentagon. They were upset by segregation policies in the off-base housing facility, the Nathan Bedford Forrest project, which was built with federal funds but was administered by the Selma Housing Authority. Blacks asserted that the barracks also were segregated. Black airmen were tired of sitting in the rear of the bus that made the 5-mile trip from Selma to Craig, and they complained that menial jobs on the base always came to them.

Colonel Ault's strategy for promoting racial harmony on the base concentrated on an official procedure to deal with racial grievances—a biracial Craig Improvement and Relationship Committee, Ault's designated "sounding board for black troops."[2] Ault believed that the committee was functional, and it grieved him that one signer of the letter to Washington sat on the committee. But blacks considered the committee to be impotent because it had met only twice in approximately five months and had not significantly altered race relations at Craig. Smeltzer suspected that the committee was too top-heavy with brass to be effective.[3]

In spite of the black airmen's frustrations, Colonel Ault, whom Smeltzer considered interested in at least minimal progress, recently had made several contributions to civil rights. Ault persuaded the housing project to give the base commander (i.e., Ault) responsibility for future housing assignments and planned to tell the neighborhood in no uncertain terms that an eligible black would get the first opening. Ault also successfully negotiated with the University of Alabama to move its Selma extension to Craig so that those classes could be integrated. The necessary enrollment for an algebra section had already been reached.

Change was much more elusive with the bus line. Also, movie theaters in Selma remained segregated, but Ault explained that Craig's blacks could see decent movies at the base theater or the black theater in town.

Although Smeltzer brought a mild-mannered, gentle personality to his mission in Selma, he carried within him aggressive determination, which he occasionally displayed without violating his role of quiet bipartisanship. For example, on Smeltzer's first visit to Craig, Ault called in the base's Protestant chaplain, the Reverend J. Walter Poorman, a Baptist, for an introduction and then stepped out briefly. When Ault returned, he asked Poorman if he had inquired about Smeltzer's purpose for being at Craig. Poorman laughed and said that he did not have to ask because Smeltzer had quickly raised the topic.

During his efforts at Craig, Smeltzer traded information and collaborated on strategy with Alfred Fitt at the Defense Department in Washington, and through Fitt, Smeltzer learned that he had earned Ault's trust. Fitt suggested that Smeltzer drop hints that Craig could be closed if sufficient progress at the base was not forthcoming. Fitt himself could not say this and, if confronted, might even deny it, but Smeltzer could use such a line effectively. Actually, there were no plans to close the base in the near future, but Fitt believed that the base was vulnerable in the next round of closings if Selma's stubbornness continued. According to Fitt, Ault lacked firmness on civil rights, but the Air Force top command did not press him because it was waiting for the Civil Rights bill to pass. Ault probably realized that he eventually would have to act; he procrastinated in order to preserve positive public relations with Selma and to enable blame for further actions to fall on the federal government.

Smeltzer's Meeting with Black Airmen

On a visit to Selma in March 1964, two black airmen asked Smeltzer to meet with a group of interested black servicemen at the Negro Elks Lodge. Smeltzer agreed, with the proviso that he be invited as a guest, not as a participant. Twenty black airmen attended the Tuesday, 6:30 P.M., meeting, plus two workers from SNCC, whose presence Smeltzer privately questioned. As he was introduced, Smeltzer carefully shook hands with everyone. He presented an update on issues and shared information that was new to the men. He told them that the off-base housing project would be integrated. He reported that University of Alabama courses, open to all, would be meeting at Craig this coming summer, and he urged interested persons to apply. In fact, the March-quarter classes held in downtown Selma were to be integrated, but Craig's blacks never got the word.[4]

The airmen were incredulous over the coming integration of the housing project. Not only had they not been informed about the extension courses, but they were ignorant of the housing project plan too. Smeltzer explained that Ault had not publicized his decision in order to avoid arousing the community before a family was ready to move into the project. The black airmen indicated their intention to apply and test the situation immediately.[5]

After the meeting, Smeltzer telephoned Ault (at 11:00 P.M.) to say that he had talked to a Craig man with many concerns who requested a meeting. Smeltzer advised the man to take his concerns to Ault's biracial committee, and he thought this suggestion would be followed. Smeltzer reported a misunderstanding about the committee; the airmen thought they should not voluntarily bring concerns to it because the group met so seldom. But, Smeltzer told the men that it was better to take problems directly to the committee and Colonel Ault, rather than have himself caught in the middle.

Smeltzer confidently concluded that this early mediation succeeded because he reassured Ault that he was not a meddler and gained the colonel's confidence. Smeltzer wrote in his notes that it "cleared me completely and really set things up." Ault thought Smeltzer's suggestion to use the committee was much better than another appeal to Washington, which, he said, would upset Selma (not to mention the colonel).[6]

The afternoon following Smeltzer's meeting with the black airmen at the Elks club, Major Ivan J. Ely scheduled a meeting for the biracial committee. At the meeting, Ely reported on the integration of the housing project and discussed the January 7 letter to Washington that many black airmen had signed. Also, Ely informed the committee about a complaint from a black airman living in the barracks, but he ruled that no action could be taken because it was not the committee's business, an interpretation that irritated black committee members. Because of the speed of developments, especially the hastily scheduled biracial meeting, Sergeant Joe Black, the leader of the black airmen, thought that Smeltzer had betrayed their confidence to Ault but conceded that Smeltzer's visit obviously produced quick results.

The first black to apply for admittance to the housing project, Airman First Class Enoch Fears, submitted his application the morning after the Elks meeting. Base authorities told him that they did not expect trouble in integrating the project, but if a problem arose, which was certainly possible, he should report it to them rather than fight. Craig's top officers called in a group of project residents and told them that blacks deserved to be in the project and that there would be no violence or hostility. Only one resident said that he would move, but he never did. Fears's new neighbors were cool toward him, and although he previously enjoyed cordial relations with some whites in the barracks, he felt they were now surprisingly stand-offish. Fears had one white friend, who ignored the housing situation and visited Fears to play chess.

Uneven Progress at Craig

In spite of the integration of the University of Alabama classes and the housing project, progress at Craig was uneven. After the Smeltzer-induced rush meeting of the biracial committee, the group did not meet again for several months; it was so low-profile that Chaplain Poorman was not even aware of its existence until Smeltzer told him about it. Sergeant Black reported that he had suffered reprisals since the meeting. Black charged that he was denied his coffee break because the authorities feared he would talk with other blacks, and he did not receive a three-day pass when his wife had to go to the hospital. A transfer to Alaska loomed in Black's immediate future, and Ault refused to approve his request to go instead to California.

By the middle of May, Ault's committee had met only once since March.[7] Ault claimed progress because of the theoretical integration of the University of Alabama courses (although the airmen still thought the extension courses were not open to them) and the placement of Fears in the housing project without negative reactions. But he had not been able to desegregate the bus from Selma because, he said, that would have to be changed in Selma. Smeltzer told the colonel that, although the black airmen lacked the courage to express themselves, they probably had deeper feelings beneath the surface, an obvious suggestion to Ault that he needed to work harder to communicate with his black troops.

Another Craig issue that Smeltzer explored was alleged discrimination by the base contractor, who hired civilians to perform unskilled jobs on the base. Although the contractor changed every year, the employees, many of them black, stayed on. Smeltzer met two black employees, both of whom were scared to be seen with him; one conversation took place in Joe Black's parked car, and the other employee left Smeltzer and Black standing on the front porch. Black employees charged discrimination; specifically they complained about the following:

- Black employees received no raises.

- Blacks were not promoted to or trained for supervisory positions.

- Supervisory positions went to whites, even whites with little training or those who worked at the base as a second job.

- At least one white, even if only a part-time employee, was kept in every job classification in order to avoid discrimination charges.

- Blacks feared dismissal if they complained.

- Moonlighting airmen were beginning to replace blacks.

Ault maintained that it was not the base commander's job to monitor the hiring practices of the contractor, but Smeltzer insisted that federal investigators might ask questions about just such a topic. Ault was reluctant to act on this issue, so Smeltzer wrote a letter to an air force industrial employment policy specialist, E. Vincent Suitt, informing him of the situation. The Air Force began an investigation.[8]

Evidently Ault was impressed with, or concerned about, Smeltzer's contacts in Washington. When Ault asked what information Smeltzer had gathered at the Pentagon regarding Craig, Smeltzer replied that Washington considered it urgent to desegregate the base and was disappointed that blacks were not yet enrolled in the University of Alabama classes. When Smeltzer hinted that the Pentagon was reviewing Craig's future, a topic of obvious interest to the colonel, Ault conversed enthusiastically and at length—"launching into a speech," in Smeltzer's words—about the importance of Craig. Ault emphasized that the base should not be used to desegregate Selma and that national security, which the all-weather, year-round base provided, was more important than integration.

To improve communication between Craig's officers and black enlisted men, Smeltzer challenged Ault with a bold initiative by suggesting that Ault meet with three black airmen as Smeltzer's guests over dinner to discuss the base's problems. After quickly giving theoretical support for the plan, Ault hedged with questions about where such a meeting could occur. Certainly any location in Selma was out, especially Smeltzer's hotel room, because the community would learn of it immediately. (Ault believed that Selma's spies knew that Smeltzer was visiting Craig at this very moment.) There were no private facilities on the base. Smeltzer hypothesized that if he lived in Selma, he could invite the group himself; he knew of several integrated gatherings of clergy. Ault wondered why the neighbors had not seen anything at the clergy gatherings and maintained that integrated meetings were illegal, which Smeltzer disputed. Ault also objected to Smeltzer's request that civilian clothes be worn at the dinner. Both agreed that it was a "strange and inhuman" situation when people could not invite whomever they wanted into their homes, but Ault never took the blunt hint to offer his residence.

Smeltzer considered his mediation attempts with Ault to be constructive. They departed as friends, and even if Ault disappointed Smeltzer by not agreeing to the suggestion for a meeting with black enlisted men, at least the colonel was thinking about new approaches and issues.[9]

Although it is impossible to measure the precise impact of Smeltzer on the Craig base, he felt his mediation contributed to several successes including the opening of the housing project and the integration of the University of Alabama extension courses. (Perhaps Smeltzer would have been more accurate in claiming that his prodding resulted in the acceleration of Ault's timetable for these steps.) Problems remaining were bus and school segregation, job discrimination, and segregation signs; Smeltzer also was disappointed when Ault missed a Pentagon training session on integration. Nevertheless, Smeltzer's visits produced results— the Craig interracial committee met in May at Smeltzer's suggestion—and Ault took Smeltzer seriously. The colonel considered Smeltzer "a pleasant chap . . . sympathetic to my position." There was increased awareness of black concerns by Craig authorities, and interracial communication had improved, although Smeltzer continued to act as a go-between. Black activists on the base supported his work and believed that he contributed to progress at Craig.[10]

Smeltzer's Efforts in Selma

Although Smeltzer concentrated on Craig during much of the second quarter of 1964, in Selma he continued working toward his goals of learning about the community and establishing himself as a neutral mediator. He hoped that in a crisis situation the police and even extremists would recognize his reconciling mission. Smeltzer discovered that although black grievances continued to build, concessions from whites, especially elected officials, were unlikely, and many whites continued to plead ignorance of any racial problems in Selma.

After several months of involvement in Selma, Smeltzer concluded that an overwhelming majority of the city's population, both black and white, would lean in whichever direction the pressure was greatest. He assumed that only a small portion of the white community, approximately 10 percent, were extreme segregationists, but many in this minority were vocal, powerful economic and political intimidators. At the other end of the spectrum, he thought that another 10 percent of the white community were moderates or genuine integrationists, and the remaining 80 percent would go along with the strongest pressure. Blacks were similarly divided. Perhaps 10 percent were extreme integrationists—vocal, educated, and courageous—and another 10 percent were "Uncle Toms" in collusion with segregation. In the middle was the vast majority, who would swim with the strongest tide.[11]

Several afternoons were spent at the *Times-Journal* office reading back copies of the newspaper and enjoying courteous treatment from the staff. (A Selma friend explained to Smeltzer that the hospitality probably resulted from the assumption that he was a federal investigator, but after the newspaper learned his true identity, the politeness continued because he was a preacher.) Smeltzer also exchanged information with John Doar at the Justice Department and others in Washington. He provided Doar with details on the Dunn case and supplied names for Justice Department attorneys to interview in preparation for a voting rights discrimination case.

Smeltzer, the Die-hards, and White Optimism

As the passing months blurred, slightly, the memory of the September 1963 SNCC demonstrations, by early 1964 many in Selma noticed the absence of public pressure, especially in the form of organized activities, and believed that tensions were easing. A March mayoral election, in which young, ambitious Joseph T. Smitherman upset the incumbent, Chris Heinz, contributed to this guarded optimism. Smitherman promised equal, professional law enforcement, code words signaling a change from the aggressive policies of Sheriff Clark, and planned to defend segregation with less strident tactics that would not discourage new industry from locating in Selma.

Forgetting the turbulence of 1963 and reassured by superficial tranquillity in early 1964, many in Selma's white establishment continued to support the traditional approach to race relations, unwilling to admit that Selma faced anything but racial harmony. Although Smeltzer quickly won the confidence of Selma's black leadership, the absence of alarm in the white establishment made it less receptive to him. In 1963, Smeltzer's ministry to white Selma had begun with discussions with the clergy (see Chapter 2), and he had progressively worked from the fringes toward the core of Selma's political and economic power structure. By June 1964, seven months after he first arrived in Selma, Smeltzer was able to introduce himself and his mission to four of Selma's and Dallas County's most important officeholders—Sheriff Jim Clark, Mayor Chris Heinz, Judge Bernard Reynolds of the probate court, and A. C. Allen, a member of the Board of Voter Registration—all of whom displayed little inclination to budge from the traditional, segregationist philosophy that made Selma infamous in civil rights circles.

C. C. Brown's assistance enabled Smeltzer to become acquainted with Clark and Heinz. Brown took Smeltzer to City Hall to meet the lame-duck mayor and, after introducing Smeltzer, Brown left. When Brown took Smeltzer to the courthouse to meet Sheriff Clark, he went in first to determine if Clark would see Smeltzer. Clark initially refused because he was tired of outsiders; Selma already had enough do-gooders. Brown countered that Smeltzer was a friend. "Won't you see my friend?" he asked. "Oh, all right, if he's a friend of yours," Clark replied.

Smeltzer explained to the white officeholders that he was there merely to get acquainted and, guessing their thoughts, denied being an agitator. Instead of creating trouble, he said, he wanted to reduce tensions. Smeltzer pointed out that the Brethren had no congregation in Selma or even in the region; therefore, he was in town not out of self-interest but only because he cared about peace. He offered quiet, confidential assistance without personal credit or publicity, adding a request that his visits be kept secret. He told Heinz he knew that the mayor was concerned about the situation and dropped the name of the mayor's pastor, Dr. Kerlin, as a source.

Smeltzer discovered that Selma's powerful white officeholders were unapologetic segregationists who believed that there was no racial problem. Selma's races got along remarkably well, at least they did until the agitators showed up. Heinz admitted to being a strong segregationist and, assuming that Smeltzer was not, advised that when in Rome, do as the Romans do. Three times, Heinz warned Smeltzer not to eat in a black home, not even Brown's, an act that violated a strong southern taboo. Clark claimed that a Department of Health, Education, and Welfare study on intelligence showed that blacks had less brain matter than whites.

Segregationists quickly pointed out that northern racial problems were more severe than those in the South, and they portrayed Selma's society as racially serene, although their descriptions of ideal racial interactions contained many condescending and patronizing attitudes. As evidence of normal race relations, Heinz offered a story about a black employee of his, whose wife had punctured his stomach with an icepick. The wound did not heal properly, so Heinz took the man to the hospital and personally paid for most of the costs of the operation. Jim Clark told Smeltzer that he never locked his house, that he had neighbors of both races, that he knew approximately 60 percent of the county's blacks by name and more by face, and that blacks brought him gifts. Judge Reynolds asserted that he gave a majority of his time to the blacks who came into his office because they required extra assistance in completing paperwork.

Responding to charges of voting discrimination, A. C. Allen maintained that the voter registration board was scrupulously fair and that blacks made unreasonable demands on the board to change or evade the law. Although the current board was being sued by the Justice Department, Allen claimed that it was the previous board that had displayed unfairness, not the present one. According to Allen, the problem was that most blacks, even some with master's degrees, were illiterate; most black teachers were just handed their diplomas by Alabama State. For example, when one black's application was rejected, he returned with a master's degree but surveillance (by whom?) revealed that he did nothing but fish in the meantime. As proof of black ignorance, Allen revealed that when black applicants finally learned to answer the "What is the Constitution?" question with, "It is a document," the board changed the question to, "Who is Vice-President and what are his duties?" Blacks still responded, "It is a document." Most whites in Selma, including the moderate–progressive minority, believed that the board was honest and interpreted the law fairly to blacks and whites alike. The law that the board enforced, not the board itself, was discriminatory, and illiterate whites also suffered from the rigid law.

Mayor Heinz suggested that time and patience would solve Selma's problems and that better education and moral uplift were the most certain paths to advancement for blacks, who should improve themselves just as Jews and Catholics had done. Heinz urged Smeltzer to advise blacks to rely on patience and improved health and sanitation standards; when he bought and rented houses, he always installed a tub, the mayor said. Heinz refused to comment on Smeltzer's metaphorical suggestion that Selma was a steam boiler about to explode and that Selma needed the steam released slowly.

Segregationist politicians occasionally expressed fear of white extremists such as the National States Rights Party and the Ku Klux Klan. Heinz emphasized the risks because he felt threatened by the white lunatics; if he did not arrive home thirty minutes after leaving the office, his wife had instructions to look for him. Smeltzer acknowledged the danger and told Heinz that all people of goodwill had to accept the risks, as Christ did.

The familiar incantation against outside agitators was a staple of each conversation with the segregationists. Clark allowed that a few local black leaders were responsible people, but he categorized several national black leaders and outside agitators (i.e., civil rights organizers sent to Selma) as irresponsible, immoral, and sexually perverted. Reynolds maintained that Selma's race relations were the best they had been for fifty years until outside agitators came a year ago, and that there would be no trouble this coming summer unless agitators created it. Reynolds repeated his concerns about agitators three times in his conversation with Smeltzer, but he graciously added that Smeltzer was not one of them. He conceded that tensions between blacks and whites had increased over the last year or two.

Smeltzer's discussions with the segregationist politicians produced mixed results. For example, Smeltzer's talk with Sheriff Clark was long and cordial. Smeltzer actually broke off the meeting; he got up twice to leave, but Clark wanted to keep on talking. Smeltzer prepared for the meeting with over a page of notes, "Agenda for Clark," emphasizing to Clark the opportunity he had to help the community, but he never got a chance to make his point.[12]

Unknown to Smeltzer, however, Clark resented Smeltzer's question about the treatment of blacks during slavery because he thought the Yankee preacher was trying to make him feel guilty. Undoubtedly, Smeltzer's reference to slavery was an attempt to establish common ground with the sheriff by appealing to the morality and sense of decency within him—within everyone, thought Smeltzer—but unfortunately Clark's response was not what Smeltzer expected. (Smeltzer probably expected Clark to acknowledge the injustice of slavery.) Immediately after Clark's talk with Smeltzer, the sheriff discussed the conversation with R. W. Head, an investigator from Al Lingo's office.[13]

Smeltzer's first meeting with Mayor Heinz encouraged Smeltzer because it went better than he expected. The two men had a friendly and open discussion, although Heinz opposed all demonstrations and promised to use fire hoses if necessary to prevent marches on City Hall. But he also criticized Sheriff Clark's methods, explaining that brutality toward animals or humans was wrong. Heinz would not see a delegation with more than

three people and refused admittance to any racially mixed committees. Heinz wanted the city to build a swimming pool for
blacks, but funding was a problem. (In an aside, he remarked
that it was odd that whites want to get darker and blacks want
to get lighter.) Heinz even struck a common chord with Smeltzer
with the thought that he was related to a Smeltzer.

Only Allen responded negatively. He broke off the meeting
after about fifteen minutes and indicated little interest in future
conversations with Smeltzer.[14]

Tensions Build

In spite of the many officials who believed that all was well with
Selma's race relations, the evidence contradicted this optimism.
Black complaints about injustice continued, and interracial
confrontations persisted. For example, Amelia Boynton charged
that when a camera crew from the National Education Association visited, the sheriff's deputies, who were alerted by Mississippi law enforcement officials, surrounded her house.[15]

As Easter approached, rumors circulated that blacks planned
kneel-ins at white churches. Clark responded with a letter, addressed to congregations rather than pastors, offering the assistance of the sheriff's department on Easter Sunday and requesting
written confirmation of any request for assistance. Although no
church wanted Clark's posse riding up and down outside their
building on Easter Sunday, his letter received a varied reaction.[16]

Even the news in Selma was segregated, and Selma's blacks
developed several grievances regarding the *Times-Journal,* especially its policy of putting all news about blacks in a separate
"colored" edition. F. D. Reese and Marie Foster met with publisher Roswell Falkenberry to urge the abandonment of the two-
edition policy.[17] Smeltzer encouraged Boynton to express black
concerns to Kathryn Windham, an open-minded reporter on the

Times-Journal staff, and to ask Windham to cover a Monday evening mass meeting. Boynton was unacquainted with Windham, exemplifying once again the communication gap between black and white Selma. Windham was a perceptive and sensitive reporter interested in fairness, a potential asset to the movement, but even the activist Boynton did not know Windham until Smeltzer suggested her name. Smeltzer was moving closer to his goal of learning to know the city better than the natives did.

The possibility of a dangerous confrontation between Clark and the black townspeople arose when the sheriff, who was never allowed to enter a Voters League meeting, let it be known that he would come to the next meeting if he had to break down the door. To prevent a probable escalation of an already tense situation, Smeltzer suggested that Clark not be locked out (in order to avoid arrest for a fire-code violation) and further advised blacks to invite FBI agents, whose presence would help Doar in his case against Clark. (Smeltzer specified that the invitation be written and hand-delivered by two couriers.) Although Boynton and Doyle distrusted the FBI, they agreed to follow Smeltzer's advice, and Clark's deputies began attending mass meetings.[18] Black leaders also announced that the coming summer demonstrations would be publicized beforehand, a strategy that, if not suggested by Smeltzer, certainly would have received his strong support.

Nevertheless, when blacks felt that the *Times-Journal* misquoted meeting speakers, the admittance of sheriff's department observers continued to be an issue. At the next meeting, two plainclothes officers were challenged at the door with a request to leave so that the meeting could go about its "business unfettered and free from all forms of intimidation."[19]

The black boycott of downtown Selma businesses continued into the spring of 1964. When several merchants proposed to answer a letter sent by boycotting civil rights activists, Citizens Council partisans were powerful enough to veto the idea. Some merchants had mixed feelings about the boycott, however, and privately refused to walk in lock-step with the council. For example, Smeltzer talked to a department store owner who felt slightly embarrassed by the boycott because he believed he had always treated blacks well by cashing hundreds of checks each week and by winning the trust of illiterate blacks. Although the store employed black porters and stockroom employees, the owner found it impossible to employ black clerks because other merchants would protest.

Inadequate interracial communication remained a crucial problem in Selma. In spite of the assertions of Selma's segregationists that they had excellent communication with the black community—much better than Yankees had with their blacks—the die-hards were usually not personally acquainted with Selma's black leadership. Black leaders were disappointed when Smeltzer told them that what Selma's whites feared most was a takeover of elective offices by uncultured and uneducated blacks.

Communication in Selma was so poor that even the establishment of a black negotiating committee, acceptable to both the black and white communities, was difficult. Not only were some names unacceptable to whites, but rivalries and misunderstandings within the black ranks also hindered the emergence of a united black negotiating team. The only name that was readily agreeable to both sides was F. D. Reese. Amelia Boynton was too militant for whites, and blacks rejected several of their own leaders for reasons such as shallowness or verbosity. C. C. Brown and Edwin Moss enjoyed more respect among whites than most blacks did, but each had lost ground recently within his own camp for irregular attendance at mass meetings. Some charged that Moss and Brown attended mass meetings only when they were to speak at them, and Brown was further burdened with a perceived lack of support for the 1963 demonstrations.

Smeltzer made several suggestions to the black leadership to enable them to communicate more effectively, and he proposed to them a black negotiating team of Reese, Brown, Moss, and

Foster. He urged black support for Brown and greater appreciation for his contributions to the movement. Smeltzer also suggested that Reese encourage Boynton to be less demanding and antagonistic toward white officials.

Reminders of Selma's dangers continued. Although one merchant was unable to suggest to Smeltzer any next steps for Selma, he reminded Smeltzer of the hazards involved and specifically asked Smeltzer if his room was bugged! Concern over secure use of the telephone mounted. C. C. Brown strongly suggested that Smeltzer avoid using the Hotel Albert switchboard for confidential calls because once Brown had a long, confidential telephone conversation from the hotel with a visiting religious executive, and shortly thereafter a Selma police official recounted to Brown major portions of the talk. Brown suggested that Smeltzer use a phone booth. In June, Smeltzer wrote a note to remind himself to emphasize to everyone not to quote him.

Unknown to Smeltzer, but surely suspected by him, law enforcement authorities had placed him under surveillance. An Alabama state investigator determined that Smeltzer was in town to "solicit Negro and white mixing," but the investigator was unable to locate Smeltzer for another day or two—until he strolled into Sheriff Clark's office for a talk. State investigators mistakenly believed that Smeltzer was paid by "the President's Committee on Poverty" and "works out of Bobby Kennedy's office, along with Sergeant Schriver, Peace Core [sic]." The state investigation concluded that Smeltzer was responsible for the integration of the housing project and the extension school courses at Craig and listed his phone calls.[20]

Although Selma's spring was quiet, blacks planned to turn up the heat during the summer. As the long-awaited Civil Rights bill ran the gantlet of congressional politics, its final passage promised to add another emotional element to Selma's unstable chemistry, and the city was now a major target of the civil rights movement. Leaders of SNCC considered Selma to be so important that they planned to send their best workers there and hoped to have twenty-five well-trained people in the voter registration line on every day the books were open in early July. Clark was unpredictable, and some members of his posse were rumored to be eager for violence.

While civil rights groups plotted their course, those on Selma's far right were similarly active. About fifty members of the National States Rights Party met June 8 in a local motel. Their threat was real enough that when Smeltzer asked a Jewish merchant to participate in an interracial discussion, he declined because he wanted to be careful about participating in public meetings. The businessman understood that the party had singled him out as a "Jew, Communist, nigger-lover," and the attack made him cautious.

As the summer sun warmed Selma, the components for a blowup congealed. The white segregationist establishment blamed the problems on outsiders; if only the agitators would go home, racial problems would disappear, and the peaceful status quo would return. Blacks planned a summer of activity; moderate whites feared the worst, but they remained silent. The city power structure quietly prepared for solid resistance, and merchants promised not to compromise.

In late June, Martin Luther King, Jr., announced that Selma would be one of several southern cities subjected to court tests as soon as the Civil Rights bill became law in Washington. The following night, while a mass meeting was under way a block down the street at the First Baptist Church, a cross burned on Sylvan Street, in front of Brown's Chapel.[21]

4

A Summer Storm

I have been a member of the [Board of Registrars] for nine years. I have not discriminated against either white or colored since being under an injunction issued by Judge Thomas about 18 months ago. I hope when I die and face God for judgment I will be as innocent as I was when I faced this federal court on this charge by the "so-called" Justice Department.

J. A. Blackburn, Perry County

The Negro help do not approve of integration. . . . They have always been happy with the present arrangement and are unhappy with the testing [of compliance with the Civil Rights Act]. One long-time cook even weeps to think about what is coming.

A waitress at the Splendid Restaurant

Selma is a tremendous and challenging social engineering job in achieving peace and reconciliation based on justice.

Ralph E. Smeltzer

This place could be a real Donnybrook.

FBI agent Robert Frye

In March 1964, Smeltzer took his laundry to Selma's Superior Cleaners where an inquisitive owner pumped him with questions. Did Smeltzer live in Selma? Why was he in town? The first reason that occurred to Smeltzer was that he was connected with broadcasting, so that was what he said. Then the proprietor asked if he was connected with the recent broadcast of Amelia Boynton, and Smeltzer said no. When Smeltzer picked up his clothing, the owner remembered him by name.

Smeltzer used the Superior Cleaners again in early July. When he delivered his laundry, the owner said hello, but when Smeltzer returned, the owner called him by name and asked why he was in Selma this time. "Church business," Smeltzer replied. The owner said, "I thought you said last time you were with an Atlanta TV station." Smeltzer said he was not with an Atlanta station and never said so; he was just working on an audiovisual project. The owner adamantly repeated his understanding that Smeltzer was with the television station, which Smeltzer again denied before quickly departing. Smeltzer wrote himself a reminder not to return to the Superior Cleaners because he felt the owner's curiosity created a security threat.[1]

The 1964 Civil Rights Act

On July 2, 1964, President Lyndon B. Johnson ended one of the most difficult legislative battles in congressional history by signing the Civil Rights Act of 1964 into law. Although Smeltzer was grateful for what the federal law gave to blacks—for example, the ending of discrimination in public accommodations such as restaurants, businesses, and transportation—he feared that the legislation created new dangers for Selma. The local civil rights movement remained institutionally disorganized and inarticulate, and communication between the movement and the white leadership was nonexistent. The correction of both these problems had high priorities for Smeltzer. Because of the inchoate movement and inadequate communication, testing (i.e., attempting to implement the new law by personal visits to previously segregated areas) involving Selma's two white movie theaters and several restaurants was sporadic and uncoordinated. Blacks who tested the provisions of the new law did not consider either white sensibilities or the potential for personal injury, and neither restaurants and theaters nor law enforcement authorities were given prior notice of such testing. Confrontations and street violence resulted, raising fears of a bloody future for Selma. The events of early July 1964 demonstrated that Smeltzer's apprehensions about Selma's situation were realistic.

Selma's movie theaters became an early testing ground for the new law. Early in the day on Saturday, July 4, a lone black youth broke the color line at the Walton Theater by sitting in the movie house for about thirty minutes. Later in the day, when blacks began sitting in the Wilby Theater's white section, a group of whites approached the ticket window, and one of them shouted, "There's niggers in the Wilby." A crowd of youths of both races gathered outside. Sheriff Clark's men cleared them away with nightsticks, but within minutes of the incident, bumper-to-bumper traffic clogged the streets; every parking spot for two blocks was occupied as curious whites, including women and children, gathered on the sidewalks to watch what would happen at the Wilby. With these developments in mind, the manager went inside and advised the blacks "to let [him] escort them outside in the interest of their safety," although they were free to remain. They were about to leave when two white men entered, one of them yelling, "Where are them niggers?" A short time later, Clark arrived, sent everyone home, and closed the theater.[2] By 6:40 P.M., Saturday both theaters were closed for the evening. A week later, James Gildersleeve, a professor at the Lutheran Academy, and a female Selma University student quietly entered a theater and viewed the movie for about an hour.[3]

Blacks also tested Selma's restaurant facilities. On Friday, blacks left quietly after being refused admittance at a downtown restaurant and a drive-in, but on Saturday, Clark arrested, on trespassing charges, four young blacks at the Thirsty Boy, a short-order establishment, when they attempted to obtain service. Clark used his cattle prod on one of the blacks because, he explained later, a prod was the safest way to move someone who refuses to move. Another of the four youths, nineteen-year-old Carol Lawson, was further charged with carrying a concealed weapon; Clark found what he called a "weighted chain" in her purse, although civil rights people said it was merely a broken medallion. (At the trial later, Clark called it a "slung shot," a weighted bicycle chain. Lawson said the "weight" was a lock that she used for her bicycle.[4])

Later that Saturday night, scores of officers responded to a reported brick-throwing incident at a restaurant that continued to refuse blacks. Although the sheriff's men found no rock throwers, again, as at the theater, traffic jams and crowds of the curious appeared. Also on Saturday night, three white teenagers were treated for cuts at a local hospital after a sodapop bottle was thrown through their car window.[5]

On Sunday night, July 5, the violence grew more serious; a riot broke out following a SNCC-sponsored mass meeting. As participants left the church, a shot was fired, and bricks and bottles suddenly were hurled through the air. The posse charged with nightsticks and tear gas into the black crowd. The melee lasted about twenty minutes. Two blacks were brought to the infirmary bleeding extensively from blows on the head, and Clark reported that several of his deputies were slightly injured. Among those attacked were two journalists from Ohio, who claimed that Solicitor Blanchard McLeod screamed at them to get out of town, and threatened that "if you stop, you'll be killed. You'll be followed." An unmarked station wagon followed them for about fifteen minutes on the road to Montgomery. Clark stated publicly, "I hate to think what might have happened if the posse hadn't been on hand to beef up the regular force of officers."[6]

Smeltzer Finds White Resistance

Smeltzer, sensing that the city would be in danger, was en route to Selma several days after the passage of the Civil Rights Act. During a layover in Atlanta, he called his contacts in Washington, who painted a perilous picture of Selma. Smeltzer learned that John Doar had spent an hour on the phone with F. D. Reese at 3:00 A.M. and that Father Ouellet, who might have been a stabilizing presence, was on vacation. (When Ouellet returned, he stressed caution to blacks but was not heeded.) Washington people told Smeltzer that some of the SNCC workers hoped to use the Civil Rights Act to escalate drastically the pressure on white Selma and force the deployment of federal troops, a development that would have confirmed the most paranoid conspiracy theories of white conservatives. Doar believed that if blacks carefully avoided violence—and the previous night there had been a rifle shot outside the police station—white community leaders would eventually turn against Clark.[7]

On his arrival there, Smeltzer found a Selma that resembled an armed camp with Clark's deputies, the posses, and state troopers (fifteen of them lodging at Smeltzer's hotel) on the streets. His first week in Selma in July was frustrating and "desperate"; he implored blacks to remain nonviolent and sought restraint and patience from both sides. He searched for business leaders willing to step into the leadership vacuum before major violence broke out, but he was unsuccessful in establishing contact between black and white leaders. Smeltzer recorded that he spent the week "trying but completely failing to establish direct communications between elected officials and Negro leaders—instead running back and forth between them."[8]

The day after the disturbance at the mass meeting, racial confrontations continued. On the afternoon of Smeltzer's arrival, Clark arrested forty-nine blacks who were demanding the right to vote on the steps of the Dallas County Courthouse across the street from the Federal Building. Clark's posse made the arrests, and the men freely used their cattle prods as they walked the freedom-song-singing marchers to jail five blocks away. Posse members also arrested adults with juveniles in their company when the youths became involved in activities such as carrying signs; and in a curious twist of law, Clark charged forty-one adult blacks with contributing to the delinquency of one minor, Claude Nelson. Clark later explained that there were many juveniles present, but authorities named only the youngest in the arrest papers.[9] That evening, the Voters League held its regular Monday night mass meeting, which, although surrounded by the posse, was violence free.

Selma's white extremists contributed to the ominous environment. On July 6, the Ku Klux Klan met, and a National States Rights Party Executive Committee planned attacks on blacks. Agents of the FBI infiltrated both gatherings. Approximately fifty people attended a States Rights rally the following night.[10]

Smeltzer learned that many whites, including moderate segregationists, remained unreconciled to the Civil Rights Act and unwilling to surrender to its authority. He discovered that many of Selma's restaurants planned to avoid, somehow, compliance with the public accommodations provisions. At Smeltzer's first meal in Selma after the bill's passage, breakfast at the Splendid Restaurant, he was invited to join a newly forming "supper club" that would make the establishment private and, it was hoped, immune from federal legislation. The proprietor, clearly harried, had been up late the previous night with his lawyer working on club plans and was printing membership cards by hand to get them in use; in fact, the owner was disappointed not to have the "club" operation ready that day. The Splendid willingly assumed a financial burden to avoid serving blacks because the shift to a private club required a new sign and entrance. The new format might cost the restaurant business, but it was also expected that some people would join the club merely to support the concept.

A few days later Smeltzer got his membership application for the Splendid Club. Included was a request to abide by the rules and bylaws of the club. Smeltzer asked for a copy of them, but the employee offering the application reacted uncomfortably and, professing ignorance about rules, told Smeltzer just to pay his dollar and bring his guests.

Smeltzer visited other eating establishments in town to discover their reactions to the Civil Rights Act but found little in the way of a pattern. Responses varied. Several restaurants evidently had no plans for dealing with the law or else were not sharing them with strangers. "Clarice," a waitress who served Smeltzer at the Selma Del, knew of no plans at that establishment in the event that the restaurant was tested, but she was confident that her boss would not ask her to serve blacks against her will. Clarice confided that she was afraid of blacks and thought that they followed her home at night. She also repeated a rumor that the Holiday Inn would comply with the law and that one waitress had left her job in protest.

The manager of Perrin's Cafeteria tersely replied that he "couldn't say" what he would do if blacks came, and Swift's Drug Store took out its lunch counter rather than face the question; the stools were removed and merchandise was placed on and in front of the counter. The owner of Tim's Cafe advocated resistance and professed amazement over why southern restaurant owners complied. If everyone resisted, he said, the jails could not hold them all, which was a page from Martin Luther King's methodology!

Procrastination—a request for several weeks to grow accustomed to the law—was the least-resistant line from one local restaurateur. One owner explained that when Selma's citizens visited large, successfully integrated cities, then they would be more receptive to desegregation. Selma would eventually accept the new ways, but tradition was stronger in Selma than in other places, and its large black population was threatening to whites. Montgomery, for example, was only 25 percent black, an important difference. The owner continued to explain that because Selma had thirty restaurants—too many for a small city—many owners felt acute financial pressure in this crisis, and a loss of business for a few weeks would be catastrophic.

To confirm rumors that the local Holiday Inn planned to comply with the Civil Rights Act, Smeltzer ran a test of his own. He called the desk to make reservations for "three negro school teacher friends of ours from the North" and booked the reservations routinely. Fifteen minutes later, Smeltzer called back to remind the clerk that his friends were black and explained that he was not interested in embarrassing them but only wanted them to have the best accommodations in town. The clerk understood that his "friends" were black. When he asked Smeltzer for his name and phone, he replied, "R. Johnson, 4-5712," which turned out to be a real phone number. Smeltzer called the Holiday Inn again on Monday to cancel the reservation and received an assurance that the calls would be kept in confidence.

While Smeltzer toiled behind the scenes to improve long-range communication, the streets continued to be active and tense. On Wednesday, July 8, Reese drove two juvenile, "one-man, one-vote" pickets to the courthouse and was arrested when he returned to his office for contributing to the delinquency of a minor. Moss began immediate action to secure bail for Reese, but Smeltzer learned from Peter Hall, a civil rights lawyer, that Reese planned to refuse bail and remain in jail for a day or two. Smeltzer informed Mrs. Reese of her husband's decision.

The voter registration campaign and the testing of the civil rights laws combined to put seventy activists behind Sheriff Clark's bars by the end of the week; accusations, counteraccusations, and ill feelings proliferated. Members of SNCC accused Clark of beating a thirteen-year-old boy, which the sheriff denied, but a jailer admitted to striking an adult, who allegedly cursed at and attempted to hit him. Two English exchange students, traveling through Selma, were detained for three hours for "making a nuisance of themselves" downtown with critical remarks about racial issues. The students claimed that police ille-

gally searched their car and confiscated film for their camera.[11]
With much of the movement's leadership in jail, activity decreased, and on Thursday, July 9, Circuit Judge James Hare shut down civil rights efforts effectively with an injunction that prohibited nearly fifty specifically named blacks and fifteen organizations from holding public meetings of more than three people, which banned everything from the steering committee of the Dallas County Voters League to the Monday night mass meetings. Heinz and Clark asked Hare to issue the injunction in the interests of public safety, and the judge agreed. Civil rights lawyers immediately appealed to the federal district court, but Judge Daniel Thomas did not hear the case until mid-September. Then, weeks and months went by without a decision, while the injunction remained in effect.[12]

As Smeltzer became increasingly familiar with Selma's white community, he discovered that the only position with public expression of support was die-hard resistance, although some influential whites—generally merchants and bankers—privately supported modest concessions, such as compliance with the Civil Rights Act. He went directly to the few businessmen who enjoyed respect across the entire white community to urge their public help, emphasizing that the situation would worsen before it improved and that personal influence was insufficient. Public action by groups and organizations was critical.

Smeltzer's appeal for public support for moderation failed to prod anyone to significant action. Moderate whites were timid and often believed that Smeltzer's position lacked the required support to begin negotiations. One business leader, Charles Hohenburg, had drafted a letter the day after the church bombing in Birmingham in 1963 that repudiated the act and offered to blacks immediate negotiations, although requesting retention of "valuable traditions." He was primed to ask sixteen of Selma's leading citizens to support the letter, but when the SNCC demonstrations began at the courthouse, no one would sign. Hohenburg asked Smeltzer several times not to mention the letter to anyone, and because of this early "fiasco," approximately one year before Smeltzer met him, Hohenburg refused to assume any leadership.[13]

Because municipal officials remained unyielding, many in Selma looked to and waited for the merchants to take the lead or to press the city government to act. But whites remained fearful of the Citizens Council, and the Merchants Association and local politicians would not act to improve race relations until the council sent favorable signals. The council did not even support discussions with black leaders, however, much less concessions or changes.

The possibility of a white boycott also threatened merchants. Business leaders felt tremendous pressure from their white customers and considered a white boycott more devastating, perhaps fatally so, than a similar black action. One merchant, exemplifying the attitude of the storekeepers, maintained that there was little more he could do to help because he already had blacks waiting on black customers, had taken down segregation signs, and had allowed blacks and whites to use the same dressing rooms. A photo of a tanned model in his store window attracted Citizens Council criticism because the model (a white) looked dark and he was asked to remove it.[14]

Smeltzer had not yet abandoned efforts to persuade segregationist officials to improve communication with blacks, and he talked with Judge Hare, a die-hard traditionalist, for two hours. Hare understood that Smeltzer was from the federal poverty program—Washingtonians were considered the most sinister outsiders—and the judge believed that outside blacks and the federal government were trying to destroy him. According to Hare, Bobby Kennedy ruthlessly forced integration on local communities, and one of the top SCLC leaders was a sex pervert. Hare theorized that Selma's blacks descended from African tribes of low intelligence, Berbers and Congolese. The judge said he refused to ride on trains or go to Washington because of uncouth blacks.

Judge Hare's top priority was the preservation of law and order, but with Smeltzer's prodding, he agreed that law and order were merely prerequisites and that Selma needed to move on to constructive measures. Hare believed that the drastic social change demanded by the civil rights movement could only come through slowly changing social customs, not through legislation. The judge prophesied further trouble for Selma, and he was under the impression that six carloads of blacks from Saint Augustine (i.e., more outside agitators) were driving to Selma. (Saint Augustine was the target of the most recent SCLC campaign.[15])

Smeltzer wanted Hare to meet with black leaders, and he struggled to find common ground with the judge by proposing that Reese, Moss, and himself meet with Hare to plan later, more formal discussions. Evidently Smeltzer extracted from Hare assurances that he would meet with "responsible black leaders"—Smeltzer's stock phrase describing black leaders to whites—because immediately after the meeting, Smeltzer suggested to Ed Moss that they visit the judge to arrange a conference. Smeltzer declined Moss's request to telephone Hare and urged Moss to do it because a Moss contact would be a small step toward improved, or at any rate initial, communication. Two days later Smeltzer had a chance encounter with Hare in Perrine's Cafeteria and said, "I mentioned to a couple of responsible leaders your willingness to see them, and one or two may contact you." Hare replied, "Well, they already know they can see me anytime."[16]

Hare's injunction against civil rights activity was so sweeping that Smeltzer feared that it might prevent the kind of private meetings he felt would be most helpful. Would a private meeting between him and three or four black leaders who happened to be named in the injunction be a violation of the order? To determine if the injunction placed his ministry in jeopardy, Smeltzer telephoned Hare at the judge's home at 9:20 on a Sunday morning. Smeltzer dangled the possibility that he might be able to help officials receive prior notice of testing, and Hare assured him that the injunction did not include anything done in private—only public and street meetings.[17]

As cordial and cooperative as Hare was over the phone, Smeltzer learned from Art Lewis that the judge distrusted him and doubted his sincerity. Hare suspected that do-gooders must have ulterior motives. Another die-hard remained unmoved by Smeltzer's appeals.

As the conservatives became increasingly determined to resist the civil rights movement, Smeltzer's relations with them deteriorated. His last visit to Mayor Heinz's office lasted only ten minutes. Heinz welcomed him and said he would talk about anything but race relations, which he could not discuss with outsiders. Smeltzer managed to comment that blacks considered Heinz inaccessible, but the mayor insisted that he would see them any time and that they knew it. Heinz grew increasingly suspicious of Smeltzer and began to say that he would only work with people he knew from his childhood.

When C. C. Brown did meet with the mayor, it discouraged him and left him feeling that further communication with the uncompromising, lame-duck official was futile. Brown told Heinz that demonstrations could not be postponed much longer and that only two or three people were holding back the marchers.

Probate Judge Reynolds was unable to offer Smeltzer any encouragement either. Reynolds refused to support the formation of a biracial committee because he considered blacks so factious that it was impossible to deal with them. If concessions were granted to blacks, he claimed, they would just ask for more. Reynolds maintained that even if the courthouse used paper drinking cups and removed Jim Crow signs on the fountains, whites would never give up segregated toilets because of the high rate of venereal disease among blacks. In spite of Reynolds's low opinion of the despised outsiders, he asked Smeltzer for suggestions. Smeltzer mentioned black police, the removal of segregation signs, and basic improvement in communication with black representatives.

A visit with Bill Speed, president of the Restaurant Association, was similarly unproductive. Based on Smeltzer's talks with officials at the Justice Department, the local FBI, and with local blacks, he thought it feasible that, with negotiations, the testings could be kept nonthreatening and limited. Smeltzer wanted to avoid the confrontations that restaurant testing had brought during the first week of July, and he tried to tempt Speed with the possibility of prearranging the details with black leaders. Speed had not met any black leaders, and even with the possibility of influencing the testing, Speed was not interested in negotiations or meetings. He spoke critically about compliance with the Civil Rights Act and said that each manager would follow his conscience. (This individualism enabled each owner to demonstrate to whites his determination to resist. Compliance would come after a court test.)

Security remained a top priority. In the midst of Smeltzer's conversation with Speed at his restaurant, a waitress appeared and without request or announcement photographed Smeltzer, who quickly questioned the picture taking, saying that he liked to work without publicity. Speed assured Smeltzer that the picture was just part of his hobby of photographing customers. Soon the waitress returned and snapped another picture. Speed made sure that he was in this one, and Smeltzer renewed his protest. Speed promised that he would use the pictures only in his personal collection, but after the visit, Smeltzer called back to complain again and to solicit a third promise that the picture not endanger his confidentiality. In another security matter, Claude Brown passed along a warning from a hotel porter that the switchboard was bugged.[18]

At Smeltzer's urging, and perhaps with some pressure from Federal Judge Daniel Thomas, the moderate business leaders became more active.[19] Their dilemma was finding a method that would bring about change but would still permit political leaders to save face because any biracial committee, or at least a group so named, would be a liability for the white politicians associated with it. Smeltzer informed his most frequent contact with the group, the lawyer Edgar Stewart, that blacks considered the lull in demonstrations to be an opportunity to negotiate but that they were concerned because there was no tangible progress. The only encouraging development was Smeltzer's word that several white leaders were working on the problem. Blacks feared that the current calm produced in whites a false sense of security, and they were anxious to continue to move forward.[20]

With the disappointing exception of the die-hard segregationists, Smeltzer's contacts increasingly recognized the value of his work. When a visiting church executive asked a small, integrated meeting of local pastors for suggestions, several replied that assigning to another community a person to replicate Smeltzer's Selma ministry would be ideal. Another group of moderate whites told Smeltzer that they were under the impression he was working hard, "twenty-four hours a day," and that they had confidence he could help. His reputation, pro and con, began to precede him through the city. Once, when Smeltzer introduced himself as "Reverend Smeltzer" to a restaurant owner, his name was already known, and the proprietor replied, "Ralph Smeltzer?"[21]

By this time, Selma's influential people began to hear more about Smeltzer, but confusion over his role persisted. Robert Frye, head of the local FBI office, "knew" that Smeltzer was in town since last fall through an auto check, and several people that Frye interviewed in Selma, plus John Doar in Washington, mentioned Smeltzer to him. Frye also heard that Smeltzer was photographing, which was inaccurate because Smeltzer never took pictures. Smeltzer concluded that Frye must have confused him with someone else.

Rumors continued to circulate, undoubtedly fed by the state investigation (see Chapter 3), that the War on Poverty program in Washington financed Smeltzer, which was a kiss of death for his mission. Art Lewis suggested that Smeltzer produce a letter from the head of the Church of the Brethren declaring that his funding was independent of any federal agency. According to Lewis, the letter should emphasize that Smeltzer's goal was "to prevent the explosion of [the] community," but, above all, the letter should not say that Smeltzer wanted to "get [the] races working together," which implied support for the civil rights movement.

Although Smeltzer picked up a variety of reports that underscored the volatile nature of Selma's racial tension, occasional optimism surfaced in the community. Frye's pessimism cast the worst-case scenario: "This place could be a real Donnybrook," with SNCC, SCLC, and the National States Rights Party here together. But Clark took a small step toward equal law enforcement by arresting a carload of white youths carrying six nightsticks, a rubber hose, and a single sheet of National States Rights Party literature. Clark called a press conference to announce the arrests. Although the entrance of white extremists into Selma inched the city closer to flashpoint, the arrests by Clark were considered by many to be a helpful sign that evenhanded law enforcement was more likely to be the rule in the future than in the past.

Another minor achievement was Craig's hiring of a black secretary—who had an M.A. in business administration! The most that Craig's scholarly typist could earn in Selma was $3,000 a year at Selma University; the air force job, at the bottom of the salary scale, paid $3,800. Several whites in the office objected, but they were told that integration was policy and that they could leave if they did not like it. Another promising trend was that the idea of black police officers was becoming thinkable and even acceptable to influential whites.[22]

Smeltzer found several whites who supported his work; his growing friendship with one of them, Art Lewis, was especially encouraging. During his visit to Selma in early July, Smeltzer talked frequently with Lewis, whom he had met in June. Lewis, a wealthy, progressive Jew, moved to Selma from New Jersey in 1941 to buy a cigar factory, which he sold in 1955. An admired man in Selma, Lewis enjoyed genial relations with many community leaders and provided Smeltzer with insights and suggestions regarding who might be able or inclined to help. At their first meeting, Lewis said that he was in Selma to conform, not reform, but that he wanted to help everyone see the issues clearly. Soon, Lewis and Smeltzer collaborated by exchanging information and names, by keeping one another abreast of their activities (although Lewis was more forthcoming about this than the secretive Smeltzer), and by discussing strategy. Smeltzer considered Lewis a "close informant."[23]

Lewis was very concerned about Selma and feared a bloody summer. Approximately one week after the passage of the Civil Rights Act, Lewis detected improvement in the restaurant situation and offered several suggestions for Smeltzer to pass along to the blacks. He thought that some whites had begun to see the inevitability of public-accommodation desegregation: "They will find they haven't died due to it." To capitalize on this atmosphere, Lewis advised testing restaurants by gently putting a foot in the door individually or in pairs, which would avoid the appearance of taking over a place, and to stay away from restaurants during the rush hour. Because proprietors feared that compliance might bring about a white boycott, Lewis suggested calling ahead and doing several restaurants at once so that complying owners would not be isolated. A few days later, Lewis felt that the atmosphere had become even more favorable for compliance and that many whites would accept "gentle" testing.

Black Frustrations Grow

While white conservatives dug in their heals and moderates fretted, black activists became increasingly frustrated. John Love, a SNCC organizer, saw black attitudes quickly becoming more bitter, and he considered it no longer safe for whites to enter the black community at night; he warned Smeltzer about the new danger and promised to spread the word that he not be molested. Love reported that now black adults, as well as young people, came to him requesting action, even violence. Members of SNCC planned to continue the pressure by testing public accommodations, restaurants first, and the "big question" was whether they would be arrested for "trespassing" by law officers even if they were served. Love was unaware of earlier (1963) talks between white leaders and local blacks until Smeltzer filled him in on them. (A committee headed by C. C. Hunter to discuss a black swimming pool and other recreation issues with Hare had met with very discouraging results.)

Father Ouellet, back from vacation, also experienced the awakening black anger when his counseling of restraint produced little but antagonism from blacks, which complemented the normal hostility he got from whites.[24] Irritation over the injunction was not confined to militants like SNCC's John Love; middle-class, middle-aged Ed Moss reported that the order had so angered and solidified blacks that older people now wanted to join the movement.

Furthermore, Reese and Moss were uninterested in talking to Hare because the black overtures made last fall were ignored; now it was the whites' turn to take the first step. After considerable effort, Smeltzer convinced Reese and Moss that it was impossible for whites to meet with blacks and yet hope to remain influential with their peers. Blacks, according to Smeltzer, needed to go the second mile.

Moss called Hare the next morning. He found that the judge was receptive to the idea of a meeting, but he avoided commitment on a date. Moss dropped Smeltzer's name in the conversation and thought it helped, but eventually the only thing Moss got from Hare was a runaround. A week passed, and Moss was no closer to an appointment with Hare. Smeltzer also asked Moss to test Mayor Heinz's declared willingness to see three blacks, and suggested that Reese, Brown, and Moss form a negotiating team to make the visit. Moss asked whether Brown was willing; Smeltzer said yes. That Moss had to ask Smeltzer about Brown's intentions demonstrates once again the poor communication among black leaders.

An emerging and critical segment of the black community

was its young people, and restraining their excesses was especially important. Thanks to the Civil Rights Act, blacks now had the law on their side; they needed to be careful that adolescent exuberance did not forfeit newly won legal advantages. Recently, Love had stopped fifteen young people on their way downtown to "test". It was pure coincidence that he saw them and averted a potentially damaging situation because, although some whites might tolerate quiet testing, almost no white in Selma defined "quiet" as fifteen black teenagers.

Efforts to Improve Black Organization

Before blacks could communicate effectively with whites, they needed to strengthen their own organizational base. Communication within the movement was hindered not only by its informality but also by rivalries between black leaders. Not only did organizational structures require development but interpersonal relations among black leaders also retarded the blacks' ability to articulate their demands and communicate effectively with whites. Smeltzer devoted much energy toward improvement in these areas.

Although white inertia increasingly disappointed blacks, the tendency of the black leadership to engage in internal bickering remained amazingly vigorous; the growing frustration with whites did not necessarily lead to black unity. Conversations during which black leaders poured out to Smeltzer their suspicions and biases about other blacks troubled him. Most of his talks with black leaders in July produced insults, rumors, scandals, etc., directed against others. Blacks charged disloyalty, overdrinking, lack of commitment, and Catholic proselytizing. Brown and Moss were especially strong rivals; and older, more traditional blacks spread rumors of homosexuality at SNCC headquarters. One prominent black criticized John Love's "mod" fashions, long hair, and jewelry; he likened Love to a Zulu—he looked for a ring in Love's nose. Another black called Love a "Fuzzy Wuzzy." Nevertheless, establishment blacks conceded that SNCC workers had made an important contribution with their influence among the youth, who had shown tremendous courage.

Although many accusations and rumors lacked substance, the "informer" barb had a point. Blacks repeated this indictment often, and federal attorney Bob Jansen confirmed the existence of a major leak. He told black leaders that their opponents knew everything they did and planned to do.

Smeltzer encouraged black leaders to be cooperative in spite of their animosities if they wanted to be effective, and he actively participated in the organization of the first strategy meeting for all black leaders. Because Moss, who was employed by St. Edmund's Catholic mission, might not attend a strategy meeting at the home of a particularly outspoken anti-Catholic, Smeltzer personally made the phone calls arranging a switch to the residence of the universally respected Reese. Also, when blacks agreed to Smeltzer's suggestion to invite Bob Jansen, Smeltzer had Reese call Jansen; Smeltzer could not issue the invitation because he was not a local man, and if a black other than Reese invited Jansen, then a rival might reject the attorney. The meeting with Smeltzer, Jansen, and Selma's black leadership wound up at Selma University, a neutral site, where a large group would be less noticeable than at anyone's residence. Smeltzer considered this meeting to be a major breakthrough because, for the first time, representatives of all the factions in black Selma came together in the same room to discuss strategy. Smeltzer's influence was very important to the success of this event.[25]

Although Selma's blacks had problems relating to one another, Smeltzer's relations with the black community continued to improve. When C. C. Brown said that he wanted to transfer his daughter to a Brethren college, Smeltzer picked up the phone and called Manchester College in Indiana. Brown also offered Smeltzer the use of his car.[26]

Another civil rights activist impressed with Smeltzer was

Marie Foster. After an evening committee meeting with Smeltzer at Boynton's, Foster accompanied Smeltzer to the front porch. Smeltzer wanted to walk in the neighborhood and talk with people to see how they felt about recent developments. It was a dark, miserable night with steady rain and muddy streets, but talking with residents as they sat on their front porches was a standard tactic used by organizers to plumb grass-roots attitudes. Smeltzer was prepared; he had on a raincoat and rubbers, and Foster watched him trudge through the rain into the night. Foster remembers thinking, "There goes a faithful soul."[27]

The Civil Rights Act and Craig Air Force Base

The passage of the Civil Rights Act not only had an impact on Selma but also on Craig Air Force Base. Fitt, in Washington, told Smeltzer that the air force now classified the testing of public accommodations as a right instead of a demonstration, and therefore black airmen engaged in such activities were entitled to official support. Air force people at the Pentagon wanted Ault to press Jim Clark for assurances that air force blacks would be safe.[28] Black airmen generally feared joining the testing of public accommodations in Selma because their service records would be adversely affected if they were arrested. Jailed airmen were considered AWOL and risked demotion; even a traffic ticket earned demerits.

Toward the end of his July visit, Smeltzer discussed with black airmen orderly ways of testing. Enoch Fears, who unofficially assumed leadership of the black airmen after Joe Black's transfer, organized the meeting, which was Smeltzer's second with Craig's blacks. Smeltzer initially refused to attend and agreed only after the men insisted. The meeting was predominantly a social, get-acquainted affair for black enlisted men to discuss mutual problems and decide how often to meet. Smeltzer made a few suggestions regarding the testing of public accommodations: He encouraged order, testing in pairs, and notification

beforehand of the FBI. He also informed the men about memos
Ault received regarding the Civil Rights Act and the rights of servicemen, and he assured them of Ault's support if they tested
public accommodations. Black airmen were especially interested
in obtaining service at the restaurants on the stretch of highway
between Selma and Craig and began testing on July 26 and 27,
several days before testing resumed in Selma.[29]

The weekend after the July civil rights disturbances in Selma,
Colonel Ault ordered a major inspection and discouraged Craig
personnel from going into town. Rumors circulated among enlisted men that everyone would be restricted to base for the
weekend. Instead, Ault ordered all men to wear their uniforms
when they were off the base, assuming that uniforms would
probably secure quicker compliance in public accommodations,
identify servicemen for law enforcement officials, and deter rednecks. An early casualty of the rule was the military men who
held second jobs in Selma; because they could not wear their uniforms at the workplace, they lost their jobs. Soon the rule was altered to require the wearing of the uniform to and from town,
but to allow men to change clothes once they arrived at work.

Meanwhile, Smeltzer's threat that Craig would close became
real when the Pentagon began to consider that possibility, and
Ault gently passed along the word to Selma. Apparently the bus
line from Craig would continue to be segregated for some time.
There was speculation that the owner feared a white reaction to
integration and, to save face, wanted to wait for legal action
forcing him to change. Reportedly, Ault worked out plans with
School Superintendent Pickard to move the University of
Alabama extension courses back to Selma's Baker Junior High;
the Crimson Tide's Selma branch functioned quietly that summer
with blacks and whites together at the airbase.[30] There was also
some thought about having a black serviceman request that his
children be enrolled in the all-white Parrish High School, but the
logical candidate for the challenge feared reprisals and did not
act.

Smeltzer left Selma on July 25 after a nineteen-day stay. He was still briefing people as he ran to catch a bus. He had found Selma so close to danger that he stayed longer than he had planned, and he canceled everything else on his calendar during that period, including a National Council of Churches conference on "The Role of the Church in Controversy" at Lake Geneva, whose July days must have been more appealing than those in the steamy Black Belt.

Smeltzer's Work in Jeopardy

No sooner had Smeltzer returned home to Illinois than he received news from Selma that his work was seriously endangered. In a phone call from Enoch Fears on Tuesday, July 28, the airman recounted a "terrible" turn of events. "We're in trouble," he said. Sheriff Clark's discovery that Smeltzer had attended an Elks meeting with black airmen convinced Clark that it was a civil rights affair in violation of the injunction. Clark broke down the door at the Elks and pulled its liquor license off the wall. Many in Selma were frightened, excited, and emotional. Although Clark learned about the meeting from an FBI report, Fears speculated that Clark's information came from bugging Smeltzer's phone calls. Craig authorities told Fears that he had violated the injunction and that they could not help him, even though jail was a possibility. The Elks were angry with everyone, Fears said, and called him to the Lodge to ask why the airmen had used their facilities for the meeting. (He replied that he had asked for and received permission.[31])

Clark brought Fears to his office to sign an incriminating statement and to identify a photo of a sitting, smiling Ralph Smeltzer. (How did Clark get the photo? Smeltzer assumed it was the Bill Speed picture.) Fears was uncooperative, did not sign the statement, and declined to acknowledge that Smeltzer was at the meeting.

"Frantic calls" from the Justice Department and the U.S. attorney, Jansen, came to Smeltzer in Elgin. Colonel Ault was distressed by the Elks raid, and the incident damaged Smeltzer's relationship with him. In Ault's viewpoint, Smeltzer had put the airbase "squarely between the county [Clark] and the Pentagon and had played squarely into Clark's hands." Ault feared that he might be subpoenaed. When Smeltzer asked what could be done to smooth the situation, Ault replied, "Nothing. I want to get as little assistance from outside as possible." Smeltzer stressed that he had not called the meeting and had attended only because he was invited. He followed up the phone call to Ault with a letter that detailed the meeting and his role there and expressed his surprise and disappointment with Ault's reaction. No one intended to violate the injunction, he said, and he encouraged Ault not to misinterpret the men's purposes "even if their choice of a meeting place turned out to be unwise." Later, Ault's anger cooled, and he and Smeltzer resumed amicable conversations.

The black airmen felt isolated. Although they received support from federal authorities, including promised legal support all the way to the Supreme Court, it was difficult to translate this support to Selma when Craig officers suggested that the men might wind up in jail. When Smeltzer briefed Bob Jansen about the raid, Jansen told him to assure Fears that Burke Marshall, head of the Civil Rights Division at Justice, would be contacted immediately and that, although this was a difficult period, no harm would come to the men. Jansen also commented that the FBI had given the Justice Department little information about the Elks incident; instead, he was responsible for informing Justice about the situation. And Jansen got his information from Smeltzer.

The crisis climbed the bureaucratic ladder in Washington until Secretary of Defense Robert McNamara contacted Ault to prohibit air force discipline against the airmen. Soon Smeltzer put Fears in direct contact with Jansen. When Jansen told Fears that Clark could not jail him, the phone went dead for several minutes. Fears cautioned Smeltzer to be careful, that "they" knew when Smeltzer came and went, and that all the information "they" had was frightening.[32]

Whites Relax, but Black Grievances Remain

In early August, Smeltzer decided to postpone another trip to Selma, chiefly because white moderates considered the situation to be encouraging. Although Reese urged him to come, several whites counseled that there was little Smeltzer could contribute to the developments they believed were under way.

Several reports supported the white moderates' contention that changes were slowly taking place in Selma's race relations. After the Elks-raid story spread throughout Selma, a member of the business leaders' group called Enoch Fears and asked to talk with several blacks from Craig. The testing of public accommodations continued. Apparently, most of the white community accepted testing, although many believed the Civil Rights Act was unconstitutional. Blacks had the right to test, but not to be served, and Clark no longer arrested testers for trespassing. Following Smeltzer's advice, blacks phoned their targets before coming, but they were still denied service. There was little danger that the testing would escalate into violence, however, and when Edgar Stewart credited Smeltzer for the testing, Smeltzer refused the compliment because his neutrality precluded support for testing. But he added that he would gladly accept recognition for the testing's being quiet and orderly, and Stewart appreciated this attitude.

Smeltzer believed there was little more he could do at the moment. In spite of the small signs of change, the business leaders' group was unrealistically optimistic about their efforts; they again mentioned the unspecified "progress." On the one hand, the moderates might resent pressure to do more if they believed they were already making headway; on the other hand, Smeltzer had not won the confidence of Clark and Hare and could not expect to have any influence over them.

Nevertheless, the absence of negotiations and the increasing hardening of positions concerned Smeltzer. The business leaders moved too slowly to be effective, and neither Smeltzer nor Art Lewis was able to get any movement from a number of other middle-of-the-road whites. Influential moderates were staying backstage, and some, who were not associated with the business leaders, became increasingly negative and pessimistic. Assurances from the business leaders that they were making progress were conspicuously devoid of specifics.

Undoubtedly, Selma had backed away from the brink of racial violence. Despite the occasional optimism, however, signs of continuing resistance abounded. Interracial communication was still so muted that Smeltzer relayed to F. D. Reese a request from the president of the Merchants Association for current black demands. Not only was the Merchants Association ignorant of black grievances, but they needed a third party, Smeltzer, to obtain that information. According to Lewis, Jim Clark, with whom he had recently met for over an hour, and his sympathizers hatched a theory that the Congress of Racial Equality (CORE) and the National States Rights Party were both communist fronts in cahoots to raise money. The YMCA board, under pressure from the national office to integrate, decided to become a private club rather than yield on this point. The white leadership believed it was stronger than ever and did not need to negotiate. Lewis reported that the die-hard faction thought they had won because the blacks were quiet and, presumably, defeated. Actually, blacks had restrained themselves but would eagerly restore pressure at future opportunities. Blacks remained frustrated, moderate whites flirted with complacency, and the die-hards remained inflexible.[33]

5

The Calm

While we rejoice in the passage of legislation designed to further justice
for all races, a civil rights law may in the early stages of its
implementation only harden both sides of the conflict and thus intensify
the struggle. We recognize that the church must go beyond law. Ours is
the task of creating the climate of understanding, goodwill, and concern
for the right without which the law can not succeed.

Church of the Brethren Statement on Race Relations, 1964

In late August 1964, Frank Wilson and Edgar Stewart, key members of the informal business group, drove to a little town outside Selma, parked behind a church, and waited for J. J. Israel to arrive. Israel, a large black man who sported flashy clothes, had recently appeared in Selma offering his services as a mediator for hire.

Members of the business group had acquaintances in Auburn, Alabama, who credited Israel with delaying school desegregation there for a semester and recommended him. Wilson and Stewart hoped that this smooth talker could do the same for Selma. Although the businessmen seriously doubted Israel's integrity and knew that his guiding star was a dollar sign, they also hoped that he had some of the contacts he claimed and that he could buy time, literally if necessary. Stewart and Wilson waited behind the church for their first encounter with Israel.

Soon Israel arrived in his air-conditioned Cadillac. The three men sat for two hours discussing Selma's race relations. At the conclusion of the meeting, the businessmen handed Israel an envelope containing $3,000 in cash. Over the next several weeks, Israel pocketed between $8,000 and $10,000.[1]

White Selma Relaxes

Smeltzer did not return to Selma until the end of the year. In the wake of the July crisis, the business leaders became more active, and Smeltzer facilitated a round of talks between them and black leaders. Once the crisis atmosphere receded, however, the pressure on whites to act diminished, and blacks were again frustrated. Finally, with little prospect of further concessions or improved communication, blacks welcomed Martin Luther King, Jr., to Selma at the end of the year.

From August through November, Smeltzer stayed in Illinois and monitored Selma by telephone, which was safer and cheaper. His telephone mediation was possible because of the fundamentally good relations he enjoyed with many people in the city. Art Lewis was especially supportive of this telephone diplomacy, which he considered very effective. When John Doar asked him to return to Selma to update the situation there, Smeltzer replied that he had all the information he needed. The next morning, a Saturday, Smeltzer was in a Washington, D.C., office with Doar and other Justice Department staff.

Smeltzer had repeatedly suggested as bluntly as possible to moderate whites that they needed to establish direct contacts with blacks, which would eliminate the need for Smeltzer to act as go-between. Although Smeltzer was an important conduit of information, part of his message often included the need to establish direct links between black and white Selma.

The business leaders continued to make unspecified claims of progress. Smeltzer tried to impress them with the urgency of the situation and told them he was uncertain how long he could effectively counsel restraint to blacks. Although Smeltzer praised the businessmen's courage and "heroism," he also informed them that blacks needed to see improvements and that it was unclear how long they would remain calm without visible signs of progress.

Working with Business Leaders

After the alarm over the passage of the Civil Rights Act in early July and the Elks raid later that month, Selma slipped into a period of calm. Moderate business leaders became much more active, but nearly all their work was done anonymously, which left black activists unsatisfied because blacks needed public signs of change. Testing continued but was quiet and uneventful; resistance to compliance with the law remained. The white establishment considered a biracial committee to be an impossibility.

The businessmen saw Judge Thomas's injunction, which prohibited civil rights meetings, as a blessing because it brought stability to Selma and provided them with time. The businessmen found progress slow, and they wanted all the time they could get. Everything from vacations to local politics to national politics hindered efforts at conciliation, but any change in public policy would be difficult until Mayor-elect Smitherman took office on October 1. The business group met about once a week, ironically on Monday nights (in place of the mass meetings), and had recently counseled a group of local politicians to stop making frivolous arrests and to be more cautious.

The formation of the business group approximately coincided with the beginning of Smeltzer's presence in Selma. During his early trips in 1963, Smeltzer had heard about this group, which was largely dormant until the Civil Rights Act crisis, but by the second half of 1964, the group's concern and activity intensified. (The previous chapter mentions increased activity by this group; the renewed concern grew in late summer 1964.) This small group attracted some of the most influential men in the community, who wanted to see Selma change but feared trying to "rebuild Rome overnight." They believed that the South had entered a new era, but that change that came too quickly, "pell-mell change," was dangerous. They understood that the times would force Selma to change, but they favored a gradual and smooth transition. Three bank officials—Sam Earl Hobbs, Charles Hohenburg, and Frank Wilson—plus Edgar Stewart, president of the school board, formed the group's backbone, but they specifically avoided naming a chairperson to spare one individual having to face the brunt of the opposition. They considered themselves "dyed in the wool" southerners—both of Stewart's grandfathers had fought in the Confederate Army—but with a broader, more sophisticated outlook than might be expected in the Black Belt. Based on comments they heard at the Citizens Council, on the attitude of Chris Heinz, who, they claimed, said he would "rather see Selma blow away than to change any of its traditions," and on their knowledge of the city, this informal, secret committee of moderates believed that under Selma's surface seethed a white anger capable of producing street violence and riots.[2] Smeltzer prodded, cajoled, and massaged this group, trying desperately to stimulate it to action because its members were so important in Selma. When they gathered, his gentle urgings must have been remembered by them.

As Labor Day and the new school year approached, the moderate business group feared that school desegregation was more than their city currently could absorb. Some whites had made threatening comments about blacks who might attempt to desegregate the schools, and the businessmen suspected that school desegregation might generate serious violence, certainly more than a random brick or a few bruises. They were desperate to avoid this anticipated disaster and therefore were willing to pay someone as suspect as J. J. Israel out of their own pockets. School desegregation did not come about in September, and although the business leaders never knew if Israel was responsible for this, they were very relieved that Selma had successfully navigated those treacherous waters.[3]

When Israel appeared in Selma, Smeltzer delicately tried to spread information about his unsavory reputation. Art Lewis asked Sheriff Clark to contact the Montgomery police, who confirmed that Israel had a long criminal record, and federal attorney Bob Jansen urged caution until an FBI report arrived. Smeltzer advised blacks to use Israel, if they could, but to be careful that Israel did not manipulate them. Smeltzer passed along Art Lewis's phrase "smooth racketeer" to describe Israel, and he suggested that Reese visit Lewis for a fuller report on Israel's record, an idea Reese accepted that resulted in another small but important step toward improved interracial communication. Blacks were suspicious of Israel, but they cooperated with him for a while because they were desperate for contacts with whites, which Israel had.[4]

That the bankers' group gave at least $8,000 of their own funds to Israel shows Selma's desperate need for mediation. Wilson, Stewart, et al. were not acquainted with black leaders and could not, or would not, approach them directly. The communication gap was so wide that highly respected businessmen willingly filled the pockets of someone they privately considered to be a scoundrel.

The Merchants Association's request for a list of black demands (see Chapter 4) was one of the few practical paths to interracial communication at this point; therefore, Smeltzer's conversations with white moderates sampled their opinion on the request. Blacks had completed a letter stating their priorities and were ready to send it, but was the time ripe for such action? White responses to Smeltzer's inquiries revealed that the moderates were insecure about their political strength and unwilling, or unable, to deal with black grievances. Edgar Stewart was inclined to receive a letter on condition that it contained no demands, but blacks also could hold back the letter for a while. Art Capell, editor of the *Times-Journal*, believed that any kind of letter from blacks, no matter how carefully crafted, would be taken as a threat; he cautioned further that if such a letter fell into the hands of the Citizens Council or the National States Rights Party, it would be damaging because it would force people to take sides. It would be better to save the document for now and use it later in face-to-face discussions. Businessman Roger Jones thought the much talked about letter would be received favorably if prepared properly, but it would be best if the letter was not sent until the following month. The business leaders wanted very much to move slowly, and they were generally acquainted with the black agenda because Israel had supplied them with a list. (After F. D. Reese told Israel about black concerns, Israel typed up a list and gave it to the whites on his own authority.)

White nervousness also surfaced at the *Times-Journal*, where there was some interest in ending the segregated news section. Capell signaled that neither a letter nor a visit to publisher Roswell Falkenberry would be useful at this time.[5] The *Times-Journal* staff had decided to offer leadership to the community, but not until after school started; the timing, once again, was not right just now.

In mid-August the courthouse drinking fountain signs came

down; drinking cups were placed by the fountains to appease sensitive whites. Judge Reynolds remained adamant about the restrooms, however. Smeltzer believed that his talks with Reynolds deserved some of the credit for the fountain development, but assumed that the business leaders' influence was the more effective. Edgar Stewart was well known in the courthouse, and primary credit for the fountain decision was his. But it was Smeltzer who informed black leaders about the drinking fountains.[6]

Stewart was consistently tight-lipped; he continued to assure Smeltzer that his group was making progress but stubbornly refused to divulge any examples of it. Were the secret payments to Israel the "progress" about which Stewart could not tell Smeltzer? Smeltzer called another member of the group, Roger Jones, who listed two achievements: the removal of segregation signs from the courthouse drinking fountains and the postponement of a major Citizens Council rally.

Although whites welcomed Judge Thomas's injunction because it removed pressure from them and gained them time, blacks became increasingly discouraged. By banning public organizing efforts, the injunction made nearly impossible the functioning of civil rights organizations.

Interracial communication remained anemic. For example, whites considered paving streets in the black residential area a major concession, but when Smeltzer suggested to Reese that he thank the city for the paving, Reese retorted that black property owners had to pay a high price for the paving out of their pockets, while whites had their streets maintained with public money.

Although unofficial talks with the bankers' group seemed imminent, communication with City Hall continued to disappoint civil rights leaders and Smeltzer. Mayor Heinz's continuing rigidity plus his lame-duck status led to an abandonment of efforts to persuade him and a concentration instead on the incoming administration. And blacks grew increasingly insistent and impatient about direct communication with Mayor-elect Smitherman.

In the fall of 1964, the Justice Department filed two lawsuits that declared the federal government's support for civil rights in Selma. One action, aimed at the Dallas County political leadership, ordered officials to stop discrimination and intimidation directed against black voter registrants. Observers thought that the suit would only solidify white intransigence. Another suit sought to force several Selma restaurants to comply with the Civil Rights Act, a move that would probably help Smeltzer's work because now he could tell blacks that his assurances about help from the federal government were correct. Also, the lawsuits would give the business leaders time and the restaurant managers a graceful, face-saving excuse to comply with the law.

Small Steps Toward Progress

Two months after the passage of the Civil Rights Act, the atmosphere in Selma had cooled, at least superficially, as small steps toward progress accumulated, although the courthouse drinking cups remained the only visible change. Blacks began to speak positively about the improving atmosphere and looked forward to future progress. Reese, Moss, and Brown moved closer toward black unity with three meetings at Brown's residence, and Reese informed Israel that he was no longer needed.

There were other bright spots. Increasingly, individual whites viewed changing race relations as inevitable. Boynton remarked that more street paving, the costs of which were split between property owners and city and state funds, had been done in twelve months than in the previous thirty years. At Smeltzer's suggestion, the Justice Department assigned a black attorney to Selma as an interviewer. "You know we always do what you suggest," John Doar remarked![7]

In October, the trial began for a Department of Justice voter discrimination case. John Doar put thirty black witnesses on the stand, including teachers, who had been denied voter registration. Some testified that they had been asked to spell difficult words: "secular, bona fide and innumerate [*sic*]." One woman testified that she was asked the duties of the Vice-President, and after she answered that he took over if the President could no longer serve, the registrar asked for specific Vice-Presidential duties. She was unable to respond correctly and was rejected. Doar also put several illiterate whites on the stand, people who were registered. They were "voters who were miserable specimens," according to Bob Jansen.[8]

Although the business leaders rejected the formation of a biracial committee, they indicated an interest in meeting individually with several local black leaders. When they asked Smeltzer for names, he again suggested Reese, Brown, and Moss and urged the committee to see them quickly. A landmark event in interracial communication occurred when three black leaders held private, individual discussions with three white business leaders. Smeltzer, at his telephone in Illinois, had done much to see that these meetings took place. His persistent appeals to whites for direct communication had been a major theme in all his conversations with them, and it was he who gave the names of Reese, Brown, and Moss to the businessmen's group. The plan called for Frank Wilson to meet with Brown, Rex Morthland with Moss, and Paul Grist with Reese. The meetings generally received favorable critiques, but it was the fact of the meetings rather than any concrete results that was encouraging. For example, Moss and Morthland each recognized the other's difficult situation. Morthland expressed sympathy for Moss's requests but claimed that his bank would go broke if he stuck out his neck. Morthland encouraged blacks to seek the support of other bankers; Moss believed that Morthland wanted to help but was unable to do so because of the severe pressures on whites. (Morthland was evidently unwilling to speak himself with the other bankers.[9]) White moderates appreciated the black under-standing of the difficulties they faced.

The Reese–Grist meeting was somewhat less successful than the other two, mainly because Grist delayed it. After a reasonable wait, Smeltzer called Wilson to inform him that Grist and Reese still had not met (Wilson thought the meeting had occurred). Grist kept his agreement to meet Reese about ten days after the other two conversations took place.

Blacks considered the talks a great step forward, contributing to an unseen movement in Selma. Smeltzer thought these conversations were the third breakthrough in Selma. (The other two breakthroughs were the July meeting of all black leaders at Selma University and the drinking fountain changes in August.) The business leaders also appreciated the discussions and gained new confidence in the quality of Selma's black leadership, but the businessmen planned no activity beyond continued talk plus support and advice for local officials.[10]

Blacks wanted very much to impress Mayor-elect Joe Smitherman that their tiny bloc of votes had gone almost exclusively to him. Probably at Smeltzer's suggestion, Lewis gave Smitherman the message, and the mayor agreed to pick up the talks with the blacks where the business leaders' discussions had left off. Influential white moderates gave assurances that blacks would be able to visit the mayor after Smitherman was settled in office.

Another signal Smitherman sent that indicated change would continue was his appointment of Wilson Baker as Director of Public Safety (i.e., supervisor of the police and fire departments). Blacks were encouraged in that Baker's duties were to include the protection of all people, regardless of race, creed, or color. Ed Moss and Claude Brown both told stories that demonstrated the encouraging changes brought about by Baker. Moss was at police headquarters with Baker when two officers brought in a black man they had arrested. The prisoner had been beaten, and right in front of Moss, Baker berated the arresting officers. If the two of them could not bring in a prisoner of this slight build without a beating, they did not deserve to be on the force. Baker released the prisoner.[11]

Brown reported police intimidation when a friend of his, a white pastor from Iowa, visited. Three police officers on motorcycles waited across the street from Brown's house; they followed Brown's friend as he was leaving and searched his car. Baker reprimanded the police officers in front of Brown: "Don't you know that we are not going to do it this way any longer? That time is past. Hereafter, you check with me regarding any surveillance of Negroes." Although blacks were thankful for the improvements brought by Baker, they knew that he, too, was a segregationist —but one with a little class.[12]

Smeltzer's name surfaced often, generally favorably, in conversations around Selma, and he began to establish a reputation in both Selma and Washington for effective work. Art Lewis and Claude Brown both credited him with breaking the ice and beginning initiatives that moved Selma off dead-center.[13] Before Annalee Stewart of the Women's International League for Peace and Freedom went to Selma, she asked Smeltzer for advice because John Doar had spoken to her about Smeltzer's "splendid work in Selma."[14] Only at the Dallas County courthouse was Smeltzer unsuccessful in winning confidence.

By the end of September, Smeltzer had no plans to return to Selma unless a new crisis erupted; he hoped to phase himself out of Selma. There were indications that Selma had changed. Several black teachers from Hudson High took approximately twenty students to a movie theater one evening to view the film *Hamlet* at a special price of a dollar per ticket. Many white students from Parrish High were also at the theater, but aside from a few young whites (whom Frank Wilson called "punks") stomping out complaining that it "looks like the Congo," there was no trouble. In fact, no police were present when the students entered the theater, and only one was present when the movie was over, a sign of the changes blacks believed had come to Selma.[15] Also, Enoch

Fears had enrolled in a University of Alabama extension class in welding. Fears was pleased because both Pickard and the Craig brass had been supportive.

Reverting to Stagnation

Although some of the news was upbeat, by late 1964 there were indications that Selma's race relations were drifting back into stagnation. The only integrated motel, a Holiday Inn, in late October reversed its policy and refused to register two of Reese's friends.[16]

Gradually it became apparent that the secret group of moderates was not able to capitalize on the injunction's period of calm. Smeltzer pressed the business leaders for a group meeting as the next logical step from the recent series of individual conversations, but they decided that the next round of meetings would again be on an individual level. The bankers' desire not to usurp the power of elected authorities slowed the movement toward a group meeting with blacks. Mayor Smitherman was also reported to be uneasy about the idea.

The long-awaited optimism over Smitherman gradually proved unfounded. Between his election in the summer and his inauguration on October 5, he had no contact with black representatives. He was not personally acquainted with any black leaders, and his lack of communication after the election disappointed them. Reese tried to see Smitherman several times, but felt that Smitherman was avoiding him. In his inaugural speech, Smitherman forcefully opposed a biracial committee, which Smeltzer considered an unnecessary statement. Smitherman explained that he had to say it in order to satisfy the extremists.[17] Hopes continued that Smitherman would engage in direct talks without the biracial committee and that opposition to the committee was meant to placate the die-hards rather than express policy. By the middle of October, about two weeks after

Smitherman took office, he took steps to meet black representatives by personally telephoning Reese, Brown, and Moss, asking them to come in for a short, get-acquainted meeting. Based on Smeltzer's warnings to Lewis about rivalry between black leaders, Smitherman carefully treated the three black leaders equally. For example, Brown requested an individual meeting with the mayor, but Lewis saw to it that the request was denied.

A week after telephoning the black leaders, Smitherman postponed the meeting with them. Smitherman called Reese and Brown personally, while Lewis looked up the phone numbers for him. The mayor said he still intended to meet with the three blacks. He asked them to discuss job qualifications with Dan River Mills personnel and then to recruit blacks for positions there, while making it explicit that they were working with him. The mayor also planned to ask the three black leaders what streets they wanted paved with surplus state road money. But Smitherman held back from setting a new date for a meeting.

As Smitherman inched toward direct biracial conversations, his talk of conciliation aroused die-hards, who viewed the mayor as a moderate who would surrender to the blacks. Smitherman's political enemy, Chris Heinz, became the new president of the Citizens Council. Smitherman, who believed that Selma's problems were unique, carried his adamant opposition to outside interference to the point where he refused to meet with mayors of other Alabama cities that had experienced a successful transition to desegregation. And although Lewis suspected that the business leaders had not even met lately, Smitherman felt that they were pushing too hard.[18]

The long-awaited meeting between the mayor and the three black leaders took place on Friday, November 6, over a month after Smitherman became mayor. That morning, at 8:00 A.M., Smeltzer telephoned Reese to ensure that blacks would enter the talks cordially rather than in a confrontational mood. Smeltzer emphasized that the mayor wanted to cooperate and shared the news that Smitherman had an "even better project he will be telling you about," probably an allusion to the street paving. The meeting between the blacks and Smitherman, Art Capell, and Wilson Baker lasted for an hour, and both sides proved cooperative.[19]

An incident at the Roman Catholic church in October reminded Selma of its potential for spontaneous racial violence. A group of black high school students had been attending Catholic Mass there regularly, sitting in a certain area, but on two recent Sundays they had spread out among the congregation. Their boldness provoked two whites to assault them while a crowd watched, but a white sergeant from Craig airbase, James Burke, grabbed the assailants by the collar and pushed them away with a reprimand. Many whites believed that the blacks had come not to worship, but to make trouble, and Burke's action brought him threats and harassment. The following Sunday, while he worshipped, his car was vandalized, and strange white men were seen and heard around his house that week. There was no prosecution, and civil rights people accused the police of refusing to allow one parent to swear out a warrant because her child's assailant was white. Instead, police gave her a lecture on the benefits of racial separation.[20]

Violence Again Threatens, and Smeltzer Returns

In the months since the July crisis, blacks had won only a single, lonely public sign of progress, the removal of the drinking fountain signs at the courthouse, plus the confidential discussions with the business leaders' committee and Smitherman. While blacks also were encouraged by the appointment of Baker and the paving of streets, the lack of direct progress on civil rights issues increasingly frustrated them. By the end of November, there were no more Smitherman meetings in the foreseeable future, and contacts with business leaders had ended. The Dallas County Voters League steering committee kept the organization alive during the life of the injunction by meeting at Amelia Boynton's home. But because these gatherings violated the injunction, they were covert, and the black rank and file assumed that not even organizational meetings were being held and that the movement was stalled. Blacks expressed concern, but the only reply their leaders could give them was a plea for patience and a little more time. Reese urged Smeltzer to tell whites that blacks needed a timetable for progress, that just asking about more time was insufficient. Reese could not tell blacks to be patient without any visible sign of progress.[21]

Whites failed to respond to black concerns. A tough speech by Baker to the Rotary Club on December 11 exemplified the failure of the Smitherman administration to live up to the progressive expectations that came with its inauguration. Baker complained to the Rotarians—with a sneer, according to John Newton—about the "inquisition" the federal government had inflicted on Selma. Alluding to Doar's voter registration suit against Clark and the county, Baker warned, "Woe be unto us if the trial goes against us. We'll have to figure out another way, another tack to keep them [blacks] in their place." He complained about the futility of trying to fight the national government: "We tried, but you can't fight the United States. We tried, but the United States is too strong." Although Baker's talk to the Rotary may have been a ploy to coax an expanded police budget out of the city fathers or to win the confidence of whites, black leaders were extremely disappointed in his hard-line approach, and moderates noticed his apparent enthusiasm and sincerity for the tough stance.[22]

With the situation regressing and danger signals flashing, Smeltzer returned to Selma in early December and quickly learned that ill feelings had grown worse. While Smeltzer was talking on the phone in the Hotel Albert lobby on a Friday evening, Sheriff Clark came in. Recognizing Smeltzer, Clark called out, "Mr. Smeltzer, what are you down here for? Making more trouble? Why don't you stay up North?" Smeltzer thought the sheriff was drunk and noticed that Clark's friend pulled him along and out the door. When the person on the other end of the phone, federal attorney Bob Jansen, heard the conversation, he asked Smeltzer if he needed help. Smeltzer gave assurances of his safety, saying, "I always agree with fellows like that."[23]

Smeltzer's December visit coincided with the beginning of a Justice Department suit against Dallas County on voting discrimination. Smeltzer attended two sessions of the trial, but after learning that one of the defense attorneys had asked if he was affiliated with Justice, Smeltzer feared that he would be subpoenaed to testify, which could damage his work. An appearance on the witness stand might publicly identify him with the civil rights movement or force him to reveal the contents of confidential conversations. At the least, he thought it counterproductive to be seen in the courtroom and thereby remind the defendants of his activities. He thought about getting a room in Montgomery for a few days, but decided that his whereabouts would be harder to trace if he stayed in a private home in Selma.

Indicators pointed toward increased dangers of interracial violence. Air Force Sergeant Burke, who broke up the attack on blacks at the Catholic church, suffered through weeks of threats that climaxed five days before Christmas with a beating by four whites, who called him outside his house by saying they had hit his car. Once he was outside, they attacked him. Burke's sixteen-year-old son rescued his father by shooting one of the assailants in the back with a .22-caliber rifle. The thugs took their wounded friend, who had recently been released from Tuscaloosa County jail, to the hospital. There, the three were taken into custody and arrested. Although Burke received a severe and painful beating about the face and head, his injuries were not reported to be serious. Later, the fourth man was arrested, and a robbery charge was added because Burke's wallet, containing $300, was taken.[24] There was some speculation that the four whites had been hired to thrash Burke.

Burke's beating stimulated several moderates to disassociate themselves publicly from the tactics of the violent segregationists. The *Times-Journal* editorialized against the "shameful brutal beating" of Burke, commended Baker for quickly arresting the "goons," and wrote that "there must be no further acts of terrorism in the City of Selma." Several letters to the editor supported the *Times-Journal*'s criticism of street violence.[25]

Interracial violence again disturbed Selma when two white teenagers assaulted a fifteen-year-old black, Fred Scot, during an argument over who should yield the sidewalk. One of the whites struck Scot, who hit his head on the sidewalk and remained unconscious for a day. The whites, whose defense was that Scot appeared to reach into his pocket for a knife, were promptly arrested.[26]

Another theater incident occurred in late December, and according to Wilson Baker, it was potentially more serious than the July 4 incident at the Wilby. On a Saturday, the Walton Theater filled with an integrated audience. A crowd outside learned that the movie house was integrated, and several members of the posse in the crowd began to create a disturbance. Wilson Baker and another officer, both in plainclothes, came and told the crowd to go home until the next show. Most of the people left, but a few of the posse had to be told to leave. After the crowd dispersed, Baker watched from the street corner, put troublemakers in his car, drove them halfway around the block, and then told them to stop making trouble and go home. This tactic proved effective, and the incident did not appear in the newspaper.[27]

The Invitation to King

With negotiations at a standstill and black frustrations building, the Dallas County Voters League (DCVL) turned to the outside for help and invited the Reverend Martin Luther King, Jr., to Selma. As blacks became increasingly desperate and whites showed little inclination to respond to their grievances, black leaders pursued a new tack, one that would considerably alter the confrontations in Selma and the nature of Smeltzer's mission. The dynamics behind King's decision to come to Selma remain shrouded behind fading memories and SCLC's dearth of records. King refused to appear without a local invitation and sent C. T. Vivian, director of affiliates, to Selma to obtain it. Vivian met with the DCVL committee in Boynton's home to get the invitation, which Reese signed. Although the SCLC board had voted to mount a major, lengthy campaign in Selma and to stay as long as necessary, there was some concern among local blacks that SCLC would desert them before the local campaign was completed. But, the DCVL was so frustrated over the lack of action that they were glad to have SCLC's help and were flattered that King, a celebrity and a hero, chose their city. Certainly progress in Selma had slowed, and the DCVL felt that SNCC had contributed all it could to Selma. Perhaps SCLC, with its greater resources, could restore momentum to Selma's movement. Reese now asserts that the invitation was his idea, that he invited King, but he told Smeltzer that he "would not stand in the way of SCLC's coming," which hardly sounds as if he initiated it. Marie Foster sums it up: "I was just so glad he [King] was coming." Leaders of SCLC considered Selma to be the quintessential hardcore area, from which they hoped to springboard into sixty-five other Black Belt counties.[28]

As soon as Smeltzer learned that SCLC planned a campaign in Selma, he telephoned Vivian in Atlanta. Vivian told him that SCLC wanted to restore the momentum toward progress in Selma and felt that pressure was needed to jolt the city forward. Blacks wanted something more than the recent "progress" (i.e., street paving, plans for flood-control projects, and encouragement to apply for employment at Dan River Mills); visible progress was vital. Smeltzer learned what it would take to keep SCLC out: voter registration and jobs. Harry Boyte, a white

SCLC staff member who spent a few days in Selma to open discussions with local whites, contacted Smeltzer, and the image of
black Selma that Boyte took back to Atlanta headquarters relied
heavily on Smeltzer's observations, especially Smeltzer's concerns
regarding divisions among the black leadership.[29]

Selma's position as the keystone of King's voting rights campaign now made it a city of national importance, and just as
Smeltzer dealt with factionalism among blacks in Selma, the representatives of the national civil rights organizations in Selma
were also divided. Members of SNCC, who had toiled in the
Black Belt since February 1963, when Bernard and Colia
Lafayette set up headquarters in Selma, had mixed feelings about
the SCLC plans. Although the fame of King would attract national attention to the dismal record of voter registration in
Alabama, and perhaps stimulate the federal government to act
against Alabama officials, King's campaign might also detract
from SNCC's long, patient emphasis on local leadership. Also,
there was a major misunderstanding between SNCC and SCLC
regarding decisions made at a mid-December strategy meeting.[30]

Locally, Love complained that SCLC had informed neither
him nor the DCVL of its plans and that the Voters League was
completely disregarding him; Reese maintained that he always
had to seek out Love, who never contacted him. To remove the
misunderstandings, at Smeltzer's request Reese invited Love to a
strategy session. Selma's SNCC and the DCVL considered each
other to be slow and unproductive.

Smeltzer believed that most white community leaders would
consider a King visit counterproductive because he was so controversial a figure. Even moderate whites disliked King, and
many civic leaders, including the newspaper editors, publicly
criticized him. Smeltzer predicted that local leaders would claim
to be undisturbed by King's visit but that it would arouse rank-
and-file whites. The day before Smeltzer left Selma, he requested
a meeting of black leaders on one-day's notice and suggested to

them that they use Martin Luther King's visit as leverage to gain visible goals.[31]

Preparations for King's Visit

Martin Luther King's projected visit to Selma added heat to Selma's social caldron, intensifying emotions. As the day of King's visit approached, all factions prepared themselves. Smeltzer made several successful eleventh-hour attempts to improve communication. He was especially pleased with the relationship he established with Wilson Baker.

Among blacks, minor dissension and rivalry continued. Black preachers were especially disappointed that the plans for the campaign had been finalized before they had been consulted, but apologies from Brown, Reese, and Bradford salved their wounded pride. The black ministers achieved about as much unity as possible. White extremists prepared activities to coincide with the SCLC campaign; a National States Rights Party membership campaign scheduled for early January was the most serious threat. The NSRP was more feared in Selma than the Klan, which was smaller. And FBI agents assured Reese that they told the rednecks to forget about King's visit because they were being observed.[32]

The city administration was also busy. Wilson Baker had a showdown meeting with county officials and let them know that the city was his turf; they had no authority there, and he would handle civil rights cases. Although King's speech would be a violation of the injunction against civil rights meetings, Baker announced that he would not make arrests under the injunction because its enforcement became a federal matter removed from his jurisdiction when it was appealed to federal court, and Judge Thomas reportedly planned to allow the injunction to die quietly.[33]

Although Smeltzer had difficulties in establishing a working relationship with several of Selma's officials—Clark and Hare were hopeless—three days before Martin Luther King arrived, Smeltzer succeeded in making a favorable impression on Wilson Baker and began a productive association that lasted throughout the Selma crisis. Art Capell brought Baker to Smeltzer's hotel room for a relaxed, one-hour chat that inaugurated the relationship.

Smeltzer praised Baker for his policy of equal law enforcement and especially commended Baker for communicating with black leaders, urging him to continue this practice. Baker invited Smeltzer to drop by his office anytime and invited him to a civil rights instruction session for city police officers.

Smeltzer's suggestion for Baker—by this time, Smeltzer had a suggestion for almost everyone—was to stop making arrests under the city's "civil rights ordinance" (likely the trespassing arrests of blacks seeking restaurant service) because this would help Selma's case in federal court. Smeltzer "pointed out the importance of timing" because action before the King visit would be a show of good faith toward blacks. Although having these cases dismissed was a small step, it is typical of Smeltzer's strategy of seeking small, visible actions to build interracial trust. The more Capell and Baker thought about it, the more it made sense. They were certain that it would influence Judge Thomas, and Baker doubted that the city could get convictions anyway.

Smeltzer was euphoric over the "almost providential" outcome of the meeting. As much as anything, Capell and Baker came to get acquainted with him, and Smeltzer appreciated that. The meeting achieved several of Smeltzer's most important goals: (1) Smeltzer established a congenial relationship with Baker and Capell, (2) Baker indicated a willingness to work with Smeltzer, (3) Baker accepted his suggestion to drop charges on one of the city's civil rights cases, and (4) Smeltzer's newly established relationship with the Director of Public Safety greatly enhanced his physical security. Contributing further to Smeltzer's elation over the meeting was satisfaction with his role in it; he thought he was "relaxed, well prepared, poised and in good form." To Smeltzer, "it seemed as if the hand of God were at work. All I could do after they had left was pray a prayer of thanksgiving and ask God's future blessing upon our work here." He was so excited that he telephoned his wife Mary and John Newton.[34]

Interracial communication improved as the King visit neared. Smeltzer gave Baker the home and business phone numbers of Andy Young, with the invitation to call anytime. On December 30, Reese and Baker exchanged information on King's visit. Baker assured Reese that Clark would be out of town and that the posse would be kept at the courthouse unless summoned by Baker, which was highly unlikely. Baker also promised not to send any of his men to the mass meeting—in fact, he would not even station his men close to the church—unless the state carried through on its plans to put men inside. Then Baker would send a man inside, to ensure that the report of the meeting was accurate. Reese was so positive about Baker's attitude that he wanted to announce to a January 1 mass meeting that the city would protect them—that the city, but not the county, was a friend.[35]

On the day of King's arrival, police were seen in the streets with billy clubs, which they usually did not carry unless they expected trouble. Jim Clark was in Miami to cheer Bear Bryant's Crimson Tide in the Orange Bowl.

6

The Fury

The basic problem in Selma is the slow pace of voting registration for
Negroes who are qualified to vote.

Lyndon B. Johnson

Selma can't heal itself until the depth of its hostility is explored.

Harry Boyte

In early 1965, the Reverend L. L. Anderson led a march to the courthouse. He took the line of demonstrators to the front door and was met by Sheriff Clark, who ordered them to move. "And moreover," Clark said as he glanced at his watch, "I'm going to give you five minutes to get the God damn hell from this door." Facing Clark's posse, Anderson was afraid.

I was worried about the wives, their children and those old ladies—grandmothers—back there, but to tell you the truth, I was worried about me, too. And we were standing there with nothing but faith in God, which in the estimation of a non-believer was in effect nothing.

And [Clark] said, "You have four minutes." He stood around, and he said, "You have three minutes." I heard a lady in the back—when he said, "You have two minutes"— she cried out, "Lawd, have mercy!"

Well, it was rough on me. I turned to Reverend Hood. And I sorta got my nerve. And I'd never asked anybody for any strength before like that. I'd prayed and whatnot, but I'd never felt that I needed to be encouraged; I was the one out there priming everything before, but at this time I needed priming. And I knew that they could knock my eyes out and I'd never see again, and he could hit me up the side of the head—enough people had already been killed and beaten and knocked here and there—the Philadelphia situation in Mississippi and numerous other situations—Medgar Evers—you couldn't help at that point but to face up to reality and make a determination, make a judgement as to whether you really believe what you say you do. The woman who cried out, "Lawd, have mercy!": that's what put my mind to work.

Clark said, "You have one minute." At that point I began to block out everything; I began to make myself unconscious. I had decided that come what may, that if I would die here that would be the price that I must pay and so I stood on. And he said—he waited longer than a minute; I knew it was longer than a minute—this was very heartening, to say the least! He said, "You have one minute;" he said it again. With a great sense of gratitude and humility to God, I said, "Thank you, Lord." And we stood. And he said perhaps some of the most consoling words I've heard since I'd learned that I was coming home from overseas during the war—he said then, "Lock them up." And I felt wonderful. This is all he's gonna do, put us in jail? Why my goodness, I could have hugged his neck, so to speak!"[1]

The Resurgence of the Crisis

The previous months of calm had not promoted social healing, and the neglect only resulted in greater harm. The business leaders' group had not met for over a month because they thought the crisis had passed. Now they were about to reap what they had not sown.

The introduction of SCLC into Selma resulted in a definite increase in the polarization, and SCLC's tactics, which emphasized confrontation, produced hardened feelings that impeded the interracial communication desired by Smeltzer. King and his aides had discovered that Sheriff Clark, with his emotional and angry responses, made a dramatic opponent and a photogenic villain, so SCLC strategy focused on Clark and his outbursts. This was not the scenario that Smeltzer had hoped for. The heightened pressures on the community brought by the SCLC campaign made his objectives more urgent but more difficult. If Selma had to live with the national civil rights movement in its streets, Smeltzer must search for ways to prevent that ordeal from becoming counterproductive to Selma's interracial relations.

Blacks were upset over a *Times-Journal* editorial on King's coming. Although they understood the pacific intent of the editorial—it asked that King's appearance be treated as a non-event—they considered the language "unnecessarily crude." The editorial called King "the controversial darkie" and quoted J. Edgar Hoover's description of King as "the most notorious liar in the country." The *Times-Journal* complained that King was interested primarily in using Selma for publicity, but granted that "this is his privilege." The newspaper appealed to Selma citizens to ignore King, a statement directed toward violence-prone white extremists as well as black activists. The editorial continued that, in recent years, Selma had experienced several circuses, Jeanette McDonald, minstrel shows, "two World Wars, a number of floods, the Democrats, the Republicans, and Colonel Bundy's rodeo. This fellow [King] just isn't in that class."[2]

Searching for Public Support for Moderation

Smeltzer warned those who would listen that King's appearance made critical the acceleration of a timetable for visible signs of interracial trust. It was vital that business leaders and clergy publicly support moderates at this time, and Smeltzer concentrated his efforts toward the realization of that goal. In the days before King's visit, Smeltzer began to prod moderates for a public statement, and immediately following King's visit, Smeltzer's efforts in this direction became more intense, climaxing with a meeting of moderates at which Smeltzer predicted tragedy for Selma unless policy changed.

Smeltzer also asked for public support for Wilson Baker. On December 31, Baker spoke to the Exchange Club and for the first time described the new city policy on civil rights. Although Baker was no integrationist, his policy would be equal law enforcement for all, and Smeltzer considered it critical that Baker be supported by names that counted, that is, the bankers, preachers, and merchants.[3]

Smeltzer asked Newton to call a special meeting of the Dallas County Christian Ministers Union and to invite Baker and himself as resource people. Smeltzer and Newton hoped that the Ministers Union could support a resolution that pledged support for Baker, law and order, and progress. Smeltzer encouraged Newton, if he felt spiritually moved, to act independently rather than follow Baker or political considerations. Smeltzer also wanted invitations issued to the local rabbi and Catholic priests, but there were too many biases among the Protestant preachers to have a productive meeting with Jewish and Catholic clergy. On the day of King's speech, Smeltzer spent most of his time in strategy meetings with blacks. He pressed them to visit the *Times-Journal* office to protest the obnoxious editorial personally. Smeltzer suggested that the black ministers' organization invite representatives of the white Ministers Union and added that Wilson Baker would come to a meeting of black preachers. Smeltzer was able to tell them that Baker, following Smeltzer's suggestion, called Judge Thomas about dropping charges against blacks and that Baker arrested two whites who threw tear-gas grenades in the black section the previous night. At the last minute, a new element was added to the situation. Rumor had it that Jim Clark, who had been vacationing in Miami, cut short his holiday and would probably be in the city when King arrived.

King's speech that evening, at Brown's Chapel, described the goals of the drive and laid down a challenge to the segregationists. He declared, "We must be willing to go to jail by the thousands. We are not asking, we are demanding the ballot." King said he would be returning to Selma frequently, to assist in the "march on the ballot boxes" throughout Alabama. The Nobel Peace Prize winner would be back.[4]

To avoid public meetings, Smeltzer never went to church in Selma and therefore stayed away from the King rally. While the meeting was in progress, he strolled around town and found calm and quiet. In front of the courthouse was a lone state trooper in a car, and the Federal Building and City Hall showed no signs of activity. There was a minimal police presence on the streets: One police car was three blocks from Brown's Chapel, and a motorcycle was on the corner of Sylvan and Selma. A deputy sheriff's car passed Smeltzer twice during his walk. People stood on the porch at the doors of the chapel, indicating an overflow crowd.

Blacks appreciated Baker's calm approach, but he requested that he receive no public praise at the mass meeting because Clark would accuse him of being too soft. (Baker's message went

from Art Capell to Ed Moss to Reese.) Several days later, Clark
cast it up to Baker that the city administration was working for
"equality for all," and Smeltzer delivered another message to
blacks through Amelia Boynton that Baker did not want to be
portrayed publicly as a black ally.[5]

Following the King meeting, Smeltzer was on the phone with
Newton, Reese, Moss, and Baker. All felt that Selma had weath-
ered the storm with no damage, and black leaders praised
Baker's professional, low-key behavior. Baker also was pleased
with the way the meeting had gone, and he appreciated the favorable reports Smeltzer relayed from Reese and Moss. After
meeting this test successfully, Baker was quite confident, even
euphoric. He predicted that his close contacts with George Wallace through Selma native Cecil Jackson, the governor's executive
secretary, would win Wallace's support for Baker's approach
rather than Clark's. But even if Wallace did not endorse Baker's
policies, Baker would continue his present course anyway: "Just
let him get in the way." Baker asked Smeltzer to tell James Bevel
of SCLC to contact him. Although Baker was tired and wanted a
vacation, he was determined to control the situation in Selma:
"To hell with anyone who tries to stop [me] or interfere."[6]

Selma survived a speech by Martin Luther King; its next test
would come in a few weeks when King returned to lead a march
on the courthouse in mid-January. In the meantime, King returned to Atlanta, and Selma became a scene of frantic maneu-
verings. Smeltzer attended a joint SNCC–SCLC staff meeting
that discussed Monday's plans to have a long line at the voter
registration office. The struggle between city and county became
increasingly bitter. On Monday, January 4, city attorney McLean
Pitts, Baker, Clark, and Hare met regarding jurisdiction of the
courthouse sidewalk, a strategic piece of cement because the registration board met in the courthouse, which was a county building, and demonstrations would probably bring lines and crowds.
Baker told Hare, Clark, and Pitts that his authority included everything in the city except the courthouse, and his jurisdiction in-

cluded the sidewalks outside the courthouse. Baker was so insistent that he stunned Pitts when he threatened to arrest anyone
who got in his way.

At a black mass meeting on January 5, the city–county split
was again evident. Clark had three cars of men at the mass meeting because he feared a Klan appearance, and with a powerful
camera he took pictures of license plates. Baker, who stayed in
his car except to make one phone call and get a Coke, told Clark
to relax, the situation was under control. Baker was at the
church only because of Clark's presence there, and he thought
the sheriff "was making a fool of himself."[7]

On January 4 Smeltzer finally met Smitherman in Wilson
Baker's office. The mayor said he knew about Smeltzer through
Capell and Baker but had avoided a meeting because Smeltzer
was an outsider, who Smitherman implied could not help.
Smitherman was self-conscious about his youth, explaining that it
was a disadvantage he hoped would be offset by his vigor and by
mature advisers such as Baker and Capell. Smitherman also felt
squeezed from several directions simultaneously because both the
Ku Klux Klan and blacks—both of whom he described as poor,
downtrodden, and seeking betterment—had voted for him.
Smitherman also explained that he had many other municipal
problems to manage besides race, which could not consume all of
his time. Smeltzer thought that Smitherman dominated the conversation and considered the mayor's apology for being frank
and straightforward unnecessary because eventually Smitherman
himself confessed to talking around the issue.

Although close advisers Lewis and Capell urged Smitherman
to meet with a biracial committee, the mayor held back from
that decisive symbol because of his perception of the political
climate and the strength of the Citizens Council. Nevertheless, he
was willing to meet with black leaders again, as he had in early
November, which, with Baker's and Capell's presence, would become a biracial meeting if not a committee.[8]

Smeltzer explored every avenue that might lead to greater interracial trust. He called the executive vice-president of Dan River Mills, a company that called itself an equal-opportunity employer, to ask for a public statement, to be issued that same day if possible. Smeltzer acted as a go-between for Reese and Capell regarding the offensive King editorial. On January 5, he arranged a meeting for Reese and Bevel with Baker, at which time the blacks gave the city officials their general plans and explained the purpose of their program. Bevel thought that King's next visit would be on January 14, but he was unsure of his itinerary after that. Bevel was silent on the question of mass demonstrations but emphasized that there would be long lines at the courthouse; Baker wanted only fifteen to twenty people on lines at a time. Baker wondered if more could not be done for blacks "by peaceful and friendly means," but Bevel replied that because of Clark and his posse, Selma was "made to order" to "open the eyes of the nation." It was a helpful, frank meeting that lasted for over an hour.[9]

Two days later Bevel and Baker met again. Bevel confirmed to the Director of Public Safety that King would return on January 14 for testing and demonstrations. "The movement is nothing without demonstrations," Bevel explained.[10]

The Monday after King departed was eventful for Smeltzer. Besides meeting with Smitherman and Boyte, he began to ask, even plead, with whites to come to an emergency meeting he wanted. As the hours slipped by, Smeltzer stressed that it was even more imperative that he meet with a small group of Selma's most influential moderates, including Capell, Ault, Smitherman, and the businessmen's group. Ault was out of town, however, and Smitherman would not be able to attend because of a Chamber of Commerce meeting. On Tuesday, Ault still was away, but Smeltzer pressed for the meeting because he had received new information since the day before. "Every day counts," he stressed. He shared with Capell the news that Harry Boyte had told him: The full power of the national civil rights movement would soon focus on Selma. Smeltzer hoped that his meeting could be held before the chamber meeting that night because he hoped to influence the second meeting.

On the morning of January 6, several of Smeltzer's key white contacts, including Frank Wilson of the business group and Art Capell ("representing" Smitherman), gathered in a room at the People's Bank. Smitherman stubbornly refused to attend because if he talked with outsiders, he suspected his support from segregationists would weaken. Capell called Smitherman "hypersensitive" on this point. And Ault still had not returned from his trip.

Smeltzer did his best to present the situation to the group as bluntly, concisely, and cogently as possible. For once he stepped out of his mediator role and presented the group with a sober analysis and careful suggestions. He said that his SCLC contacts—Boyte and Bevel—had informed him that Selma was chosen as the site to launch an Alabama voting rights campaign because of its reputation for having the toughest resistance in Alabama. The SCLC had at least ten organizers from across the state working in Selma for several weeks or longer to educate and prepare black voters. When black voter applicants were rejected, their example would be held up to the nation as a symbol of resistance to civil rights and as proof of the need for lower voting standards so that all citizens could be enfranchised. King would return at least once, maybe more often, and other nationally known blacks might also come to Selma.

Smeltzer told the group that although civil rights organizations considered voting rights their top priority, compliance with the Civil Rights Act of 1964 would also receive attention. Every major southern city had complied, but not Selma, and blacks were considering importing several hundred volunteers from around the state and nation to test the law. More outsiders!

Furthermore, pressure was building from the direction of Craig Air Force Base. Because of Selma's reputation for discrimination, the Department of Defense was considering putting the city off-limits to Craig personnel. Smeltzer did not have to tell the local business people how that would affect their profits. Smeltzer predicted that the coming scenario would so damage the city's reputation that new industry would bypass Selma, and the companies already in town might close or refuse to expand. Perhaps even Craig would close. "I don't want to be an alarmist, but a realist," he warned.

Unless something was done fast, Smeltzer advised the group, Selma would probably become a regular on evening news programs, and he offered a few small suggestions that he thought would deflect the coming civil rights juggernaut. To remove the focus from voter registration, he proposed that Governor Wallace take a low-key step to speed up the registration process or announce that he was undertaking a study of registration procedures. Also, the county registration board could streamline its process significantly. Voluntary desegregation of Selma's public accommodations, without waiting for a court ruling, would demonstrate good faith. If the city could let local and national civil rights leaders know that they sympathized with the Civil Rights Act and with the voter registration drive, Selma's cause would be helped: "Attitude counts." The city had already improved its reputation with civil rights people because of the way it had handled the King visit on January 2.

Although the meeting lasted two hours, Smeltzer's warnings failed to stimulate the group into action. He tried three times to get them to summon Harry Boyte, whom Smeltzer had standing by at the Holiday Inn, but the group did not respond. (Smeltzer was able to tell Boyte that, according to Capell, blacks who tested public accommodations would not be arrested for trespassing.) Although Smeltzer's prophecies were remarkably precise, these city fathers probably already knew that Selma would receive the brunt of the civil rights movement. King's briefcase had been stolen in Anniston in late 1964, and the FBI had told Wilson about King's "battle plan." For example, it was common knowledge among white officials that King wanted to be arrested. The problem for the moderate whites was not a limited view of the future, although they consistently underestimated the strength and legitimacy of black demands, but finding the community support for change and the individual courage to lead the city in new directions. They probably agreed with Smeltzer's analysis but fatalistically saw no way to avoid the impending civic disaster.[11]

Undaunted by the disappointing reaction to his appeals, Smeltzer resumed laboring for improved communication. On the day following the People's Bank session, January 7, Smeltzer persuaded Wilson to meet with Boyte by delivering a final, this-is-your-last-chance appeal to Wilson. Boyte and Wilson talked genially for an hour in Boyte's Holiday Inn room. Boyte shared the SCLC plans for testing public accommodations and large demonstrations, to which Wilson remarked, "Of course, it would be better for Selma if the SCLC doesn't come." They disagreed over whether the city administration had Clark under control; Wilson was confident, but Boyte was dubious. The meeting left the door open to continued discussions, and Boyte gave Wilson his unlisted home phone number. Smeltzer had struck another blow for better communication.[12]

Smeltzer thought that a public statement supporting compliance with the Civil Rights Act might relieve some of the growing pressure, and he pushed for quick action so that moderates could avoid the appearance of being blackmailed by, or caving in to, a second Martin Luther King visit. When he heard that several businessmen were considering such a document, he telephoned the local SNCC office and asked them to call headquarters in Atlanta to obtain a copy of the McComb, Mississippi, statement and read it back over the WATS line. (The statement came through in a few days.) Although moderates could always be found who privately supported a public declaration of compliance, at this point such statements never attracted substantial support; although statements were drafted, none survived to reach the public.[13]

Art Capell understood Smeltzer's reasons for requesting a

public statement, but felt that any statement now came too soon after King's first visit and would be too close to his next. According to Capell, tensions had heightened; a statement might have been possible at an earlier point, and even useful, but it was too late now. Capell believed that strong, careful editorials in the *Times-Journal* could replace a public statement, without moderates exposing themselves to public pressure. On that day, for example, the *Times-Journal*'s editorial instructed its readers that "the only sensible course left for our citizens to follow is to face-up to the inevitabilities of the future," which implied the need for change. The editorial called for law and order and praised Wilson Baker.[14]

Smeltzer's hope for a public statement from white preachers also went unfulfilled. In hopes of producing a declaration, John Newton called a meeting of the Ministers Union and asked its president, Paul Grist, who was also president of the YMCA, to invite Baker. Newton sat beside Grist at a Rotary meeting and told him that although he had not talked to Baker, Baker expected to be asked, which drew a quizzical look from Grist. (Smeltzer was the intermediary between Newton and Baker.)[15]

The white Protestants gathered on January 11. Baker's moderate words were similar to the recent Exchange Club presentation, and he backed away from his hard-line Rotary speech. Baker advised the clergy to keep their distance from the demonstrators, but he offered no constructive suggestions. When Newton asked for specific advice, he and Baker saw heads shaking. Perhaps this deterred the director of public safety from becoming more specific. His talk was received favorably by the Protestant ministers.[16]

Although abstaining from public action, blacks took steps to increase their support among the grass roots in time for King's next visit. Organizers from SNCC and SCLC leafletted the city and knocked on doors to persuade blacks to attend ward meetings on Thursday, January 7. As they went door to door, the staff people received a mixed reaction. Some residents eagerly promised to attend, but often the canvassers saw those most likely to be home during the day—the old, the sick, and the chronically unemployed—who sometimes responded with bewilderment, negativism, or ignorance. Many replied with unemotional ambivalence.

The first ward meetings covered concerns from the dramatic to mundane—in one ward the topic was garbage removal—but they were landmark events because black citizens now publicly complained about their treatment. At another ward meeting, James Bevel expelled sheriff's deputies, and when one of them raised a camera, Bevel further ordered that no pictures be taken.[17]

King's Return

As the SCLC campaign progressed in Selma, it attracted an ever-growing number of outsiders of various ideological persuasions, and this tended further to destabilize the community. The SCLC tactics and Clark's response to them polarized Selma and gradually pushed the community farther from Smeltzer's goals of interracial understandings and reduced tension, with tragic results. While Smeltzer worked to close the gaps between black and white Selma, SCLC and Clark combined to widen them.

King returned to Selma on January 14 to tell a mass meeting that he would head a march to the courthouse on Monday, January 18, and that squads of volunteers would test public facilities. King himself would lead the testing by registering at the Hotel Albert, an antebellum structure modeled after a Venetian palace. City–county cooperation was smooth in policing the mass meeting, and the large press corps that had followed King to Selma in early January was absent.

Baker believed that Monday's march would be important for another reason: If the events did not produce enough public attention, then SCLC might shift its project to another Alabama town. This was exactly what Baker wanted. So far, the SCLC campaign had produced few sparks, and Baker knew that the despised "outside agitators" would go somewhere else if another non-newsworthy day occurred.[18]

Municipal insiders were optimistic about Freedom Day, which was what blacks called the day of planned marches and testing. There were minor misunderstandings between blacks and Baker, but from his phone base in Illinois, Smeltzer helped remove them. Baker had expected blacks to pass along information regarding their plans, but with only a few days left until the march, black leaders had not talked with Baker. (Smeltzer told Reese about this.) Baker offered to take black leaders into his office and review Monday's walk in order to assist blacks to avoid violation of a local ordinance; Reese and Bevel spent over an hour with Baker. The Clark–Baker relationship was about as good as it would get, although a newspaper photo of Baker, hanging in the sheriff's office, had horns and a mustache doodled on it. Judge Thomas was sending federal marshalls to observe Clark and the state troopers, and Love and SNCC were cooperating to keep students in school.[19]

Although the editors remained opposed to the Civil Rights Act, another *Times-Journal* editorial strongly urged compliance.[20] Restaurant owners still waited for the federal court to rule on their noncompliance so that they could gracefully yield, but some observers believed that only one restaurant really wanted to resist. If owners insisted on calling for the arrest of blacks, Baker would have to follow through, but he hoped to talk them out of it.

At the last minute, Smeltzer canceled his trip to Selma. Everything was set for Monday, and there was little he could do. Although interracial communication fell far short of his goals, he believed that the contacts he had worked so hard to build between black and white Selma had paid off. Capell suggested that he could come after Monday and help pick up the pieces, if necessary.[21]

In spite of all the precautions and preparations, on the morning of Monday, January 18, Smeltzer received a phone call in Illinois from Harry Boyte, who said that it was essential for Baker to talk with King that morning because of a possible misunderstanding. Boyte thought they had an agreement that blacks could walk from Brown's Chapel to the courthouse, but on the previous day, an Associated Press story had quoted Baker that he would arrest King if he led a march. When Smeltzer telephoned, Baker was in a patrol car, so a lieutenant radioed Baker with the message to call Smeltzer immediately for a message from Martin Luther King.

Baker was willing to have King drop by his office, but Smeltzer pointed out the difficulties with this and suggested that King, Baker, and Reese talk briefly in front of the church before the meeting began. Also, Boyte wanted to talk and would take Baker's collect call. Baker agreed to contact King and Boyte as suggested, but he added that he would not be seen calling the SCLC group from his office.[22]

The Baker–King caucus cleared away any misunderstandings about city ordinances and parades; there were no arrests, and the first day's demonstrations of the Alabama Project were peaceful, if inconclusive. King led about four hundred blacks—they followed Baker's advice and walked in groups of threes and fours on sidewalks and obeyed traffic signals—to the courthouse where Clark and Baker posed for a picture as jurisdiction passed from city to county.

As the blacks came to the courthouse, they were met by a menagerie of notables; besides Baker, Clark, and a media contingent of approximately eighty, there were George Lincoln Rockwell, leader of the American Nazi Party, and Jimmy George Robinson, of the National States Rights Party, confronting King. Rockwell dared King to let him speak to the mass meeting that evening. After hesitating, King granted Rockwell and Robinson fifteen minutes each to present their doctrines that segregation was best for all. With that done, the marchers focused on gaining admission to the building, while Rockwell and Robinson turned on each other.

At the courthouse, Clark directed the marchers through the Lauderdale Street entrance, past the registrar's office, and out the back door into an alley, where he had strung a rope. He left them standing in the freezing temperature for the rest of the day. None of the blacks in the alley was called into the building that day; the only applicants processed were forty whites, who arrived there early, an effort probably organized by Clark or his supporters. The press saw almost nothing because Clark shunted them across the street as soon as the King–Rockwell dialogue began.[23]

The testing also went quietly. Several establishments closed rather than comply, but only one, the Carter–Walgreen drugstore, refused to serve blacks. Reportedly, the drugstore had white toughs hanging around to handle the situation. (Smeltzer called the national headquarters of the Walgreen chain to ask them to pressure the local outlet.) There was a small incident when one of Rockwell's Nazi colleagues showed up at the Selma Del, an expensive restaurant, wearing blackface, carrying a doll, and claiming to be a cannibal. He planned to parade in front of any black demonstrators in blackface. Baker arrested him for disorderly conduct, and he made him wash before his arraignment.[24]

The most disturbing incident occurred when King arrived at the Albert where the manager, who sympathized with integration, registered King smoothly. States Rights Party leader Robinson followed King's entourage into the lobby and approached King, requesting a conference with him. As soon as King came abreast of the man, Robinson hit him on the temple and tried to kick him in the groin. King doubled over, and aides struggled to subdue Robinson, upsetting a lamp as they did so. A white woman, in tight slacks and a leather jacket, at the opposite end of the lobby yelled, "Get him! Get him!"

Baker was only a few feet away. He lifted Robinson off the floor by his thunderbolted lapels, asking, "What are you doing in here anyhow?" He put Robinson in a police car, under arrest. Robinson's kicks had missed their target, but for several days thereafter King suffered a severe headache from the blow to the temple. That night, a Ku Klux Klan rally on the outskirts of town attracted approximately twenty tough-looking whites.[25]

Baker's control of the situation and the absence of any antics by Clark were major topics at a midnight SCLC staff meeting. Although the day had gone quietly, and would be so noted in the press, King was amazed at Clark's uncouth behavior. Clark was not even civil to whites, much less blacks, King observed. If Selma remained too calm, the press would quickly desert them; with nothing to write about, the reporters would go home. The staff decided to try another march the next day in Selma; if it, too, went quietly, they would find a new location. Alabama had plenty of candidates for a voter registration campaign: perhaps nearby Marion in Perry County or Camden in Wilcox County where, despite an 80 percent black population, there was not a single black voter. If Selma failed to live up to its reputation, there were many other fertile fields for publicity in the Black Belt.

There was a spy at the staff meeting, and Wilson Baker soon learned that if he could repeat the day's serene scenario, the SCLC campaign would leave Selma.[26] But Baker's chances for success dimmed when Smitherman called him down to the jail for a meeting in the wee hours. There, Sheriff Clark angrily vowed to arrest the marchers and ignored the pleas of the mayor and Baker to practice one more day of restraint.[27]

The Demonstrations Gain Momentum

The marchers again gathered at Brown's Chapel and walked in small groups to the courthouse. This time, they went to the Alabama Avenue entrance because they wanted to go through the front door. They would not wait in the alley today. Their boldness paid dividends: Clark responded as expected.

The sheriff arrested the marchers. One of the first to be seized was Amelia Boynton, and when her pace to the sheriff's car was slower than he liked, he grabbed her behind the collar and pushed her down the street in full view of astonished marchers and newspeople.[28]

Following the day's activities, there was another SCLC staff meeting, and it was agreed that activities would increase the next day. In provoking Clark, the civil rights people had found Selma's soft spot. Clark's treatment of the dignified, middle-class black woman demonstrated that he could personify to the nation and, more specifically, to Congress the violence of segregation and provide persuasive publicity in the drive for national voting rights legislation.[29]

Were it not for Clark's arrests or even his treatment of Boynton, Selma might have been off the hook. After George Lincoln Rockwell's case was dropped in city court, he stomped out of town complaining that the city police had "cut my heart out with this harassment, so I'm going to leave and let Martin Luther Coon [King] take over your city."[30] Very few mourned Rockwell's departure. In city court, Jimmy George Robinson, King's assailant at the Albert Hotel, received a $100 fine and sixty days at hard labor, but charges against Robert Lloyd, the blackfaced Nazi, were dismissed. Baker had contained the right wing, and if Clark could contain himself, the SCLC campaign might leave.

The following day, January 20, with King in the north for speaking engagements, there were more arrests, and the Baker–Clark feud became public. Blacks sent three contingents of fifty each to the front door of the courthouse. John Lewis, the national chairman of SNCC, headed the first squad. Clark gave the marchers one minute to disperse, counted down the seconds, and then arrested them.

The second group was similarly arrested, but when the third wave arrived, Clark baited Baker, who watched with obvious disapproval. The sheriff addressed Baker as "Captain," his old rank, and requested him to clear the marchers off the sidewalks. Instead, Baker lined up the marchers in front of the main door and down the sidewalk for a block and a half, and two plainclothesmen carried whispered messages between the sheriff and the Director of Public Safety. After posse members pushed the blacks off the sidewalk, Baker put them back on the sidewalk again, this time in single file. Then Clark, seizing a bullhorn, gave the crowd one minute to leave and arrested them, too. The *New York Times* reported the division between city and county law enforcement and pointed out that the only people arrested by the city (i.e., by Baker) were white extremists.[31]

The week's demonstrations climaxed on Friday when F. D. Reese, a science teacher and former president of the Selma Teachers Association, led almost all the city's black educators to the courthouse steps for a confrontation with School Board President Edgar Stewart, Superintendent J. A. Pickard, and Sheriff Jim Clark. A teachers' march surprised many because black educators enjoyed a measure of financial security and had more to lose than most from white economic retaliation. The teachers expected to be arrested and chose to march on Friday afternoon so that they could be bailed out in time for Monday's classes. They were dressed in their best clothes, with high heels, hats, and gloves for the women and suits and Stetsons for the men.

Pickard and Stewart spent three hours at the courthouse trying to persuade Clark to allow the teachers to walk through the courthouse, which was all they wanted to do. When the teachers arrived, Pickard and Stewart tried to talk them into turning back. Stewart reminded them of the good relations that had always existed between black and white educators and then told Reese that the teachers had made their point, so now they could turn around. Of course, if the teachers were arrested and held over the weekend, then the students would be out of class and probably in the streets on Monday, which was the last place white Selma wanted them.

Stewart went into the courthouse to confer with Clark, but the sheriff brushed past him and gave the teachers one minute to move off the courthouse steps, where twelve of the educators stood. Several times Clark and his deputies used nightsticks to jab the teachers off the steps and onto the sidewalk, but each time the teachers quietly remounted the steps. Before the teachers had even arrived, Clark was visibly nervous, and by this time his anger was substantial. Clark told the teachers that they would make a mockery of "my courthouse" if they did not move and that "some of you think you can make it a Disneyland." He followed these remarks with the now-familiar one-minute ultimatum. The teachers were prepared for arrest—each carried a toothbrush, toothpaste, and any necessary medical prescriptions—but about halfway through the countdown, solicitor Blanchard McLeod pulled Clark into the courthouse for a huddle. When the sheriff returned, his deputies once again shoved the teachers off the steps.

Stewart repeated a request for the teachers to leave, adding that the sheriff "has been most forbearing." After about a twenty-minute wait on the sidewalk, Reese realized that Clark would not arrest the teachers and led them back to Brown's Chapel where a youth mass meeting was in progress. (The FBI account of this incident says that Andy Young "reportedly" told the teachers that they had made their point and could return.) Reese and 105 solemn-looking teachers walked up the aisle as wild cheering continued until all of them stood in the front. It was a high point of the campaign and a moving moment as students cheered their teachers, pillars of middle-class respectability, who, by challenging their white employers, had risked their professional and financial security. Teachers, students, and veteran civil rights workers all sang an enthusiastic "This Little Light of Mine," and some wept. The middle class had joined the revolution.[32]

After only one week of the SCLC campaign, the movement gained considerable momentum with the involvement of the teachers and the national exposure produced by Jim Clark's outbursts. But the movement's tactics widened Selma's racial divisions. Some nonextremist whites felt that blacks had goaded Clark into making arrests; moderates acknowledged that Clark snapped at the first bait offered, but had blacks behaved less irresponsibly and had they gone home when not permitted through the courthouse door, problems would have been avoided. Instead, an incurable wound had been opened. Communication between

Baker and Clark was at a standstill. The white community was bitterly divided by misunderstandings and hurt feelings. Innumerable meetings now were taking place, but they were counterproductive. The business leaders met into the early morning with no results and began to feel pressured personally. Although some whites understood that blacks were trying to make a point about going through the front door of the courthouse, they were unsympathetic because many whites, even blue-blooded Selmians, used the side entrance on Lauderdale Street. The moderates had developed a measure of trust in Reese, but they were uninterested in building communication with SCLC organizers and only wished that they would leave.[33]

Smeltzer urged Reese to keep in contact with white leaders and made specific suggestions on whom to call and visit. He talked each morning with Reese on the telephone, before Reese went to school, and his suggestions were generally followed.

Exposing Selma's Hostility

In the next round of demonstrations, the SCLC tactics of confrontation, intended to force segregationists to reveal their true nature, were matched not only by Clark's tempestuous responses but by an increasingly irascible Wilson Baker. On Monday, January 25, King was back in Selma. A line left Brown's Chapel for the courthouse, but this time, Wilson Baker's behavior changed. He was more abrupt and shorter-tempered than before, and demanded that the marchers walk in two's (as the teachers had done) and not jam the intersections while waiting for traffic lights to change. Staff workers were stationed at intervals to assure the proper spacing.

At the courthouse, Sheriff Clark patroled the sidewalk to keep it clear and shoved people who did not move quickly enough. At the end of the line was Baker, warning staff people to stay away from the line. When one civil rights worker, Willie McRae of

SNCC, refused one of Baker's commands, Baker grabbed him by the shoulder, placed him under arrest, and dragged the limp McRae to a police car.

As the line watched the commotion and Sheriff Clark elbowed his way through the blacks, pushing them back into line, Annie Lee Cooper, one of the Dunn Rest Home women whose firing had brought Ralph Smeltzer to Selma in 1963, ran out of patience. When Clark moved past her, she cursed and hit him in the head with a punch so powerful that he fell to his knees. Then, before he realized what had happened, she struck him again. By all accounts, including the sheriff's, he was stunned. Law enforcement officials rushed at the woman, but the fifty-three-year-old Cooper was sturdy and, although outnumbered, put up a competent defense. With deputies holding her down and Clark bending over her, she struggled with him for control of his billy club and told him, "I wish you would hit me, you scum." He obliged her with a whack that was audible clear down the street. In the scuffle, Clark lost his green tie, his "scrambled-eggs" hat, his badge, and momentarily his nightstick—not to mention his dignity. Mrs. Cooper left in two pairs of handcuffs and with a wound over one eye. Deputies suffered bruises, bites, and torn buttons. After the action, Baker ordered all blacks without voter registration numbers to leave, and Andy Young took them back to Brown's Chapel.

The reaction to the Cooper–Clark bout was as important as the event. When asked if Cooper was married, Clark replied, "She's a nigger woman and she hasn't got a Miss or a Mrs. in front of her name. She says she's a secretary at a motel, but I think she's a bouncer. . . . She knocked hell out of me." After King watched the battle, he told reporters, "We have seen another day of brutality." A picture of Clark sitting atop Cooper appeared on the front page of the *New York Times* and the second page of the *Washington Post*. The photo reinforced the image of Deep South police brutality because it showed a southern lawman, with billy club raised, while two deputies pinned a black person, a woman, to the ground. Local whites generally believed that the press mishandled the incident because Clark was only trying to recapture the club from Cooper's grasp—the picture shows Cooper's hands on the club—and to Selma's segregationists the wide publication of this picture was classic evidence of the media distortion they considered an everyday occurrence.[34]

Reactions to the violence at the courthouse illustrate the polarization that the SCLC campaign brought to Selma. The *Times-Journal* responded to the violence on the registration line with harsh words, signaling a shift away from moderation. Its lead sentence implied that King's return had stimulated Mrs. Cooper's action and cast doubts on the validity of his Nobel Prize for peace.

> Violence erupted in a voter registration line at the Dallas County Courthouse late this morning shortly after the arrival on the scene of Dr. Martin Luther King. Until the 1964 Nobel Peace Prize winner appeared at 11 A.M., there had been no disorders except several verbal exchanges between civil rights workers and officers supervising the procedure.[35]

Smeltzer found it increasingly difficult to get his white contacts to be receptive to his message. One of the bankers angrily complained that the "situation [has] gone to hell!" and wanted local black leaders to get rid of SCLC. Whites felt that SCLC used local blacks for its own needs, probably financial, and one source reported that now no local whites would talk with black leaders. Moderates were fatigued and disillusioned, and whites generally failed to understand the depth of black concerns and the unity that King had brought to black Selma. Art Capell shunned Smeltzer's phone calls, and Frank Wilson remembers many "sad meetings" because he was not as effective as he had hoped to be. He knew that, under the surface, there was tremendous potential for more street violence.[36]

Meanwhile, blacks were unified as never before, and SNCC and SCLC organizers cooperated smoothly. One local black ac-

tivist observed that one of King's greatest achievements in Selma
was the unification of the various black factions, the bringing together of the "Pharisees and Sadducees." Speaking at the mass
meeting the night after Cooper and Clark fought, Ralph Abernathy pointed to an antenna-like instrument attached to the pulpit and announced that he had been warned to watch what he
said because Wilson Baker's police had installed a "doohickey."
Abernathy seized the instrument, which allegedly transmitted to
the outside, and to the delight of his listeners preached directly to
it on the evils of segregation. He told Baker's "doohickey" that
there would be no more going to the courthouse in widely spaced
groups, "and the next time we go we're going to walk *together*."
It would not be a parade. "When we want to have a *parade*,
doohickey, we'll get the R. B. Hudson High School Band and take
over the town!" Abernathy's audience roared with laughter. After
his speech he put the "doohickey" back in its place with exaggerated care. Abernathy's rousing speech so scared city officials that
they summoned Al Lingo's state troopers for support.[37]

Blacks who were afraid to march contributed by delivering
bail money during the night to Ed Moss. Marchers did not mind
going to jail, but they were unenthusiastic about staying there,
which was understandable considering the conditions. If there
had been no way to bail out those arrested, the movement would
have been injured severely. Locals quartered civil rights workers
in their homes in unprecedented numbers.[38]

Blacks were disturbed by the change in behavior of the city
police and an apparent tilt toward Clark by the *Times-Journal*.
Reese noted to Smeltzer that marchers were in groups of five or
six, 10 feet apart, when the demonstrations began, but without
warning, Baker made them walk in pairs and 20 feet apart.
Reese's reply to the white accusation that the SCLC people
blocked understanding was to complain that Jim Clark was the
source of Selma's problems. The sheriff had no understanding of
blacks, and without Clark's intransigence, the simple public right
of access to the courthouse would be available. Reese told Smelt-

zer that he could find no other blacks to accompany him on visits to white leaders at this time.

Harry Boyte predicted to Smeltzer that now that the tension had increased, the pressure would be turned up and the overwhelming pattern of discrimination in Selma would become apparent. Selma's "residual hostility" would be brought into the open. "Selma can't heal itself until the depth of its hostility is exposed," he warned.[39]

Communication Becomes Increasingly Difficult

Smeltzer believed that Selma would be wise to recognize its position as the focal point of the civil rights campaign and to make the best of it by becoming a symbol of compliance rather than resistance. He encouraged Baker and Capell not to "get sucked into the courthouse mess," which would be a political liability in the next election, and he emphasized the black unity to whites.[40]

During the brief period of relative quiet between King's departure on January 26 and his return on January 31, Smeltzer discovered that positions had hardened. The pressures and emotions of the SCLC campaign had eroded his carefully crafted interracial communication and trust. The *Times-Journal* urged Selma blacks not to follow "The Path of the 'Judas Goat' " and complained about the "continuing harassment of Dallas County officials by ill-advised Negro groups." The editorial revealed that many in white Selma believed that blacks had been "coerced into participating," and it called the civil rights organizers "hypocritical" and "professional hatchetmen [committing] intemperate harangues."[41]

While whites, including the centrist *Times-Journal,* united in criticism of King, blacks became more bitter toward white Selma. In a conversation with Smeltzer, Reese used "conniving" three times to describe the courthouse people and stated his willingness to die in the attempt to register blacks. He complained that, after all this effort, only fifty-seven blacks had made it to the registrar's office, and they were beginning to receive letters of rejection. Reese was more cynical than ever. According to him, the city administration had changed its attitude and no longer kept in touch with him. Reese suspected that he had been used by the city for political advantage and that the earlier phone conversations with him had been insincere.[42]

"Baloney" was Baker's response when he heard from Smeltzer that blacks thought he was not interested in communication. He assumed that it was blacks who no longer wanted to talk and that their attitude had changed, not his. According to Baker, Reese had lost control to outsiders; King was in town for financial reasons; and SNCC workers were dirty, unkempt outsiders. He warned against using students in demonstrations.

Smeltzer told Baker that he was sure that the civil rights people had much more in store for Selma than Baker realized. Reese wanted to meet with Baker, and if blacks thought he was fair, they would share their plans with him. Smeltzer informed Baker that Reese was on the spot because he had stuck his neck out to persuade other blacks to talk with the city government; now blacks said to Reese, "We told you so." Smeltzer told Baker that there were misunderstandings on both sides and that it was impossible to correct them because everyone was too busy.

Smeltzer returned to Reese to say that there was a large misunderstanding between blacks and the city. Each side felt the other had quit communicating and had demonstrated bad faith. Reese rejected the notion that local blacks had lost control and claimed that he could veto any objectionable movement plans; he had personally chaired the last two staff meetings. Whites were not close enough to the situation to know the relationships among blacks. Reese did not feel as though he was "being taken for a ride [by SCLC]; he felt part of the ride." In spite of his feelings of distrust, Reese was still willing to renew talks with Baker.

Smeltzer acquired an ally and colleague when A. M. ("Mac") Secrest of the Community Relations Service (CRS), a Department of Commerce agency, arrived. Representatives from CRS could only come to Selma if they were invited, and Smeltzer told the business group about them, which probably was the stimulus for their invitation. Some of the mayor's supporters asked the CRS officials to prevent King's return on January 18, but when the CRS men were unable to grant that request, the mayor's people were no longer interested in cooperating with them. Smeltzer suggested contacts for the CRS men, shared his analyses with them, and thought that he might be able to phase Secrest into replacing him.[43]

7

Enter King — Exit Smeltzer

The cunningly calculated torment of Selma and Dallas County is the biggest, cruelest and most unjust publicity stunt staged in a long time.

Representative Armistead I. Seldon (D –Ala.)

We're going to turn Selma upside down and inside out in order to make it rightside up.

Martin Luther King, Jr.

There can be no remission of sin without the shedding of blood.

Martin Luther King, Jr.

When you pray, Be not as the hypocrites are, Standing in the Street.
Matthew 6:5.
Signboard on the Selma Avenue Church of Christ

What do these niggers want?

A white saleslady in Selma

We had every screwball in the United States down here.

Roswell Falkenberry

I'll never forget the day early in 1965 when I shuttled back and forth between Police Chief Wilson Baker and his officer on one side of the line and Andy Young, Dr. King's assistant, leader of the marchers, on the other side of the line trying to negotiate the rules for a march down on the courthouse.

Ralph E. Smeltzer

Here you have hundreds of preachers who decide to march against a federal court injunction, against an edict by state and city, and against the will of President Johnson as expressed in the newspapers. . . . Can they, in their prayers to God, say that they were without sin that morning?

Seymour Palmer, Selma department store manager

When the Reverend Joseph Ellwanger proposed bringing his white parishioners from Birmingham to march in support of the SCLC campaign, several of his Selma friends, including the reporter Kathryn Windham, tried to dissuade him.

> I just didn't think it was wise. I thought the presence of those white people here was going to stir up feelings of people who had best not be stirred. But he [Ellwanger] wouldn't listen to me. I called him more than twice. I did everything I could to keep him from coming down here. And that Saturday that he came was the only time I was ever frightened during that whole period of demonstrating. I was also on the newspaper here—I'm a newspaper reporter—and so I had been in all of it and I had never been frightened, not one time. I never changed my regular habits of anything that I was doing. The shortest way to town from home is through the black area. I drove it day and night and it never occurred to me to be frightened.
>
> But that Saturday I was frightened. The officials, for reasons which I do not quite comprehend, called off the law enforcement; you know they were pretty obvious all around.

There weren't any in town that day, and that white mob got completely out of hand.

Windham was especially frightened because her teenage son was with her. He was fifteen years old, and before this, she had never allowed him to attend the demonstrations. He went to all his activities, but he had not been permitted to be at the demonstrations. "But he wanted to go see," she said. "So we went and he had a camera and we were on the courthouse steps. The white mob got bigger and bigger and angrier and angrier. They overturned cars and fired them. Women were screaming, 'Kill 'em; kill 'em.' "

Windham and her son became separated in the crowd, and she feared that his camera would misidentify him as a member of the press. Although her son was still in high school, he was a six-footer and probably unaware of his danger. Windham was unconcerned about herself because most people recognized her, but she was very worried about her son.

It was as terrifying a thirty minutes as I've ever spent. I'll never forget the expressions on some of those faces: pure hatred. Some people you do not provoke any further than they can bear, and they had had just about all of it they could stand. It was just more than they could bear. The women were especially angry.

After approximately one half hour of searching for her son, Windham found him, unharmed.[1]

Smeltzer's Difficulties Increase

The transformation of the Selma movement from a local to a national event made more difficult Smeltzer's peacekeeping mission. The arrival of the SCLC campaign and national newspaper headlines took control of events away from local blacks, municipal authorities, and Smeltzer. Lyndon Johnson, Martin Luther King, and George Wallace became the important decision makers affecting Selma.

During the SCLC campaign, two specific developments worked against Smeltzer's goals of better communication and less tension: Sheriff Clark's violence and the tactics of SCLC. King was interested primarily in using Selma to bring national attention to the specific injustice suffered by southern black voters and to the general disgrace of American racism. Organizers at SCLC often considered Smeltzer's minor compromises for reducing tension and building trust to be counterproductive because they blurred the national spotlight on bigotry. In the streets, Jim Clark's behavior reinvigorated the movement several times and helped sustain emotions at a high level. Events snowballed; black strategy, fixed on a march to the state capital to bring Black Belt injustice more sharply to national notice, and the violent response by law enforcement officers played right into the hands of the demonstrators.

The SCLC campaign diminished Smeltzer's ability to influence events. Although he made several visits to Selma and monitored developments closely by telephone, especially with Reese, his visits became less frequent and more ineffective than previously. His voluminous notes are silent on what must have been disappointing frustrations, but in this case, his lack of action speaks as definitively as his beloved notes.

King's Arrest

Rather than relax pressure, King wanted to escalate tension. The SCLC methodology included nonviolent probing for a community's tender spot, and when it was located, the SCLC leaders applied pressure to the weakest link. In Selma, this was Jim Clark and his courthouse. King believed that only exposure would cure injustice but that the violence infesting segregation was always hidden in the alleys, backrooms, and jails. Therefore the movement needed to bring that violence into the streets where it could be unmasked (preferably on television) and healed. King did not believe that his campaigns created violence and tension; instead, they forced already existing conditions to become public so that the world could witness the evil of racism. King sought to replace the massive violence endured daily by innocent victims with the minimal violence now directed toward movement volunteers. A few rocks and nightsticks were preferable to the violence of undereducating thousands of black children. According to the blacks, blaming King and his suffering servants for the violence was like blaming Christ for being crucified.[2]

From the beginning of the campaign, the SCLC game plan included Martin Luther King's arrest and a "Letter from a Selma Jail" on voting rights modeled after his famous "Letter from a Birmingham Jail." A special SCLC executive staff meeting on January 28 decided that Selma's stage was now set for King's arrest. Field staff were ordered to mobilize the largest crowd possible, including high school students, for a march that would lead to King's arrest, and local black reluctance to encourage students to skip classes was overcome.

The city's policy of restraint had put King's arrest approximately two weeks behind schedule.[3] Although many contributed to the formulation of the city's strategy, Smeltzer's emphasis on nonconfrontation and interracial communication, and his assistance to the business group, must receive some of the credit. Certainly, assertive personalities such as Wilson Baker, Frank Wilson, and Edgar Stewart were not Smeltzer's pawns, but the moderates listened to him and took some of his advice. And the communication he nurtured contributed to a more sophisticated approach than SCLC expected from the hard-core Black Belt city.

Local authorities learned quickly about King's decision to be jailed and maneuvered to force one another to do the actual arresting. High-ranking state troopers reportedly pressured Baker to enforce his no-parade policy, but city leaders hoped to avoid making the arrest. One reason for this was that the Hammermill Paper Company of Erie, Pennsylvania, had recently announced the construction of a new mill in Selma. It would hardly be in Selma's interests for its jails to be bursting with Hammermill's new labor force.

Although King had little concern for his personal safety, top SCLC staff members worried about what might happen if Clark arrested King and got him away from the public view. They wanted very much to have Baker make the arrest, and this turned out to be surprisingly easy to arrange. King delivered a rousing speech to the mass meeting on Sunday evening, January 31, and the next morning headed a column of 250 marchers out of Brown's Chapel and downtown. As they approached an intersection, Wilson Baker sat in his car and watched the marchers walk in a large group, defying his requests for pairing and spacing. Baker got out of his car and, surrounded by a horde of reporters, rasped out (he had laryngitis) his demand that the parade ordinance honored for three weeks be obeyed today. Baker gave King's column an ultimatum: Break into groups or be arrested. King replied that the city's parade ordinance violated the constitutional right of peaceful assembly and resumed the march by walking right past Baker, who could not tolerate this blatant defiance and drove ahead of the column to stop its progress. After Ralph Abernathy led the demonstrators in prayer, Baker led them to the city jail.[4]

Also arrested that day were about five hundred students. The use of students, another escalation by SCLC, especially troubled whites, who regarded it as manipulative and as final proof that King's campaign did not have the good of the city, black or white, at heart because children were being taught to disrespect law and order. The use of students even disturbed whites with some understanding of black demands, and it generally increased the interracial mistrust that Smeltzer was trying to reduce. Whites had difficulty dealing with student marchers and could not find an alternative tactic to the students' arrest.[5] Blacks thought student participation to be anything but manipulative because they were not coaxing the kids onto the streets. On the contrary, black adults had to restrain them. Students had been an important part of the movement from its inception in 1963, and teachers had already marched, so why not the youth? Blacks considered the white concern over student demonstrators to be another example of white ignorance of the black community.

Many more marchers were arrested over the next two days, including three hundred students who serenaded Clark with freedom songs at the courthouse (e.g., "I love Jim Clark in my heart"). Some students eluded police for a short time but were chased down by squad cars; the classic goal of civil disobedience (i.e., to fill the jails) was achieved. At this point, more than twenty-six hundred people had been arrested since the beginning of the campaign.

The new prisoners were not docile and kept the jail corridors ringing with enthusiastic singing. Conditions, however, were anything but humane. At one camp, beds were thrown outside the cells before the marchers arrived and were piled in the halls; the prisoners slept on the concrete floor. Windows were jammed open throughout the February night. Other prisoners were housed on a wetted-down concrete floor with no heat.

The latest wave of arrests rejuvenated the movement at a moment when the campaign was losing steam. Most of those arrested with King were released the first night, and in spite of a bitter cold snap, many returned the next day to Brown's Chapel to demonstrate again.[6]

With King in jail, events in Selma increasingly became national rather than local. At a press conference, President Johnson, as part of his prepared remarks, gave his support to the voting rights campaign in Selma. He commented that "all Americans should be indignant when one American is denied the right to vote. . . . All of us should be concerned with the efforts of our fellow Americans to register to vote in Alabama."[7] Members of SCLC placed a large ad in the *New York Times* and headlined it

A *Letter from* MARTIN LUTHER KING *from a Selma, Alabama, Jail.* King's letter quoted a racist comment by Selma's villain, Jim Clark, and complained about discrimination in voter registration. In large letters King proclaimed, "THIS IS SELMA, ALABAMA. THERE ARE MORE NEGROES IN JAIL WITH ME THAN THERE ARE ON THE VOTING ROLLS."[8]

While King was incarcerated, he kept in touch with the campaign's progress and was disappointed that his assistants called off the marches on Thursday. King's aides had canceled the demonstrations because Judge Thomas issued an injunction granting black voter registration applicants a few minor concessions. At first reading, the injunction sounded conciliatory, but after closer scrutiny, SCLC staff members decided more or less to ignore it. Instead of being pleased with the concessions, some movement leaders were disappointed because the injunction robbed the campaign of momentum.[9] In instructions to Andy Young written from his cell, King suggested a variety of ways to keep Selma in the news, including a personal phone call to President Johnson, a visitation by a congressional delegation, and a telephone call to Sammy Davis, Jr., asking him to do a benefit in Atlanta ("I find that all of these fellows respond better when I am in jail or in a crisis").

To maintain the movement's momentum, King advised Young: "By all means don't let them get the offensive. They are trying to give the impression that they are an orderly and good community because they integrated public accommodations. We must insist that voting is the issue. And here Selma has dirty hands." He instructed Young to "consider a night march to the city jail protesting" his unjust arrest and to send night marchers to the courthouse "to let Clark show [his] true colors."

If daytime demonstrations risked violence, night marches carried much greater danger. The darkness made the marchers an easy target for snipers and provided greater temptations to those already violently inclined. Yet blacks thought that whites feared night marches more than they did. Who would be in the march, where would the marchers go, and who might take advantage of the march? "You talk about really gettin' some people's hairs up!" recalls F. D. Reese. King's request for a night march was a call to enhance substantially the probability of violence. King had won the 1964 Nobel Prize for peace; was his calling for a night march a deliberate attempt to provoke violence? (The march never occurred because King's request came when SCLC staff had called off all demonstrations in order to study Judge Thomas's injunction.[10])

King's messages to Young underscore the fact that Smeltzer and the civil rights movement were not working in tandem. Smeltzer believed that Selma had very real potential for random and spontaneous street violence, and one of his priority goals was to remove conditions that threatened the peace. As a strong adherent to the Church of the Brethren's traditional belief in resolving conflicts through peace and reconciliation, Smeltzer wanted the civil rights revolution to come about without violence, whether private or public. Although Smeltzer strongly supported civil rights goals, his mediation made more difficult the SCLC exposure of the hidden violence within segregation. Conversely, SCLC's confrontationist strategy hindered Smeltzer's peacemaking. Smeltzer certainly agreed that segregation was a violent system, but he hoped to see injustice end without the creation of victims of other forms of violence.

Smeltzer found Selma more divided than ever during King's imprisonment. Wilson Baker, with his laryngitis, was short-tempered and accused Smeltzer of being in league with SNCC, a major insult in Baker's vocabulary. Both sides were uninterested in negotiations and considered them fruitless. Outside observers such as Bob Jansen and John Doar believed that Smeltzer needed to let things run their course for a while before he could be of help.

On Friday, February 5, King left jail and met a delegation of fifteen northern congressmen committed to voting rights legislation, who had come to Selma to examine the situation firsthand.

The politicians talked with local blacks and whites; Smitherman told them that his city was none of a northern politician's business. According to Smitherman, the congressmen were in Selma only "to seek personal publicity in a manner which very readily could produce added criminal provocation in an already near-explosive situation." At the courthouse, Clark arrested five hundred more demonstrators. King then left town and flew to Washington for appointments with Vice-President Hubert Humphrey, Attorney General Nicholas Katzenbach, and, he hoped, President Johnson. When he arrived, however, the meetings had been canceled because of the attack on the American airbase at Pleiku, Vietnam.[11]

Clark's Actions Reinvigorate the Campaign

As the excitement stemming from King's arrest dissipated, the campaign's enthusiasm slackened. The declining size of the demonstrations, which were increasingly composed of students on a holiday cutting classes, encouraged the city administration. Student demonstrators showed up at the courthouse on the Monday and Tuesday following King's Friday release, but there were no arrests. To reinvigorate the movement, SCLC planned to explore Lowndes County, where they expected a sharp reaction from local whites.[12]

As was to happen so often, however, when the Selma campaign needed a boost, Sheriff Clark contributed with a new outrage. His rough handling of Amelia Boynton at an early demonstration had encouraged SCLC leaders to believe that Selma had the potential for a national drama, and his bout with Annie Lee Cooper had made front pages across the country. Now, with the campaign losing steam, Clark's brief period of restraint ended on Wednesday when he arrested a group of student demonstrators, and his posse literally ran them out of town. As posse members with prods shuttled between riding in cars and running beside the students, they kept the youth moving at an alternating run and rapid walk. Two miles outside of town, a road blockade stopped reporters, but the students and posse continued. Lawmen joked that the kids wanted to march, that this was their chance. The forced run ended about a mile beyond the blockade when students began collapsing into ditches and vomiting. The posse ended the chase, and many students escaped into the fields of a black-owned farm.

Criticism of the event was harsh, and the posse's action put new vigor into the movement. King spoke to two packed churches that evening, lambasting "Jim Clark's downright meanness in the handling of the boys and girls in our community." The *Times-Journal* also reacted, with a front-page editorial, and although it rebuked the demonstrators as "a cast of irresponsible actors playing to a worldwide audience," the paper found "no reasonable explanation" for Clark's action. Without mentioning Wilson Baker by name, the *Times-Journal* endorsed his policy of ignoring demonstrators, noting that when this tactic was employed, the marchers with their "crumpled homemade signs . . . eventually drifted away." The editorial urged Selma's citizens to step forward and "seek realistic solutions to our problems." On Thursday, when four hundred students and two hundred adults came to the courthouse, Clark's posse resumed its passive tactics.[13]

On Friday, the sheriff entered Vaughn Memorial Hospital with chest pains. "The niggers are givin' me a heart attack," he complained. As word of his hospitalization spread, two hundred students knelt in the drizzle outside the hospital, praying for his full recovery—mental as well as physical.[14]

On Tuesday, February 16, Clark apparently struck again. After enduring taunts, including cries of "Hitler" and "brute," from C. T. Vivian, Clark allegedly reached through the swinging doors of the courthouse with a punch that sent Vivian sprawling with his lips bloody. Vivian, still bleeding and talking about the rights of citizens, was arrested for criminal provocation and contempt of court. The confrontation began when Vivian led about a hundred blacks to the courthouse to sign the appearance book. A light rain began to fall, and Vivian sought shelter for them in the courthouse. Clark refused to let them enter, setting off the verbal exchange.

Blacks worked themselves into an outrage over this latest violence. One SCLC staff member remarked to a reporter, "Every time it appears that the movement is dying out, Sheriff Clark comes to our rescue." Although Clark had a sore finger from the encounter, he later claimed not to remember hitting Vivian. Clark remarked, "One of the first things I ever learned was not to hit a nigger with your fist because his head is too hard." In fact, a deputy, not Clark, struck Vivian. The press had an obstructed view that allowed them to see only a fist flying through the doorway, and they assumed that the assailant was Clark, especially since he took credit for it. A few hours after the incident, two SNCC organizers were beaten in front of the library by three whites and suffered facial cuts.[15]

Clark's latest outburst prompted a front-page *Times-Journal* editorial that appealed for calm and moderation. Although the *Times-Journal* had harsh words for King and Vivian, the former for exploiting and insulting Selma and the latter for provoking Clark, the editorial also appealed to community moderates to come out of hiding. The newspaper maintained that

> the responsible mainstream of acknowledged lay leaders in our white community must become unhesitatingly more vocal in supporting the course of action which most clearly represents their own views if we are to maintain community harmony and avoid continued harassment. . . . These expressions must be voiced candidly and openly, with the outspoken courage of each individual's own convictions. They must not be veiled in a shroud of anonymity, or in softly whispered tones of timidity and lack of purpose.[16]

Smeltzer Searches for a Concession

In spite of the discouraging trends emerging and the negative contributions of Clark and King, Smeltzer was back in Selma trying to extract from whites a concession that would demonstrate good faith. After talking with Reese, Smeltzer told Art Capell that the February 9 demonstration (on the Tuesday after King's Friday release from jail) could be stopped if the courthouse made several concessions. Black leaders could negotiate with the voter registration board to open an appearance book in which applicants would sign their names and be called in later. If there was an overflow of names, the board could ask for extra registration days. An appearance book would show good faith to blacks and eliminate the need for lines at the courthouse, where so many of the problems had been occurring. Smeltzer told Capell that an appearance book might stop demonstrations and that an announcement of more days for registration had an even better chance of ending the marches. Smeltzer also advised that blacks did not want to halt demonstrations on Monday in order to capitalize on King's visit to Washington, but if they could announce at the Monday night mass meeting that there would be an appearance book—or some other conciliatory announcement—they would have gotten their mileage out of the King trip to Washington and could call off the Tuesday demonstrations. Smeltzer speculated that there might be one more day without violence.

Nevertheless, after black leaders thought about the appearance book, they rejected it. Local blacks were initially receptive to Smeltzer's compromise, but SCLC staff members, especially James Bevel, considered the book to be another trick, just a stall. If the board could be open to put out a book, why not to register people? The black demand continued to be immediate and total registration, and King requested that registrars work evenings to clear up the backlog of applicants. The movement was unwilling to relinquish momentum to gain a minor compromise.[17]

On Monday, the appearance book was in place, but most blacks refused to sign it, prompting both Baker and Clark to accuse blacks of bad faith for allegedly requesting the appearance book and then boycotting it. After being refused at the voter registration office, Bevel led a number of blacks to the end of the line, where they started to go past the registrar's office again. Clark rushed outside, "shaking with anger," and Bevel was the first black he encountered. When Bevel disobeyed Clark's order to leave, the sheriff repeatedly hit him with a billy club and then ordered him and fifty others arrested.[18]

Attempts to renew talks between black and white leaders enjoyed lukewarm success. The CRS mediators arranged an informal meeting, which many of the top local blacks attended, but only two whites stayed for the entire meeting. Several arrived late, and Wilson Baker left early. No SCLC staff members attended the CRS meeting, and changes in strategy did not occur without King's approval. Smeltzer tried for a meeting between three blacks and three whites but had trouble finding three interested whites.

Nonetheless, a secret meeting at the Albert Hotel between black leaders and white businessmen produced an understanding about events scheduled for Monday, February 15. In exchange for the return of black students to their classrooms, the city granted a parade permit. The result was a line of adult voter registration applicants that stretched for five blocks, from the courthouse to a white neighborhood replete with magnolia trees and majestic oaks draped with Spanish moss. In spite of the agreement regarding the students, about nine hundred of them marched to the courthouse to observe the line and then returned to the First Baptist Church. On learning of the student march, Baker shouted bitterly at a King aide, "You aren't keeping your promise." Baker asked Harry Boyte, "All I want to know is whether you can control your people and if you intend to act in good faith by doing it?" When Young heard that the students were marching, he ran the length of the line looking for King, but before the SCLC leadership could respond to the situation, the students arrived. Young explained to the press that the students "had worked so hard in getting their parents up here that they insisted on filing by and seeing them in the line." Blacks also agreed to sign the appearance book because, after making the point that whites did not have to sign, they were willing to use the book to get a small step closer to the polling booth. Five hundred persons signed. Clark remained inside the courthouse most of the day.[19]

In spite of the apparent calm, the atmosphere remained charged, but some Selmians appreciated that the campaign had not provoked further violence. Several gave Smeltzer credit for the shaky peace that prevailed. The belated use of the appearance book was the only compromise Selma could muster, however, and the community edged closer to disaster. Mac Secrest was unable to persuade the registration board to set up a second appearance book or to go down the line getting signatures.

Smeltzer found the gulf between black and white Selma to be widening as the emotional level of the crisis rose. Blacks understood that someone in the voter registration office had quipped, "There's more niggers on the books now than I'll ever let pass." Reese was discouraged because he advised blacks to sign the appearance book, but they remained unregistered, which left him out on a limb. Further embittering Reese was his assumption that after the kids returned to school, there would be negotiations to set a timetable for dealing with black concerns, but he now doubted that talks would occur. Reese distrusted whites more than ever and cynically suspected that whites had acted in bad faith during the informal meetings early in the campaign. Reese was ready to take the kids out of school, call a general strike, close Dallas County, and march at night.[20]

Warning of a Plot to Murder King

On Saturday morning, February 13, Smeltzer received an alarming phone call from a Selmian who warned of a plot to assassinate Martin Luther King. The conspirators hoped to shoot King during his upcoming trip to Marion; Smeltzer's contact claimed to have a friend in Marion who had witnessed four men planning the crime. Smeltzer was asked to notify the proper people, and he passed along the information to Mac Secrest of CRS and Harry Boyte. The attempt failed because King's short stature and quick movement into the church prevented the conspirators from getting a good aim at him.

Smeltzer returned to Elgin on Sunday, but the next day his Selma source on the King plot telephoned with a desperate message about an SCLC press release that included the Selmian's name as an informant. Did Smeltzer betray the confidentiality of his source and give the name to SCLC? The Selmian was anxious to get his name out of the story. He believed that his career, his future, and Smeltzer's work in Selma were all in jeopardy.

Smeltzer called the SCLC office and got the man's name removed from the release. King's staff had received notice of the plot from another source besides Smeltzer, and the use of the name probably resulted from a misunderstanding with Mac Secrest.

Close to Disaster

The unfolding of events in Selma soon demonstrated that the situation was worsening; the tactics of King and Clark were bearing fruit, sweet or bitter depending on one's point of view. Although the worst-case scenario of massive street riots with multiple deaths never occurred, Selma came perilously close to this several times, and violence on city streets eventually claimed one life. Added to the growing national attention directed toward

Selma was an unprecedented influx of outsiders, including north-erners, who came to assist the movement.

Black Belt violence made headlines on February 18 when state troopers attacked a column of night marchers in Marion, 30 miles northwest of Selma, where the voting rights campaign had branched out to neighboring Wilcox County. Marion was much more rural than Selma, however, and had few advocates of moderation; Marion lacked both a Wilson Baker and a Ralph Smeltzer. During the melee at Marion, one person was shot, a black, twenty-six-year-old Jimmie Lee Jackson, who lunged at a state trooper after his mother was assaulted. Jackson ran out of the café in which he was shot, and troopers outside clubbed him down. The state troopers also struck reporters at the scene; NBC's evening news showed their man, a bandaged Richard Valeriani, giving his report from a hospital bed. Jim Clark was in Marion that night and explained that "things got a little too quiet for me over in Selma tonight and it made me nervous."[21]

The Marion riot substantially escalated passions in Selma. A large contingent of state troopers arrived in town the day after the Marion incident, and Wilson Baker heard reports that the Ku Klux Klan and other violence-prone extremists also had slipped into town. Early on Friday, February 19, King led about two hundred marchers to the courthouse where, for the first time, state troopers assisted in policing the lines. Some white people, noticeably more hostile-looking than before, watched the march-ers.[22]

Blacks decided to test the atmosphere with a night march. Before the marchers departed from Brown's Chapel, Reese re-minded them that the movement was nonviolent and called on those with weapons to put them on a table up front. All kinds of weapons appeared—a "regular arsenal," in Reese's words. Blacks expected trouble.

Baker believed that the only way to prevent a bloodbath was to prohibit any marches and restrict blacks to their area of town. He met the column as it left Brown's Chapel, and over a bullhorn declared that there would be no night marches in Selma. As Baker pleaded with the blacks not to march, Clark's posse and Al Lingo's block-long line of state-trooper patrol cars waited at the courthouse. No one knew who hid in the shadows.

Baker arrested King's aide Hosea Williams, put him in a police car, and them implored the demonstrators to turn around. "You say you are nonviolent people, so go back into the church," he told the would-be marchers. Several shouted back, "We're gonna march!" Behind Baker stood a wall of city police, wearing helmets for the first time. If the marchers were to pass Baker's police, Baker feared he could not protect them, but they quietly moved back into the church, after which Baker released Williams.

The hair-trigger atmosphere spurred the city administration to seek a temporary compromise. Later that evening, Baker entered the office at the back of Brown's Chapel to inform movement leaders about his readiness to reopen negotiations for the city. Blacks called off demonstrations for a few days, and the weekend was quiet. On Monday, however, the grace period and black patience expired. King, back in action after being bedridden for a few days with a fever, announced that he would defy a recent Wallace ban on night marches by leading one. But civil rights workers had received a warning of an assassination plot against King, and a personal phone call from Attorney General Nicholas Katzenbach further dissuaded King from marching.[23]

While SCLC leaders pondered whether to march or not that night, another event took place across town. The Citizens Council had a large rally with former Mississippi Governor Ross Barnett, a nationally recognized die-hard, as rally speaker. All the local officials except Baker attended, and Clark and Smitherman joined Barnett and Selma's native son, "Bull" Connor of Birmingham fame, onstage. Chris Heinz, the Citizens Council president, introduced Barnett with "we have arrived at that point when all white people must stand up and be counted." The evening was filled with similar white-supremacist rhetoric, and Barnett's speech was interrupted eighteen times for applause. What with King, Barnett, and the state troopers in town, the black mass meeting, and the Citizens Council rally, it was a tense evening.[24]

Reese, who believed that community relations were on the verge of irreparable damage, urgently sought a conference with city officials. But when Reese telephoned City Hall, Smitherman was unavailable and told Baker to handle the call. Reese and Baker had a difficult conversation, there was no conference, and interracial communication remained at an unhealthy stage.

Black strategy maintained the pressure. On Tuesday, February 23, Baker halted another night march—this one spontaneously organized by black youths—to the courthouse to avoid a clash with Clark, Lingo, and the state troopers. The following day, blacks announced a boycott of white businesses. Whites also applied their traditional weapon of economic coercion; blacks counted fifty retaliatory firings by white employers. Many of those dismissed were in need of food, clothing, and rent money.[25]

On Friday, February 26, the SCLC Alabama Project acquired its first martyr: Jimmie Lee Jackson. Still in the hospital a week after the shooting, Jackson developed breathing difficulties, fell into a coma, and died. He was buried on Wednesday, March 3. A memorial service filled Brown's Chapel, and well over one thousand onlookers stood along the street. Eleven hundred Hudson High students skipped classes, the highest absentee figure thus far.[26]

The most tangible sign that Selma was slipping closer to violence was the reaction to the march of the Concerned White Citizens of Alabama, seventy integrationists. The Reverend Joseph Ellwanger, a Lutheran minister from Birmingham with relatives in Selma, headed the delegation, composed mainly of ministers, professors, and their wives, many of whom had moved to Alabama from other states. Ellwanger's Selma friends warned him not to bring his group, but they came anyway. FBI agents in Selma described Ellwanger as "fanatical" and advised the military and the secret service of the potential for a "breakdown in law and order." At the Selma assembly point, the Reverend L. James Rongstad, local pastor of St. John's Lutheran, confronted Ellwanger's group and implored them not to march.[27] Clark was out of town, and Baker persuaded Clark's deputy, L. C. Crocker, to ignore the march. Therefore, when Ellwanger's courageous little band arrived at the courthouse to read a declaration supporting the civil rights campaign, law enforcement was minimal.

Downtown Selma bustled on Saturday afternoons when rural folk came to town, and the Concerned White Citizens quickly attracted a crowd. Hostile whites struck up a chorus of "Dixie," Ellwanger's group countered with "America," and a group of blacks sang "We Shall Overcome." The mood was extremely ugly, even by Selma's recent standards, and a small spark could have ignited a bloody street riot. If the situation continued, it could only worsen. Baker arrived, but with only an assistant as support. He sent the Concerned Citizens back to the church and dispersed the crowd. There were two violent incidents, one of which resulted from the reappearance of Jimmy George Robinson, King's hotel-lobby attacker, who was back in town to make his unique contribution. Baker arrested Robinson again.[28]

The Decision to March to Montgomery

The legal source of the voter registration problem in Dallas County was Alabama's election laws; it was state law that limited the number of days the voter registration office was open. Revision of the laws governing registration would clear the logjam at Dallas County's Courthouse.

Consequently, SCLC leadership decided to march from Selma to the state capital at Montgomery, 50 miles to the east, along U.S. Route 80, to dramatize their determination to vote and call national attention to the drive for a federal voting rights law.

Furthermore, there was little mileage to be gained from continuing activity in Selma. In retrospect, it is clear that the pattern of recent events—the Marion riot, the threat of night marches, and the frenzied reaction to Ellwanger's Concerned Citizens—pointed toward a violent eruption. It came with the attempt to march to Montgomery.

On Thursday, March 4, Wallace, Lingo, and others met to devise a strategy for dealing with the threatened march to Montgomery. Doubting that the marchers could complete a 50-mile walk, Wallace considered calling King's bluff by allowing the march to proceed, but eventually Wallace decided that the march would have to be halted. In a meeting with legislative leaders, the governor pounded his desk and declared, "I'm not going to have a bunch of niggers walking along a highway in this state as long as I'm governor."

Baker was away for a rest and Mayor Smitherman, left to his own judgment, agreed that the city police would cooperate with the state troopers in stopping the march. On returning, Baker objected vehemently to the governor's plan and the mayor's order that the city police assist the state and county. Baker had worked hard to keep troopers away from the action, and now Smitherman agreed to a plan that gave Lingo's men a major role. Baker did not want the perpetrators of Marion to swing into action on Selma's streets, and he doubted that once Clark and Lingo had their hands on the marchers, they would just allow the line to turn around. Baker still believed that the best way to deal with the march was either to arrest the blacks as they left the church or to let them march. How far could they get? Nevertheless, Smitherman, who had been assured by high-ranking Wallace aides that the governor wanted the march halted peacefully, overruled Baker, who then threatened to resign rather than have his men participate in a bloodbath. Several City Council members intervened and arranged a deal with the mayor to station only two city police as observers at the Pettus Bridge, where the marchers would head out of town. Clark and Lingo promised Smitherman that they would follow the governor's orders and stop the march peacefully.[29]

The Battle on the Bridge

On Sunday, March 7, a column of 525 marchers filed, two by two, out of Brown's Chapel and headed downtown. But instead of heading for the courthouse or another of Selma's civic buildings, as they had during other demonstrations, the line turned left on Broad Street, passed a group of about thirty possemen, and began to climb the slope of the Edmund Pettus Bridge, a steel-girder construction arching high over graceful bends of the Alabama River. A few blocks from the bridge, law officials halted several ambulances with volunteer doctors from New York. Many of the marchers were prepared for a long trek with bedrolls or knapsacks, but others wore church clothes; some women were in high heels and a number of men wore suits. F. D. Reese knew that the march would not go far; he wore a suit and overcoat and was without a blanket or toiletries. The mood of the demonstration lacked the festivity of earlier marches. Although marchers knew that authorities had declared their intent to halt the march, blacks were unsure what tactics would be used, and recent events predicted an increased probability of violence. Blacks knew violence was possible, but they wanted the confrontation.

At the top of the bridge, the leaders of the column, John Lewis and Hosea Williams, looked down the other side and saw Al Lingo's state troopers, shoulder to shoulder, wearing their gas masks and holding nightsticks ready, blocking the highway. Members of Jim Clark's posse stood behind them; his mounted posse waited between buildings. Hundreds of spectators watched. As Lewis and Williams came off the bridge, they stopped in front of the state troopers. Their commander, Major John Cloud, announced that the march was illegal. Williams asked for a word with Cloud, but the major replied, "There is no word to be had." After Cloud and Lewis repeated that dialogue twice, Cloud gave the marchers two minutes to disperse and then commanded, "Troopers, advance."

State troopers charged the column with billy clubs and tear gas. (Witnesses disagree on whether Cloud waited the full two minutes before attacking the marchers.) Initially, the troopers pushed at the marchers with nightsticks, but when troopers and marchers began falling over one another, more serious violence broke out. Screaming marchers were pushed, shoved, and clubbed to the ground and streamed back to the church, while whites watching along the roadside whooped and cheered. None of the spectators, however, left the sidelines to join the attack. Although four troopers herded members of the press to the side, reporters caught a clear view of "fifteen to twenty nightsticks . . . flailing at the heads of the marchers." Clark's mounted posse chased after the marchers, and posse members at the rear of the column struck the marchers as they retraced the route to Brown's Chapel. No attempts were made to arrest the marchers, and as the troopers and posse pursued the blacks, the mounted posse rode onto porches and through yards.

Back at Brown's Chapel, Clark's posse tried to force blacks into the church as bottles and bricks flew toward them. Wilson Baker intervened to persuade blacks to enter the church and to dissuade Clark and the posse from charging again, but Clark replied, "I've already waited a month too damn long about moving in." Approximately thirty minutes later, the posse and troopers left, and the police resumed normal patrolling.

The Brown's Chapel parsonage became an emergency first-aid hospital with moaning patients, some of them hysterical. Seventeen blacks were hospitalized, including Lewis with a fractured skull, and another forty to fifty received emergency treatment. As the battered blacks recovered at Brown's Chapel, there was "hate, bewilderment and doubt" in their eyes, and many doubted the value of continued nonviolence. Reese's preaching that "vengeance is mine saith the Lord" fell on deaf ears. King called from Atlanta and talked to Reese: "Mr. [Voters League] President, I understand you had a—a little—a little trouble down there." Reese answered, "Doc, that's an understatement. We have a whole lot of trouble down here."[30]

"Bloody Sunday" struck the national consciousness. Graphic footage of the riot appeared that night on an ABC news bulletin, interrupting "Sunday Night at the Movies." Monday's newspapers ran extensive stories with pictures, and congressmen condemning the attack portrayed segregationists in more diabolical images than before. Protestors picketed the White House and staged a sit-in in the attorney general's office, demanding quick action on a voting rights bill.[31]

Why the confrontation on the Pettus Bridge became violent remains mysterious. Most whites in Selma today quickly point their fingers at Clark; only his staunchest supporters dissent from this feeling. The day after Bloody Sunday, Governor Wallace called Smitherman, Clark, and Hare on the carpet in his Montgomery office to chastise them, but before the meeting, a Wallace aide tipped off Smitherman that the gubernatorial wrath was meant only for Clark. Yet Wallace had made clear that the march would be broken up by using "whatever measures are necessary" and without arrests, and the New York Times reported that the decision to use tear gas and nightsticks had been worked out in the governor's office before the march. Perhaps Clark and Lingo decided on their own to use force against the marchers, perhaps to embarrass Wallace, Smitherman, or Baker. Another possibility is that the rank-and-file posse and troopers spontaneously went out of control. Mayor Smitherman says that he knew what was going to happen because of his assumptions about Clark's and Lingo's personalities.[32]

Interracial communication hit a new low point, and the breakdown brought Ralph Smeltzer's return to Selma. Smeltzer characterized Selma as a series of peaks and valleys: "two steps forward and one backward," and "Sunday's episode was a real setback." In the increasingly polarized community, segregationists still monopolized the public debate, and although the courageous *Times-Journal* editorialized against the troopers' action, white moderates remained skittish. The quiet, confidential interracial meetings that had been going on for some time were no longer held. The day before the battle on the bridge, Mac Secrest and Art Lewis failed to persuade several moderates to meet with the Concerned Citizens, Ellwanger's white liberals.[33]

More Outsiders and Another Confrontation

Like no previous event, the battle on the bridge rallied not only national sympathies but also tangible support in behalf of the civil rights movement. King's call for a pilgrimage of his supporters to Selma to join the march to Montgomery was heard. Around the nation, doctors, professors, clergy of every creed, civil rights officials, and assorted celebrities flocked to Selma. After learning of the Pettus Bridge attack, many SNCC workers set aside their rivalry with SCLC. Four carloads of SNCC workers, meeting in Jackson, Mississippi, left a staff meeting and drove to Selma in autos assigned to the Mississippi Project. A group attending a SNCC executive staff meeting in Atlanta chartered a plane.

In the days that followed the Pettus Bridge attack, the immediate issue became the right of blacks to mount another march. As scores and then hundreds of supporters and dignitaries converged on Selma, King felt he could not delay a march attempt, even though it meant defiance of the federal courts, which had ordered a delay. After the Sunday battle, emotions were so strong that some blacks might march without King if SCLC decided to obey the court order. Local youths stated that they would return to the bridge no matter what their elders decided, and with SNCC in town in greater numbers, the youths undoubtedly had someone to lead them. Leaders of SCLC were concerned that the rank and file would retaliate with violence, and both Bevel and King reminded a mass meeting that the movement's tactics were nonviolent.[34]

When it became obvious that King had made the difficult decision to march, President Lyndon Johnson sent to Selma the head of the CRS, former Florida Governor LeRoy Collins, with the assignment to prevent another battle on the bridge. Collins arrived at Craig airbase on a presidential jet early in the morning and met with King, who was still in his pajamas. Then Collins saw Clark and Lingo in a Pontiac dealer's office and got them to promise not to molest the marchers if they stopped when ordered and turned around. In a tense reenactment of Sunday's actions, the marchers again confronted Major Cloud's wall of blue-jacketed state troopers soon after crossing the bridge. On Sunday, the front ranks of the march had been filled with locals, but this time, King himself led the mile-long line through the silent streets, and a collection of out-of-town ecclesiastical personages followed close behind. Hundreds of white spectators filled the parking lots along the highway, and 150 journalists watched. Attorney General Katzenbach received a live, play-by-play report from John Doar, and Governor Collins stood with the troopers. If there was another attack, the president's man would be in the middle.

Although this scene easily could have produced bloodshed similar to Sunday's, the tension eased as Cloud and King followed the script devised by Collins—with only one exception. After the long file of marchers knelt in prayer, they slowly rose to return to the church, as agreed, but Cloud suddenly turned and, like Moses parting the Red Sea, cleared his troopers off the road, opening the way to Montgomery. If King really wanted to defy the court, all he had to do was lead his people between the rows of troopers and down Route 80.

King did not accept the challenge. As Andy Young stood in the middle of the road, turning the line around, King led the marchers back as they sang, "Ain't Gonna Let Nobody Turn Me Around." Although some marchers were disappointed with the compromise, others remembered Sunday's bashing and were thankful to return safely. In King's formal remarks, back at the church, he spoke grandly of greater things to come, rather than of what had just happened.[35]

The Death of James Reeb

Although the confrontation on the bridge was resolved peacefully, that evening a spontaneous scuffle outside a bar resulted in a fatality. After the line of marchers returned, one of the white preachers in the march, James Reeb, a Unitarian minister from Boston, decided to stay in town one more day. With two white friends, Clark Olsen of Berkeley, California, and Orloff Miller of Boston, Reeb had supper in a black café. After dinner, they headed downtown and toward Washington Street, perhaps taking a wrong turn. It was nearly dark, and the route they chose took them past a bar called The Silver Moon, a hangout for white toughs with a reputation so ugly that it had not yet been tested for compliance with the Civil Rights Act. As Reeb and his companions strolled past, four whites, shouting, "Hey, you niggers," attacked them from the shadows with a club or pipe. The assault lasted only a few seconds, but Reeb was unable to stand by himself. Although only a small scratch was visible on him, he suffered blurred vision and acute pain. The other two ministers were unhurt. Reeb's pain intensified, and at the infirmary he slipped into a coma. William Dinkins, one of Selma's two black physicians, ordered Reeb to the university medical center in Birmingham, but about 10 miles out of town, the ambulance threw a recapped tire and had to return. Reeb arrived at the Birmingham hospital four hours after the attack with a massive skull fracture and blood clot. There was nothing that could be done, and he soon died.

The outpouring of national sympathy for Reeb was overwhelming. President Johnson sent yellow roses and assigned *Air Force One* to fly Reeb's widow to Selma. Telegrams from politicians and citizens all over the country arrived. The contrast in reactions to the deaths of Reeb and Jimmie Lee Jackson disappointed blacks because the death of Reeb, a white man, clearly touched the nation more than the murder of the black Jackson.[36]

White Selma's response to Reeb's death was much less sympathetic than the national outcry. The Silver Moon bar was in the kind of neighborhood where respectable whites did not walk after dark, and many whites held the attitude that Reeb had "asked for it." What would you expect? Although the *Times-Journal* encouraged local clergy to hold memorial services for Reeb, John Newton did not know one white pastor willing to participate; there was no sympathy from local white clergy for northern ministers who came to Selma. The City Council did send Mrs. Reeb a telegram of condolence.[37]

Following Reeb's death, city authorities took stronger actions to prevent further marches. The day after Reeb's death, blacks attempted a march to the courthouse to protest the assault, but they were stopped after a few blocks by Baker, the city police, and Smitherman, who told the demonstrators that he was banning further marches. Perhaps Smitherman finally followed Baker's advice to cut the Clark–Lingo crowd out of the action by preventing blacks from marching to them.[38]

That evening, the marchers were back on the street in front of the chapel, where they planned to stay until the city withdrew its restriction on marches. Sleeping bags and air mattresses testified to their determination, and Baker responded by stringing a chest-high nylon rope across the street. Blacks quickly christened Baker's rope "The Berlin Wall" and created new freedom songs, using the tune "Joshua Fit the Battle of Jericho":

> We've got a rope that's a Berlin Wall, Berlin Wall, Berlin Wall.
> We've got a rope that's a Berlin Wall, in Selma, Alabama.[39]

Baker's rope became Selma's latest symbol. Blacks kept a twenty-four-hour vigil by the rope along the unpaved street and proclaimed that they would remain there until permitted to march again.[40] The parade of religious dignitaries into Selma continued, and because each was eager to participate, the situation remained fluid. Amid a pushing and shoving crowd, Baker debated with the former president of Notre Dame University, the Reverend John J. Cavanaugh, on the morality, or lack of it, of the civil rights movement as determined-looking nuns stood behind the priest. Movement leaders moved through their ranks encouraging nonviolence: "We must not hold any hatred for these men. It is the system we are fighting, not them."

While the city's ban on all marches remained in effect, civil rights people continued the pressure to demonstrate and managed to mount a few small marches to harass law enforcement officials. Several demonstrators broke through the police line and made it to the courthouse, where they were pushed back by Clark's posse and threatened by a crowd of whites. Baker arrived and escorted them safely back to the church. On Monday, March 15, blacks held a memorial service for Reeb in Brown's Chapel because they still were not allowed to march to the courthouse; a joint statement by Smitherman and Clark emphasized the authorities' position. Moments after King completed his oratory, a message came that Federal Judge Thomas would allow a march to the courthouse, and a march was quickly organized with a line three abreast and stretching from the church to the courthouse steps.[41]

Small marches continued for the rest of the week following Reeb's service, including two by visiting white preachers to Smitherman's residence, deep inside Selma's white territory. Baker gave the white marchers, whom he called "misfits and mentally ill," a stern lecture on provoking violence and stretching the limits of law enforcement. Women and children in the area became frightened, and husbands hurried home from work to confirm their families' safety. Police rushing to the scene of marches were involved in two accidents.

On the evening of Reeb's funeral, President Lyndon Johnson delivered his long-awaited speech on voting rights. In one of the great moments of his presidency, Johnson spoke to Congress and the nation in his soft Texas accent about the need for voting rights. "There must be no delay, or no hesitation, or no compromise" in giving blacks the right to vote, he said. He compared Selma to Lexington and Concord, and left no doubt that the Selma campaign had encouraged him to support strong voting rights legislation. "Their cause must be our cause. . . . And we *shall* overcome."[42]

As Johnson rallied the national conscience with his passionate address, divisions within white Selma became increasingly emotional and bitter. At midnight in the county jail, Clark and Baker almost came to blows. Clark was upset that Baker's police had superseded the posse at a march that afternoon, and he threatened to arrest the police if they interfered like that again. After a sharp argument, the two prepared for a more physical exchange, but Smitherman intervened.[43]

Smitherman often felt caught between the various factions within white Selma, and the strain affected him. Pressures on the mayor were intense, and although his close supporters insisted that he would hold up, others observed that his nervous demeanor suggested otherwise. One night a local reporter spotted Smitherman standing by the rope, just staring dejectedly at it as the pouring rain rolled off his umbrella. Today the mayor remembers his job as being very taxing during the crisis and emphasizes that he had to keep the water running, the garbage collected, and the sewage treated, and had to meet with various groups, at the same time that he faced the civil rights problem. According to the mayor, Clark could go to the Elks to unwind and Baker to a relative's home for a vacation, but he was stuck in his office, working overtime. There were marches every day.

Smitherman recalls, "It would tear you up because you had never seen things like this."[44]

Smitherman's allegiance was the object of daily battles between Baker's moderate and Clark's die-hard factions, and the mayor felt he had to "[walk] a thin line between" blacks, moderates, and the Citizens Council. Smitherman recalls that he had many disagreements with Baker. The more the national media praised Wilson Baker, the more locals directed pressure toward Smitherman to fire him.

> Wilson [Baker] didn't have to answer to the politics of it. I'd get fed up and order him just to arrest [the marchers]. He'd tell them to stop; and they'd just walk on back home. He made statements to the press that were too liberal; they sounded good to outsiders but did not play well locally.

The strains on Smitherman were especially emotional because most of his friends from childhood were, in his words, "ultraconservative segregationists." Old friends urged him "not to give in. Stand your ground. Don't let 'em march. Don't let 'em take over. Arrest them. Turn your head and let the posse get 'em." From day to day, Smitherman's popularity seesawed, and the nighttime crank calls and hate mail hurt him. He remembers that "it went back and forth—one day you were a hero; one day you were . . . a nigger-lover."[45]

White Selma's leadership bitterly pointed fingers of blame at one another. The moderate banker faction assumed that Clark and the uneducated whites were responsible for most of the problems, but Clark's supporters thought the businessmen were unrealistic and inaccurate. The moderate business leaders attempted to cajole and coerce Clark into adopting milder tactics. Once they apparently were close to persuading Clark when he suddenly lost his temper and angrily said he had to do what he had to do. At another meeting, Sol Tepper, a strong Clark supporter, "tried to explain it" to the bankers' group when one of them blurted out, "Aw, shit, that ain't true." It was the first vulgarity Tepper had heard from this man. Smitherman thought that business leaders were intimidated by die-hards and failed to support him sufficiently; merchants "wanted their cash registers ringing and they knew [the demonstrations were] affecting it but they would not come forward." The mayor considered the bankers naive, and Clark thought they were much quicker with criticism than with practical, positive suggestions. "That was a joke," is Clark's bottom-line assessment of the moderate bankers' group.[46]

Although communication was increasingly muted, Smeltzer believed that there was still time for whites to build trust with blacks. Smeltzer considered it imperative that the city signal blacks that it was still interested in gaining their respect, and he suggested that the city offer its stadium for the Reeb funeral. Blacks might ask for it anyway. Smeltzer hoped to use the Reeb service as a reconciliation tool, and he wanted city people to attend. He told white moderates that the courthouse had become a symbol to the movement, but if Smitherman's intransigence continued, the focus might be shifted to City Hall. Blacks were reluctant to ask the city for any favors, however, and the city was nervous about the political overtones of integrated worship there. Smitherman thought that the service ought to stay in the church, the most appropriate place. Pastor John Newton told Smeltzer that his was "the only voice speaking across the great abyss"; the CRS group in Selma was too inexperienced and only Smeltzer could help.[47]

While the cat-and-mouse games over small marches frayed badly fatigued nerves, priority efforts went toward preparation for the march to Montgomery. President Johnson authorized the use of two thousand regular army troops plus the Dixie Division of the National Guard. The troops were to be flown secretly to the city at night, but thirty C-130s thundering through the darkness are hard to hide in a city of Selma's size. By Saturday, army jeeps and bayonet-fixed rifles were added to Selma's landscape.[48]

White Selma During the Crisis

The unfolding events produced considerable stress among Selmians, polarized the community, and made Smeltzer's goal of communication all that more difficult. In its wake, the racial crisis not only produced physical violence on Selma's streets but also resulted in considerable violence to interpersonal relations. Selma's social stage was strewn with stress, vicious harassment, and torn friendships. In the heat of the controversy, tolerance died. Men who became publicly identified as moderates were ostracized, and their wives suffered socially.

Whites, regardless of their ideological position, were upset with the national press, and moderates as well as segregationists believed that the outside media mishandled the story. According to one white Selmian, even the best reporters were not in town long enough to learn the real story, but thoughtful whites admitted that local antipathy for outsiders made it more difficult to acquire local news sources than it might have been. The right wing was livid over distortions they detected—the press "didn't even print the truth about the weather"—and most whites were disturbed over the redneck image they thought Selma received in the national media.[49]

Many whites were unable to understand the preoccupation of outsiders with their city. Large northern cities had demonstrations and crime. Why was Selma always in the news? Blacks had recently broken the grip of segregation on public accommodations, a major victory; what more did they want? There was sorrow for Reeb, but there was also the feeling that all these Yankee preachers deserved some of the responsibility for his death by inflaming the violent elements.[50]

Selma found it understandably difficult to absorb the sudden influx of outsiders, crusaders, press, dignitaries, and reformers. All kinds of good-intentioned "flakes" appeared to "help" Selma. One young Californian seminarian showed up at the Presbyterian church and announced that he was there to "turn your church around"; he asked to speak to all the Sunday school classes.[51]

The windshields of school board members' cars were shot out during a board meeting; no one even knew which side did it. (Kathryn Windham left her windshield unrepaired for months to remind the offender, whoever he was, of what he had done.) Crank calls were common, and two prominent women, Windham and Muriel Lewis, received late-night phone calls during which nothing was said; they heard only heavy breathing. Lewis handled her 2:00 A.M. heavy breather by breathing back into the phone. "I breathed longer than he did. Just put the phone down and breathe and go back to sleep. It got so, it was just part of life, pick up the phone and breathe." Eventually, she deduced from background noises that the caller was a night watchman. Lewis usually won the confrontation because he had to hang up to continue his rounds.[52]

The *Times-Journal* publisher, Roswell Falkenberry, considered himself caught in a no-win situation, squeezed between extremists on both sides. Blacks thought the local newspaper was unfair to their drive for justice, but die-hards considered the *Times-Journal*'s moderate editorial positions to be appeasement. Falkenberry also suffered frequent evening phone calls and angry mail.[53]

Pastor John Newton received both hostile and supportive phone calls from all over the country. Sometimes the callers were old friends, but at other times his name was picked out of the phone book.[54] Jim Clark's daughter received a minor stab wound, his mailbox was blown up, and his house was shot full of holes.[55]

With daily dramas unfolding on the streets between Brown's Chapel and the courthouse, the rest of Selma functioned normally. Unless one was on Green Street or Alabama Avenue, there was little change in one's life. Schools held class, the Boy Scouts met, the Girl Scouts sold baked goods, all ten lanes at the Echo Bowling Alley were full, and a women's clothing store sponsored a tea and fashion show. According to one news reporter, Selma looked as it always did—provided one avoided Brown's Chapel. Those seeking action had to search for it, although everybody knew where to look.[56] For local whites, the situation was unnerving. The marchers, whether deliberately or not, did all sorts of things that whites found troubling. As a newly arrived group of white demonstrators were told, in spite of the "holiday atmosphere" around Brown's Chapel, "the community is very tense." Whites carried black babies, and nuns walked beside black men; Selma had never seen anything like this.[57]

The March to Montgomery

On Sunday, March 21, approximately two thousand blacks and whites lined the route out of town as Martin Luther King, Ralph Abernathy, SCLC and SNCC members, movie stars, professors, impoverished Alabama blacks, and the national civil rights focus marched out of Selma on the road to Montgomery. In the forefront with King and Abernathy were the Right Reverend Richard Millard, Suffragan Bishop of the Episcopal Diocese of California, Cager Lee, the grandfather of Jimmie Lee Jackson, John Lewis, SNCC president, Deaconess Phyllis Edwards of the Episcopal Diocese of California, Rabbi Abraham Heschel, professor of Jewish mysticism and ethics at the Jewish Theological Seminary in New York, and F. D. Reese.

The parade attracted a variety of segregationists, whose responses reflected the diverse views of Selma's whites. Hecklers in cars with racist slogans whitewashed on fenders and doors harassed the marchers, waved Confederate flags, and shouted, "Nigger King go home." A shopkeeper said farewell with a loudspeaker playing "Bye, Bye Blackbird." A well-dressed white woman stopped her Chrysler, popped out, stuck out her tongue, and drove off. A man in front of a roadside diner thumbed his nose for the entire twenty minutes it took the marchers to pass him. A special target of the hecklers was James Letherer of Saginaw, Michigan, who had only one leg but intended to walk the entire 54 miles on crutches. As the celebrities marched across the Pettus Bridge, a structure Jim Clark helped make famous, the sheriff complained to a modest audience of about fifty whites on the courthouse steps that "the federal government has given them everything they wanted." Smitherman told the press he was proud of the "great restraint" demonstrated by Selma's citizens.[58]

The march to Montgomery lasted five days. The route through the Black Belt took marchers through the varied central Alabama landscape: past a shack serving as a black school, past stern-faced whites, through a Spanish-moss swamp with perfect camouflage for would-be snipers, and past knots of waving blacks. When the route came to a two-lane section of the highway, the number of marchers was limited by Judge Johnson to three hundred. At night, many marchers rode buses or a special train back to the city for lodging, but others slept in the mud and cold. A crew of seminarians from San Francisco, helped by entertainer Gary Merrill and "Bonanza's" Pernell Roberts, tore down the camp each morning, trucked it down the highway to the next campground, and waited for soldiers to minesweep the field before setting it up again. Food was cooked by black women, who labored sixteen hours a day in a Selma church; a squad commanded by a Pittsburgh professor of theology hauled the food in a Hertz truck. The final night's campsite featured an all-star entertainment lineup including Joan Baez, Harry Belafonte, Tony Bennett, Sammy Davis, Jr., Mike Nichols, Elaine May, the singers Peter, Paul, and Mary, Nipsey Russell, and Shelley Winters.[59]

Although Governor Wallace predictably refused to meet the marchers in Montgomery, a rally in front of the state capitol drew the largest collection of civil rights notables since the 1963 March on Washington. Besides King and the SCLC staff, there was John Lewis of SNCC, Roy Wilkins of the NAACP, Whitney Young of the National Urban League, A. Philip Randolph, Ralph

Bunche, Bayard Rustin, and Rosa Parks (whose landmark arrest on a Montgomery bus in 1955 made King an international celebrity). King delivered one of his more memorable speeches, after which a group of twenty dignitaries took a petition for voting rights into the capitol, and the thousands dispersed.[60] Many of those at the Montgomery rally carpooled back to Selma. One of those shuttling marchers was Mrs. Viola Liuzzo, a mother of five from Detroit; beside her sat a black teenager, who helped with the driving. On Mrs. Liuzzo's second trip between Selma and Montgomery, a carload of Ku Klux Klansmen chased her Oldsmobile at high speed down Route 80 and then pulled alongside and shot her. She died instantly, and the Selma campaign had a third martyr.[61]

The Impact of the National Campaign on Smeltzer's Work

The SCLC Alabama campaign changed the terms under which Ralph Smeltzer would work, and the national attention that descended on Selma made his work more difficult than before. Although Selma's problems were as acute as ever, during the most intense period of the SCLC campaign, Smeltzer was less active than previously. Voters League officials maintained that they controlled events, but they yielded at least partial autonomy to the national campaign. Harry Boyte warned that King would disapprove if Smeltzer negotiated an agreement between SCLC and the city, and the merger of local Voters League interests with the national campaign limited Smeltzer's options. His closest attempt at achieving any agreement—the appearance book compromise —was vetoed by SCLC staff members. Furthermore, heightened tensions widened interracial rifts and made communication more difficult. Reese was inclined toward continued dialogue with whites, but the SCLC group frowned on such contacts in favor of increasing the pressure.[62]

The Community Relations Service people overlapped Smeltzer's work, and he felt that with them in town, perhaps he could phase himself out. Smeltzer's superiors in the Brethren hierarchy suspected that he was too personally committed to Selma to evaluate the project objectively. With the "war on," and given the CRS presence, Smeltzer's Selma project had altered substantially from its original concept. His bosses encouraged him to take fewer notes, to do less research, and to read fewer newspapers. They also suggested that the major goal of his work was merely to get people acquainted with one another in Selma, and that goal had been accomplished. Smeltzer believed that Selma still needed his services, but he could not devote the necessary time, so he explored the possibility of sending another full-time Brethren volunteer. Smeltzer still had contributions to make, but they would have to wait.[63]

8

Returning to Normalcy

We note with gratitude that our own church has responded in some measure of concern and creativity to a healing ministry of reconciliation in the Civil Rights struggle. We commend those who have spoken and acted courageously and creatively. We commend and encourage the work of mediation and reconciliation which has been carried on by a few of our Brethren in crucial tension areas.

General Brotherhood Board Resolution on Race Relations,
March 19, 1965, Church of the Brethren

This is almost the end of the ninth week of racial demonstrations in this locale, and for most of that time we have been walking on eggshells, balancing on a very thin tightrope while trying to do what we believe is right and just. But we must act differently, and think differently because Selma is our home, we love it and its people and we want to continue to live here.

Muriel and Art Lewis

It is a miracle that there has been only one death in town.

Muriel and Art Lewis

With the departure of Martin Luther King, the cameras and notepads, and the thousands of demonstrators, Selma, suddenly left to itself, rapidly reverted to pre-King conditions. Although fundamental alterations in race relations were inevitable and in progress, change came slowly, and postcrisis Selma in many ways resembled the old Selma. The civil rights revolution had descended on Selma suddenly, but after the torrent subsided, change came only by the gradual erosion of segregation. The local civil rights movement lost its unity and momentum with surprising suddenness.

Biracial talks resumed, a positive sign, but they soon broke down, and Smeltzer returned to promote new negotiations. By the summer of 1965, however, the talks had collapsed; lines of communication had been established, but whether or not they were to be utilized was up to the Selmians. What Selma needed, Smeltzer thought, was a full-time mediator, and therefore he ended his role there.

Selma After the March

Following the March to Montgomery, with white Selma no longer sharing the city with the national civil rights movement and its enormous entourage of outsiders and members of the press, the city was noticeably different. Two days after the Montgomery rally, James Orange returned to Brown's Chapel and discovered several hundred out-of-towners hanging around and looking for a way to help because they had arrived too late to march to Montgomery. Two weeks earlier, it had taken court orders to get a march under way; now, Orange led an improvised band to the courthouse, City Hall, and back without notice, even though it was Saturday afternoon and downtown was crowded.[1]

Although Selma was no longer a regular feature on the evening news, the celebrity status bestowed on several of its citizens lingered and dissipated roughly at a half-life rate. Selma's headliners traveled all over the country telling their story, and a few weeks after the March, a group of Selmians went to Washington to videotape a David Susskind show. During the broadcast, Smitherman and Baker defended their evenhanded law enforcement, but Hosea Williams dominated the discussion and badgered Smitherman for mispronouncing "Negro" (Williams demanded "knee-grow" instead of the insulting "nigra").

The trip to the big city brought bittersweet memories for Smitherman because he and the attorney Joe Pilcher lost $107 to a black con man offering to "show them the town," and the national press picked up the story. According to Smitherman, when he returned to his room from taping the Susskind show, the two hours of debate had left him with a "severe tension headache." While the others went out for dinner, Smitherman took a nap, and when he awoke, it was midnight and all the restaurants were closed. Out on the street, a black man overheard Smitherman and Pilcher discussing their predicament and offered to get them into a private club patronized by members of Congress. The man took $7 from Smitherman and two $50 bills from Pilcher, and left them standing on the sidewalk while he went to arrange things. He never came back. Smitherman explained that he did not call the police because he was afraid that the press would discover the story and distort it. Later that night, the con artist bragged about his conquest at a dice game, and someone in the game called the police. Back in Selma, Smitherman confided to the *Times-Journal,*

> Fate plays some strange tricks.... All of Selma, in fact the entire nation, has been flim-flammed by the so-called civil rights movement for more than ten weeks. Then when I went to Washington to tell the real truths in the Selma story, we got taken by a glib-tongued Negro con man.[2]

The black man said that Smitherman and Pilcher gave him the money to find "entertainment" for them.

Smitherman also complained that the television studio flew them to Washington but left them stranded after the show was

over. Mac Secrest squeezed them into his car for the trip to the
airport, with Smitherman sitting on Boynton's lap for a while
and Hosea Williams on Baker's.

F. D. Reese went to Washington, D.C., to present his Selma
story to a National Education Association convention, and Jim
Clark was a favorite of far-right audiences, including the John
Birch Society, for several years. Others, such as Amelia Boynton
and William Ezra Greer, also spoke to out-of-state groups.[3]

In the days following the march to Montgomery, several key
Selmians, including Art Lewis, John Newton, and F. D. Reese,
plus Mac Secrest of CRS, urged Smeltzer to return to Selma.
That people at the center of Selma's conflicts encouraged Smeltzer to come back attests to their confidence in his usefulness.
With no marches in the foreseeable future and the kids back in
school, the atmosphere encouraged productive talks and Smeltzer's emphasis on communication. While the *Times-Journal* bitterly criticized Martin Luther King's call for a boycott of
Alabama, it also pointed out a truism:

> What Alabama needs now is to prepare itself for the changes
> in racial relationships which are being forced, with increasing
> speed, by present civil rights litigation and the pending new
> voter registration law. Anyone except the town idiot knows
> that these changes are inevitable—and they will come more
> smoothly if reason is allowed to replace emotion.[4]

Moderates Slowly Go Public

Art Lewis still complained that the "Selma situation stinks," but
when he and his wife, Muriel, began to speak out, Smeltzer's
long search for a centrist with fortitude had ended. The first expression of the new public posture of the Lewises was Muriel's
letter to *Time*, in which she asserted that local moderates and
liberals had been too quiet but were working "uncounted hours"

for long-range peace and obedience to the laws, including the Civil Rights Act. She told *Time*'s national readership that "there are in Selma, as everywhere, people of good will and good intentions who were heartbroken by the acts of violence here."[5] Although she received wide-ranging comments from all over the world, there were surprisingly few remarks from Selma. "I'm afraid not too many people in Selma are intelligent enough to read *Time*," suggested one local observer!

The Lewises also communicated their feelings locally. When they were accused of being rednecks, they sent a letter expressing their true feelings to close friends and relatives. But the letter was stolen and read publicly on the courthouse steps in a slightly altered form that intentionally ignored edited corrections and quotation marks.[6]

The pirated letter was only the beginning of the Lewises' trials. When a racist poster was placed on their property, Muriel Lewis had it taken down the same day, an action that precipitated a flood of hate mail. The theft of their letter, crank calls, and other forms of persecution angered her and made her more outspoken. She confesses, "I'm a hothead. And I'm not very diplomatic. And when I get mad, everybody's gonna know it."[7]

The Lewises encouraged community leaders to support a public statement, but they achieved little success. They hoped to persuade friends to sign a moderate document calling for negotiations and communication, and to that end invited to their home twelve of Selma's most powerful (although covert) moderates. After the first meeting, the Lewises planned another, but on the morning before the second gathering, several friends called Art downtown to say that the theft and subsequent publicizing of his letter made the Lewises too controversial to be effective. The Lewises were asked by their friends to withdraw temporarily from discussions on racial issues. Art Lewis said they would have to tell Muriel themselves, and so a close friend, obviously uncomfortable, visited her to make the request. "It was an experience that I don't wish on anybody," remembers Muriel Lewis. Art agreed to remain quiet for a week or ten days, but his friends backed down. Lewis complained that while moderates reverted to inactivity, the Citizens Council gained strength because it was again unopposed.[8]

For several weeks, the Lewises' public witness remained an isolated example, and the business community continued to shy away from a public statement. Smeltzer learned that Roswell Falkenberry had been working for a statement similar to that which appeared in the March 28 *Anniston* (Alabama) *Star*, but like activists before him, Falkenberry found that many "good people" assured him of their signature but excused themselves at the last minute because of the timing. It seemed as though the time was never right for a public statement about moderation. Part of Falkenberry's problem was that his commitment to moderation made him too controversial to win broad-based support for an Anniston-like statement.[9]

In mid-April, Smeltzer made a number of suggestions to a moderate–liberal group of private citizens, who approached the civil rights crisis from a religious perspective. The group held several meetings in a private residence, but they produced no substantial action. Smeltzer emphasized the need for interracial communication and suggested that the group invite several blacks to their meetings. He recommended visiting and writing to city officials to urge support for a public statement, a biracial committee, and a list of black objectives. This citizens' group lacked strength in the community, especially since its members were not native to Selma; nonnatives were defined as those who "had not dug the river." Also weakening the group's community support was the membership of several Catholics. "In Selma there's nothing lower than a black or a Catholic," remarked one long-time resident. The group met covertly, but each meeting attracted fewer and fewer people. The members had very little effect and soon stopped meeting.

Other attempts to achieve a public declaration of moderation also were unsuccessful. Several white preachers and lay leaders considered inviting Billy Graham to Selma during his summer Alabama crusade, but that was thought to be too touchy because the popular southern evangelist insisted on integrated audiences. Although the Ministers Union supported an invitation to Graham, the proposal eventually died. The Ministers Union also approved a letter to Mrs. Reeb, and that vote was more controversial.[10] A Chamber of Commerce committee visited Smitherman to urge negotiations with blacks, but the mayor was noncommittal. Smitherman apparently was unwilling to disclose a meeting a few days earlier with black representatives.[11]

As so often happened in Selma, the actions of outsiders forced white Selma to deal with its most distasteful issue. When the state's Chamber of Commerce adopted a moderate civil rights statement in mid-April and invited local chambers to sign it, Selma's business community could no longer publicly evade civil rights. (The statement supported the right to vote for all citizens and called for equal law protection, obedience to all laws, and improved communication.) The state chamber's action unwittingly forced Selma's white leadership to discuss racial relations publicly, which unmasked the deep divisions in the white hierarchy created by the civil rights campaign.

The Selma chamber's board of directors rejected the civil rights statement in approximately fifteen minutes by a vote of 12 to 7, explaining that their organization was an inappropriate vehicle for such a statement. Contributing to the negative majority was Smitherman; several prominent moderates were absent, or the statement might have passed. Today the mayor explains his vote by saying, "I didn't think it was that big of an issue at the time, and it was too easy to go along with the Chamber under the prevailing conditions." One board member conceded that he did not speak in support of the statement because he felt intimidated.

Infamous Selma was conspicuous by its absence from the list of cities that did adopt the statement, and there were repercussions. Hammermill, plus several other industries, placed concerned phone calls to several local businesspeople, and Selma's moderates worked hard to overturn the board's decision. Frank Wilson, who was president of the chamber, and Charles Hohenburg invited fifty people to a meeting in the Hotel Albert, each of whom had signed a petition endorsing the state chamber's statement; the City Council, with Smitherman's strong backing, also approved it, 8 to 0. Smeltzer thought that an apparent liability (i.e., the rejection of the state chamber's statement) was becoming an asset as community leaders mobilized to support it. He considered this to be a potential major breakthrough.

The chamber's board reconsidered its decision in a stormy meeting attended by approximately a hundred persons. According to a local reporter, "Names were called, tempers flared and voices became impassioned" at Selma's first public debate of racial issues. In an opening statement, McLean Pitts related the concerns of executives of Dan River Mills and Hammermill, who "feel that Selma is letting them down." Others speaking for the endorsement were Paul Grist, Frank Wilson, and Edgar Stewart. Die-hard segregationists retorted that to yield a fraction of an inch was to invite widespread mass integration, and Joe Pilcher named the individuals in the moderate business leaders' group, which he described as a "self-appointed" group, plotting to "compromise" on race. During the course of the meeting, Smitherman acknowledged that he was meeting with black representatives. The chamber's board reversed itself, 21 to 8.

The local statement was run prominently in the *Times-Journal* on Easter Sunday, along with the City Council endorsement and a petition of support bearing eleven hundred names. An accompanying editorial, "A Mistake Rectified," aligned itself with the statement by declaring that there was "no other reasonable approach" but to adopt the statement. The following day, the newspaper added that Hammermill and Dan River endorsed the chamber's action. The city raised $10,000 to run its statement in the *Wall Street Journal*.[12]

The Resumption of Biracial Negotiations

After the cataclysmic events of the SCLC campaign, Smeltzer found that interracial communication remained disappointingly minimal. Blacks, the CRS men, and Smeltzer all felt that weekly biracial meetings were vital. Negotiations were a major black priority, along with voter registration and jobs. In the weeks following the Montgomery march, biracial dialogue became possible again, and Smeltzer worked to ensure that talks were undertaken and successful.

But meaningful interracial dialogue had not yet entered the white mind set; white leaders still pondered requests for interracial meetings. Contributing to white reluctance to negotiate were assumptions that Reese represented Martin Luther King rather than local blacks and Smitherman's perception that much of his political support came from die-hards.

Blacks were more sensitive than ever about procedures for creating a biracial committee. They wanted to select their own negotiators and would no longer recognize invitations from whites, who might pick blacks who were weak negotiators. In postmarch Selma, Reese promised to be a much stronger bargainer. All the water that had flowed over the dam the past few months gave him a new self-confidence and faith in his leadership skills. He was impatient for action and less inclined to be forbearing with whites. Black Selma's spokesperson knew he could play several strong cards by calling demonstrations and bringing students out of school.[13]

Wilson Baker initiated the new round of talks by inviting four blacks, including F. D. Reese, to meet with Art Capell and Mayor Smitherman on Wednesday, April 7. Reese accepted Baker's invitation, but he wanted to choose the other black negotiators. It was Smeltzer who told Reese the names of the other blacks invited, and Smeltzer also talked to Baker. After conversing with Smeltzer, Baker called Reese again and listened to

Reese explain why blacks needed to pick their own representatives. It is probable that Smeltzer was the catalyst responsible for Baker's quick call to Reese.

The day before the negotiations, Smeltzer counseled blacks to develop specific goals with a timetable and to demand regular meetings with city authorities. He encouraged them to set a specific date for the next meeting. Smeltzer acknowledged to blacks that their voter registration goals were unrealized, but he pointed out that there was little that the city could do to help on that issue because election laws were controlled by the state. Instead, he stressed that blacks should concentrate on local problems and that they should pick an easy issue, such as black police officers, because any successful negotiation would establish good faith.

Hours after Baker's meeting ended, Smeltzer was on the phone with Baker and Claude Brown to discover that the meeting had gone well. Smitherman had joined Baker for an open, productive hour with Reese, Moss, Brown, and Anderson. Commenting that blacks had not lost hope in the mayor, Reese handed him a copy of demands and asked the city to help decide which ones to work on first. Reese did most of the talking and, as Smeltzer suggested, challenged the city to hire qualified black police officers. The group agreed on a time and date for the next meeting and established three goals: a meeting for blacks with business leaders regarding jobs, the hiring of black police, and a request to the voter registration board for longer hours in which to register.[14]

Blacks were encouraged during this period. When the next Wednesday interracial meeting was held, on April 14, Smitherman and three councilmen met with six blacks: Reese, Brown, Moss, Anderson, Foster, and Bradford. This meeting concentrated on the city's bus line; blacks wanted the city to hire black drivers and its white drivers to act courteously. Smitherman promised to talk to the bus company's owner. Other topics involved the fire department and black employment. The city offered to employ a black firefighting unit, but black negotiators wanted the entire department integrated. Whites asked for a cooling-off period before hiring store clerks, but blacks stressed the urgency of jobs. The whites evidently were unaware of the approximately two hundred retaliatory firings during the demonstrations.[15]

Smeltzer's Efforts to Preserve Calm

Smeltzer believed that the relatively quiet period contributed to improved relations and that the absence of demonstrations enabled leaders to engage in private but potentially productive talks. He labored to preserve this atmosphere.

The greatest threat to the short-lived calm came in mid-April when the school board instituted a retroactive policy to penalize students for absences. According to the directive, students absent for fifteen days or more failed for the marking period, and thirty absences meant an *F* grade on the year. School officials maintained that Superintendent Pickard softened the proposal before sending it to the board and that the policy was more lenient than the one in force at all-white Parrish. Insisting that their only motivation was academic integrity, the board passed the order on March 12 and reaffirmed it at the April 8 meeting. Blacks considered the new attendance policy to be in retaliation for student participation in the demonstrations. Reese claimed that, as a teacher, he too was concerned about the education of black youth and that he had worked hard to get the students back in school. Now, the board threatened to undo all his efforts. Reese called Smeltzer, who was in Selma, and asked him to help. There were rumors of boycotts, marches on Parrish, and a teacher walkout. Smeltzer thought this crisis showed the need for a biracial committee, and he joined with Mac Secrest of CRS to resolve the situation before it damaged interracial relations severely.

Smeltzer met with school administrators John Masterson and Allen Cleveland to discuss the new rule. After their conversation with Smeltzer, Masterson and Cleveland received permission from a board member to talk with blacks, and they asked Smeltzer to go along. The three of them conversed in a hallway with the Hudson High principal, Joe Yelder, and two student leaders, all of whom confirmed that there would probably be a walkout the following day. Yelder added that absences the past few days ran at about 170, a high figure; presumably some students had already begun the boycott. Cleveland insisted that Pickard had told him directly that absences and grades on report cards would be strictly checked. Yelder had passed along that interpretation to student leaders and a teachers' committee within the last twenty-four hours. Cleveland and Masterson were both certain that the board would not back down. A student walkout seemed imminent.

White Selma was especially touchy about black teenagers being on the streets in large numbers. A walkout would have been counterproductive for all parties, except perhaps the radical segregationists, who could have pointed to a student strike as evidence of black irresponsibility and bad faith. Optimism remained that the biracial meetings with Smitherman would bring results, and one of the blacks' biggest bargaining chips was the absence of demonstrations.

Smeltzer suggested that a walkout could be avoided by agreeing to Cleveland's proposal that the rule be interpreted as a "guideline" that permitted teachers to use their discretion. Report cards would not be checked for implementation of the "guidelines." Cleveland, Masterson, and Yelder agreed with Smeltzer's suggestion. They asked Smeltzer to help explain the situation to the black teachers' committee, and then Yelder and the committee would explain it to the students.[16]

The avoidance of a student walkout and demonstrations preserved an atmosphere that allowed the Wednesday biracial negotiations to continue. Race relations remained unstable, and an event as threatening to whites as a student walkout could easily have scuttled the negotiations. Both sides respected Smeltzer, and his mediation was helpful in avoiding a crisis at Hudson High School.

During the week of the absentee-policy crisis, Smeltzer extinguished another flashfire when black youths threatened to march on the public playground facilities. Smeltzer visited Comer Sims, the Recreation Association's director, who took Smeltzer's advice to telephone Reese that same day. Sims wanted to avoid a confrontation with blacks and appeared eager to reach an agreement; therefore, the demonstration was called off. About two weeks later, Sims met face to face with a black committee, which presented him with a list of grievances.[17]

With communication under way, Smeltzer planned not to visit again unless communication collapsed but to monitor progress periodically by telephone. To replace his personal presence, Smeltzer found a young Presbyterian seminarian from California, Dave Smith, and assisted him in becoming a full-time mediator.

The Collapse of Biracial Negotiations

The course of successful revolutions does not plot gracefully like an upward sloping parabola but moves unevenly toward its destiny. When the biracial negotiations collapsed and the movement simultaneously suffered major internal problems, Selma's revolution in racial relations sputtered.

Events soon proved that expectations for major changes in Selma were unfounded and that in spite of the promising start of biracial talks, race relations still relied heavily on tradition. Whites appealed publicly for support for the beleaguered city bus line, and the Chamber of Commerce distributed a letter, which it somehow hoped would remain confidential, stating that the bus line was about to go bankrupt because of a black boycott. The chamber maintained that if the bus died, a city contract with Craig, guaranteeing bus service, would be broken, and then perhaps Craig would fold as well. The letter did not have to explain the terrible consequences this would bring and appealed for whites to ride the bus. "Under no circumstances, can we afford to let this boycott succeed. We are just going to have to have a darn sight more stamina than those who would persecute us and our determination to patronize the bus lines." Before the month ended, the bus company went out of business.[18]

The mayor's biracial meeting on April 22 went poorly and resulted in deadlocked negotiations and black frustration. The dominant item on the agenda was the bus line. The minimum black demand was the employment of one black driver, but whites offered only to accept applications for future hirings. The bus company also asked blacks to end the bus boycott and offered courteous treatment, but it would not agree to drop its lawsuit against boycotting civil rights organizations. Reese was very disappointed with the meeting's lack of results and the absence of specific agreements. Some in the black community contemplated demonstrations as the only way to bring about progress.[19]

The impasse grew more serious. Whites disputed black claims of retaliatory firings and complained that many of the unemployed blacks did not look for jobs but lived off the relief that arrived almost daily. Whites also maintained that the city was powerless on many issues, such as the black demand to be addressed with titles of respect (Mr., Mrs., or Miss), which heretofore were reserved for whites. Reese predicted to Smeltzer that there would be demonstrations if there was no progress at the next biracial meeting.[20]

As black patience wore thin, the May 5 mayor's meeting took on a critical aspect. While right-wing pressure pushed Smitherman toward a hard-line position, mass meeting attendance declined, and some observers thought that blacks needed progress or demonstrations to maintain unity. The impact of the state's Chamber of Commerce statement was not as significant as had been expected; some thought it was window-dressing to attract industry rather than affect local race relations. On May 2, the black community placed a large ad in the *Times-Journal* that listed black demands: voting rights, titles, an end to police brutality, jobs, and interracial communication. The ad included a lengthy list of black supporters. Smeltzer suggested to the CRS then that Smitherman inform influential whites that pressures on black leaders were severe and that action ought to be taken before time ran out.[21]

At the May 5 meeting, the progress Reese hoped to see was missing. A Committee of Four, two whites and two blacks, was created to investigate police brutality, and Reese successfully held out for seven blacks on a fifteen-person local committee for the Office of Economic Opportunity (OEO). But Wilson Baker, although professing support for the concept of black police, pleaded that there were currently no funds to pay for additional personnel. Reese produced a list of 50 "bona fide" names and addresses of people who had lost their jobs because of civil rights activity; he had another 179 names in his pocket, but kept them there because they were unverified. The meeting was so unproductive that Reese decided to begin laying the groundwork for demonstrations at the mass meetings, although he would wait another week before actually calling out marchers.[22]

The May 12 meeting went worse than that of the previous week. Blacks complained that none of their demands had been met. Reese pointed out that although there was no money for black police, the city could afford new police cars. Although blacks had never asked for a police brutality committee or an OEO committee, they suspected that Smitherman hoped they would settle for those crumbs and avoid real issues. Blacks also wanted the chain stores in Selma—Winn-Dixie, Sears, and Penney's—to increase their hiring of blacks because local merchants said they would follow the lead of the chains.

When blacks left the May 12 meeting, they said they would not return unless they got a call saying that the whites were serious. No one called.

Blacks were extremely disappointed and considered the biracial meetings to be a runaround. C. C. Brown, an old-school moderate, had boycotted the last two meetings because of the lack of results, and Moss reportedly was also discouraged. Blacks accused whites of not negotiating in good faith, but whites charged that blacks demanded everything at once. Dave Smith worked with Reese, while Art Lewis advised Smitherman to resume the discussions.[23]

Black frustration continued with the recreation commission, which did not meet any of the black demands. The city planned to close its swimming pool in the coming summer rather than integrate, and Reese understood that the recreation commission wanted to reorganize little league baseball into a church league to avoid integrating the players (churches were strictly segregated). Reese was upset that federal officials had approved the school board's integration plan to desegregate grades 1 through 4 because of the glaring omission of the high school. White merchants were unmoved by the boycott and offered Smitherman no encouragement for conciliatory steps with blacks. Downtown merchants scheduled a Friendship Day for non-Selmians to patronize boycotted white businesses, which did more to split black and white Selma than it did to help business.

By the end of May, Reese and the Voters League were interested in another negotiating session. They were willing to name people to the police brutality and OEO committees and would settle for partial fulfillment of their demands as long as some immediate steps were taken and a timetable was set. Although Smeltzer did not return to Selma, he nevertheless contributed by relaying to whites Reese's message that blacks were ready to talk if whites were willing to engage in serious negotiations. Also, Smeltzer's idea for an interracial ministers' meeting was accepted. Twenty white preachers showed up at Craig Air Force Base for a meeting, but only eight blacks attended, and the only prominent black was Anderson. Brown, P. H. Lewis of Brown's Chapel, and Reese were all absent.[24]

In another attempt to further the negotiating position of local blacks, Smeltzer tried to establish direct links between the

Voters League and Hammermill. Smeltzer believed that SCLC had been representing local blacks in discussions with Hammermill and that it was in the best interests of the community if the Voters League did its own negotiating. He was disappointed that Hammermill's president had been in Selma and met with whites, but not with blacks.

Dave Smith had trouble establishing himself as a neutral mediator. Smitherman refused to see him; no outsiders, no errand boys. Smith complained that whites "yes me to death and do nothing." He believed that the police had questioned black youths in the hope of discovering incriminating or embarrassing behavior on Smith's part.[25]

The mayor's meetings briefly resumed in early June when Cap Swift took the initiative to call the blacks. Smitherman was absent with a cold. The meeting agreed to use titles for blacks at future meetings, and the whites said they would try to persuade merchants to do the same when sending bills. Then the Wednesday discussions ended as the civil rights movement suffered several damaging internal upsets.[26]

The Unraveling of the Movement

The white stalling stemmed partially from expectations that the civil rights movement would eventually self-destruct. Whites traditionally had little confidence in black organizational abilities, and even at the height of the SCLC campaign, many whites doubted rank-and-file black commitment to the movement's goals. Then, too, black unity had a very tenuous hold. The celebrity status of Martin Luther King and the trials of the struggle went far toward the unification of local blacks, as did Ralph Smeltzer's more subtle contributions toward the same goal. Nevertheless, three stunning events in the black community were to disrupt black harmony and encourage white assumptions about the movement.[27]

The first bombshell was the announcement that F. D. Reese

would be fired from his position as a science teacher. Reese's civil rights work often kept him out of his classroom, and although his dismissal surprised others, he expected it. Throughout the school year, Superintendent Pickard had warned Reese about excessive absences; at the end of one such conversation, Reese added, "By the way, Mr. Pickard, I'm gonna be out tomorrow too." Some days, Pickard thought Reese was in school and then saw him on the evening news leading a demonstration. Although Reese acknowledged that some of his absences were unexcused, he argued that many of his absences were legitimate; he missed several days because he was subpoenaed and other days in order to attend a National Education Association (NEA) convention in Washington. And on some of the days missed, said Reese, most of the students were absent too.

There was talk around town that if Reese was not rehired, Selma would see its largest demonstrations yet, and Reese warned the board that there would be widespread reaction to his firing. The board moved cautiously because they knew that many would perceive Reese's dismissal as retaliation for his civil rights work, but they believed that Reese needed to choose if he was going to be a teacher or a civil rights leader. The board felt compelled to act.

Smeltzer called Kathryn Windham, a board member, to warn that the NEA, civil rights organizations, and national wire services all were after Reese for a press release. Smeltzer persuaded Reese to delay issuing any statement until the board reconsidered its decision at a coming meeting, and he predicted that Reese's firing would be covered by national news media. But after the board refused to reinstate Reese, the story was not picked up, perhaps because the board's case against Reese was strong or perhaps because Selma's local affairs were no longer national news.[28]

About the same time that Reese's dismissal became public, another long-festering problem among blacks reached its boiling point. Unlike the Reese firing, however, which some ascribed to white vindictiveness, this problem was more difficult to blame on vengeful segregationists. The problem revolved around the distribution of relief supplies donated to Selma's blacks. When all the outsiders finally went back where they came from, their experiences in the bowels of the Black Belt were sources of curiosity and admiration, and they retold their tales to friends and audiences, who responded by sending money and supplies to Selma's downtrodden.[29] As the weeks following the march to Montgomery passed, the flow of materials became increasingly large, a stark contrast to the days in 1963 when Smeltzer's relief supplies from Church World Service had to be slipped into town!

Although no one in black Selma had the training or experience to handle emergency relief of this size, almost immediately someone volunteered, a "mystery man" named Elder William Ezra Greer. Greer had appeared in the vigil beside the ("Berlin Wall") rope and immediately showed that he knew how to give orders and speak with authority. But he was vague about his background, wore what appeared to be clerical clothing, and hung from his neck an official-looking but unidentifiable medallion on a heavy chain. In the constant milling in front of the chapel, people who spoke with authority were assumed to have authority, and by the end of the march, Greer was a person of influence in black Selma.

Under Greer's direction, the Selma Emergency Relief Fund (SERF), which he organized with himself as executive director, became a one-way avenue that allowed large amounts of supplies to enter the basement of the First Baptist Church but only permitted a trickle to exit. Shipments came from the far corners, but most of them stayed in the First Baptist basement, although Greer's officious assistants collected a stack of applications for relief aid. An impressive amount of food, clothing, and other material accumulated—including 10,000 pounds of food, plus clothing, toys, Easter baskets, and medical supplies from Detroit delivered personally by Congressman John Conyers. Rumors began to fly when it became obvious that the "pick of the lot"—the newest and most stylish clothing and the canned hams, for example—had been culled from the rest. No one knew who received these things, but it was rumored that black pastors or influential middle-class blacks or perhaps Greer's unpaid assistants had compensated themselves handsomely. An uglier version had middle-class people peddling the loot out of car trunks in the countryside.

By June, grumbling about Greer and the mess at First Baptist became widespread, and a new SCLC staffer, Harold Middlebrook, spoke to Reese several times about Greer. No action was taken. Voters League leadership finessed the criticism by attending ward meetings, but not to answer questions. Instead, high-ranking League officials glided into meetings like celebrities, sat on the platform, and gained control of the agenda with pulpit-pounding speeches that sparkled with generalities.

Greer's undoing came, not from his own community, but from the city administration. Baker heard reports from blacks about a misuse of money and developed a long list of questions. He arrested Greer on June 24 for using obscene language and possessing obscene literature. Before Baker could interrogate Greer, however, Ernest Doyle and James Gildersleeve, first vice-president and treasurer of the Voters League, respectively, bailed Greer out. (Reese was out of town.) Soon, Baker had another warrant, this one from an irate black father who alleged that Greer had made obscene remarks to and fondled one of the man's attractive daughters. Blacks quickly put Greer on the first bus heading north, but Baker climbed aboard the idling vehicle and arrested Greer right out of his seat. This time, Baker asked his questions, and Greer answered them.

Greer was fined $25 and sentenced to six months at hard labor for swearing in the presence of a young girl. The six months' sentence was suspended when Greer's lawyer told the judge that his client intended to leave Selma. The *Times-Journal* reminded its readers of the allegations of "sex activity" during the vigil at Brown's Chapel and on the march to Montgomery.[30] A few days later, the integrity of another civil rights leader became a public issue, but this time it was not a mysterious newcomer but one of Selma's native sons, F. D. Reese, who was arrested by Wilson Baker—for embezzling civil rights funds. The city that could not afford to hire a black police officer sent Baker and other officials to California, Ohio, and New Jersey to interview contributors to the Voters League, who stated that their contributions were for the movement and not for Reese's personal needs. Complaints evidently were filed by rival blacks, and Baker reportedly had photocopied checks written on a bank account in Montgomery in Reese's name to pay house and furniture bills. Reese was accused of signing over Voters League checks to his Montgomery account. Baker and Smitherman called a press conference to present their evidence, accompanied by pious statements about the protection of black citizens, with Smitherman adding for good measure that most of Reese's civil rights demands were unreasonable.

The press widely reported the scandal, some in a self-righteous tone, and after seeing Reese on television and reading about him in the newspapers, Smeltzer telephoned him. Reese was reticent, explaining that he did not want to talk over the phone. The evening after his release, Reese spoke to a mass meeting and emotionally accused whites of a history of embezzlement of blacks: "The white man embezzled my mother, my grandfather, my grandmother." Reese's explanation was that after he lost his job, the board of the Voters League was concerned about his well-being and approved his personal use of League funds. Only the board knew about this decision; the rank and file and even SCLC staff members were not informed of it. When Reese wrote checks on the Montgomery bank account, Baker and Smitherman found out about it, and according to Reese, spread the story throughout the black community to create suspicion and divide blacks.

Many blacks remained convinced of their leader's innocence,

but black leaders privately conceded that there was "a rotten apple" in their ranks. Reportedly, all local SCLC staff and members believed the charges were true. Jealousy resurfaced among blacks, and one observer noted that those who were most active in spreading the rumors were those in the best position to move up a notch in the local pecking order if Reese was ruined. The SCLC office in Atlanta sent Ralph Abernathy and Program Director Randolph Blackwell to Selma on the same day as the Reese arrest to support him at a mass meeting, although Abernathy later acknowledged that accounting practices may not have been professional and that any mistakes made were "mistakes of the head and not mistakes of the heart." Competing factions trekked to Atlanta to meet with Andy Young.[31]

The End of Smeltzer's Ministry in Selma

Toward the end of April, Smeltzer began to terminate his ministry to Selma. His position description on the Church of the Brethren General Board staff did not justify his devoting full-time to Selma, and other duties pressed. There were hopes that the city was ready to face its problems, and although the mayor's meetings had not produced concrete results, communication had been established, which was a novel enough development in Selma's interracial history. Smeltzer had achieved his initial goal, and there was little more that he could do if Selma's black and white leaders did not use the available communication channels. The likelihood of violence had diminished, and Selmians, in their conversations with Smeltzer, no longer expressed fears of riots or street bloodshed.

When Smeltzer visited the Pentagon, he learned that Colonel Ault was moving with assertiveness and enthusiasm toward equal rights at Craig Air Force Base. Ault faced considerable pressure at Craig, including telephone conversations with Secretary of the Air Force Zuchert and the watchful eye of Vice-President Hubert

H. Humphrey, but the base contractor was not integrated, and blacks were given careful treatment in civil service jobs.[32]

Therefore, during the summer of 1965, Smeltzer disengaged from Selma. Dave Smith kept him informed, but at the end of the summer, Smith also left. Smeltzer recommended that his denomination continue its neutrality by not assigning Brethren Volunteer Service workers to Dallas County until the crisis ended; Brethren workers could be placed elsewhere in the South. Smeltzer also kept close touch with CRS personnel, a number of whom telephoned him for information and tips on contacts in Selma. He turned down a CRS request to help in another community.[33]

Many of the problems Smeltzer found in Selma remained after he left. Smeltzer thought that as a first priority, the meetings with black leaders should be reinstated. He suggested small but public changes: hiring two black police and two black firefighters; putting two blacks in responsible positions with the city government, such as receiving water-bill payments; filling existing vacancies on city boards such as the Housing Authority and City Water Commission with blacks; desegregating recreational facilities, including the pool, step by step; and adopting the use of the titles "Mr." and "Mrs." for black adults.[34]

In July, Fred Miller and Dave Smith tried to set up a biracial meeting in Montgomery, but whites refused to cooperate because they were afraid that someone would find out about it. Black internal bickering was rampant; late in September, a rival black organization, the Dallas County Independent Free Voters Organization, was created. By October, the local movement's most widely respected figure, F. D. Reese, was knotted in legal problems and wrote to King asking for financial assistance to cover his attorney fees. That summer, Charles Fager, an SCLC staffer working with students at Selma University, wrote to Atlanta headquarters that the Voters League was a small but "fledgling bureaucratic morass, which makes up for its small size with monumental inefficiency."[35]

Nevertheless, Selma had changed forever. Although the violence of the civil rights campaign had bloodied Selma's image, the violence could have been worse. Terrible as the assault on the Pettus Bridge was, there were no fatalities there, and only the tragic death of Reeb happened on Selma's streets. Moderate whites still faced considerable pressure and were fearful, but they had spoken out publicly several times; the Chamber of Commerce and Art Lewis are two notable examples. White moderates slowly became more visible, and the heavy-handed methods of the die-hards were increasingly discredited and seen as ineffective. Perhaps most important, blacks were registering to vote, which would provide them with unprecedented leverage to have an impact on Selma's power structure.

In August, when the Voting Rights Act took effect and voter registration rolls finally became open, it was an emotional event for blacks, who stood in the long lines at the courthouse. On the first day of registration, Sheriff Clark commented to the *New York Times* that "the whole thing's so ridiculous I haven't gotten over laughing at it yet. In fact, I'm nauseated."[36]

9

Rainbow

Everything has changed and nothing has changed.

Joseph Lowery, president of SCLC

It is time for a change in this town. Selma is much better off than it was in 1965, but underneath it all, there is still racism.

F. D. Reese, 1984

Martin Luther King ruined Selma's way of life. We had a way of life we liked.

Jim Clark

We need to cut out all this foolish race baiting.

Joseph T. Smitherman

I have been in jail 115 times and have bled in thirty states and all that will have been in vain unless you remember the past.

Hosea Williams

They put "Mr." and "Mrs." on your letters now. They used to call me "P. H." Now it's "Reverend Lewis." That might not seem like much in Chicago and New York, but down here it's important.

P. H. Lewis, pastor of Brown's Chapel

I've been to Copenhagen, Denmark. I've been to Stockholm, Sweden, and Helsinki, Finland. I've been to Tel Aviv, Israel, and Amsterdam, Holland, and wherever I've gone, Selma is known. Why would this little town have become a landmark for freedom all over the world?

L. L. Anderson, pastor of Tabernacle Baptist Church

[Smeltzer] loved people, and it was perfectly obvious in his dealing with them. He was a gentle man.

Kathryn Windham

Dr. Milton Eisenhower once said, "Those who make peaceful revolution impossible, make violent revolution inevitable." One of our Christian tasks is to facilitate communication between conflicting parties, to help each understand the other's goals, to suggest alternative solutions for their consideration, and to enable them to resolve their conflicts without violence.

Ralph E. Smeltzer

And men will come from east and west, and from north and south, and sit at table in the kingdom of God.

Luke 13:29

By 1970, the civil rights revolution had brought small but significant changes to Selma. Juries were integrated, almost eleven thousand blacks were registered to vote, ten blacks were clerks in downtown stores, six blacks were on the police force, about 15 percent of the black children attended integrated classes and total integration was imminent, and two black sheriff's deputies patrolled the courthouse. The title "Mr." was used for blacks, and the few blacks who could afford it ate quietly in restaurants. The number of moderates and their sensitivities had improved. Whites shook hands publicly with blacks. In contrast, many segregationists pointed to riots in Newark and Detroit and expressed gratitude that Jim Clark had saved them from similar anarchy in Selma.[1]

One of the early signs of change was the defeat of Sheriff Jim Clark for reelection. As the spring 1966 elections approached, Dallas County blacks zeroed in on Clark. By the anniversary of the battle on the bridge, thousands of blacks were registered and primed to oust their most public adversary. Rival Wilson Baker challenged Clark. In 1964, Smitherman had appointed Baker as director of public safety on the condition that Baker pledge not to run against Clark, but as the campaign season approached, the sheriff eyed bigger fish than Dallas County—some say the governor's chair—and released Baker from the pledge. Clark's dreams of moving up to the big leagues ended when George Wallace ran his wife, Lurleen, as a stand-in, however, and Baker and Clark wound up in a nasty campaign for the office of sheriff.

Clark campaigned for the black vote, even throwing a barbecue for blacks, but won little black support. There was a black candidate, Samson Crum, but Reese and the Voters League considered him a Black Panther whose candidacy would only divert votes from Baker and reelect Clark. Therefore they pressured Crum into withdrawing; he was a postal worker close to retirement, and they allegedly got to him through his job. Also, five blacks ran for lesser county offices with little chance of winning.

The Reese embezzlement charges, which were allowed to hang without trial for almost a year (June 1965, to March 1966), became entangled in politics, and Hare and McLeod dismissed the charges. According to rumors, Baker dropped the charges in exchange for Reese's endorsement, but Hare and McLeod were Clark's men and never would have cooperated on a deal to help Baker.[2]

Baker defeated Clark in the primary, but the next day Clark went before the Democratic Executive Committee to challenge six ballot boxes from black districts that gave Baker enough votes to win an outright majority and avoid a runoff. The committee chair was Alston Keith, a fervent segregationist, and the vice-chairman was Chris Heinz; to no one's surprise, the committee quickly accepted Clark's challenge. But Baker went to federal court, bypassing Clark's local ally, Hare. In mid-May, Judge Thomas gave the election to Baker. Baker had sued under provisions of the Voting Rights Act, which he had fought so much more intelligently and effectively than Clark, but now the act gave Baker his victory. The court decision resulted from the first Justice Department intervention in a local primary in history. Clark ran as a write-in in the November election, but lost 7,249 to 6,712.[3]

Divisiveness continued to plague black Selma, and the black power–Black Panther phase of the national movement was especially difficult. A white SCLC staff member, Shirley Mesher, who had arrived just before the march to Montgomery and had stayed in Selma, personified the black-power philosophy in Selma and within a year had become a highly controversial project director. Mesher enjoyed considerable success in organizing uneducated blacks and acquired a measure of popularity among the grass roots, but local black leaders wanted her out. They accused Mesher of creating class antagonisms by encouraging hatred of educated people and by turning the laity against the clergy. Black leaders also charged that Mesher told people not to vote. Appeals for her dismissal came to Atlanta SCLC headquarters from black leaders, and petitions of support arrived from Mesher's friends.[4]

In 1968, blacks edged closer to electoral equality but with considerable internal divisions. Three of their seven City Council candidates, including Ed Moss, survived to face runoffs, although Smitherman handily defeated challenger L. L. Anderson, who was angered when F. D. Reese and other blacks leafletted against him. The Voters League endorsed Smitherman plus a white City Council president and several white council members, based on the assumption that black candidates could not win. All black candidates were defeated by 5-to-3 margins in the runoff. There was a heavy voter turnout, which followed racial lines. Reese considered the election to be counterproductive because it destroyed most of the positive relations that had developed, and he laid the blame at the feet of Anderson's camp for allegedly supporting a candidate solely on racial considerations. Anderson, on the other hand, was embittered by the opposition of his black colleagues.[5]

Reese was elected to the City Council in 1972 and supported Smitherman for years in exchange for concessions, especially on municipal jobs. Amelia Boynton and three other blacks also won seats on the ten-member council. The key to the emergent black political power was the election of council members from wards rather than at-large, a change that prevented whites from using their citywide edge in registration to deny black neighborhoods representation on the council.[6]

Although Selma never again experienced demonstrations of the magnitude of the 1965 events, civil rights difficulties surfaced throughout the 1960s. In November 1966, Stokely Carmichael was arrested by city police when he set up a sound truck downtown. Carmichael, whose work in isolated rural areas of Lowndes County became the genesis of the Black Panther party, was charged with attempting to incite a riot and with lunging at a police officer in an attempt to provoke the officer into hitting him. He was sentenced to sixty days at hard labor and fined $100.[7] In 1968, a Poor People's Campaign caravan marched through Selma. When its leader, Ralph Abernathy, arrived in town, he decided to extend the march's route across the Pettus Bridge, a "sacred spot," he said, but the city relented only after Abernathy announced that he was ready to go to jail.[8]

In 1970, a Selma police captain, Nolan Chambers, was indicted for murder when a black man, arrested on drunk and disorderly charges, died in a local hospital. Mayor Smitherman explained that the prisoner suffered "certain wounds" because the police had to use force to make the arrest, but after street demonstrations, charges were brought against Chambers.[9]

Smeltzer's Effectiveness

Charles Fager writes that Smeltzer's "influence shaped the situation subtly yet profoundly, perhaps even decisively."[10] Ralph Smeltzer's goals were modest—to create lines of interracial communication and prevent violence—but Martin Luther King's decision to target Selma significantly altered Smeltzer's mission and increased its difficulty. Although he greatly admired King, both before and after Selma, Smeltzer did what he could to keep SCLC out of town. At the People's Bank meeting, he made several helpful suggestions to the moderates early in the SCLC campaign; had those suggestions been implemented quickly, SCLC undoubtedly would have moved on to another location. Even though the city fathers did not adopt Smeltzer's suggestions in January 1965, SCLC still almost left the city because Selma was not producing the clear-cut definition of racial issues that the campaign needed. Smeltzer took the lead in suggesting the appearance-book compromise, which SCLC leaders initially declined to accept, preferring instead to maintain an air of confrontation. The SCLC organizers found the going harder because of Smeltzer's work, but Jim Clark's behavior added life to the campaign at several critical moments. The polarization generated by the civil rights movement set back Smeltzer's patient construction of communication; biracial talks stopped midway in the campaign, not to be resumed until SCLC departed and Smeltzer returned to contribute to their resumption.

Smeltzer was especially helpful to blacks in establishing with both whites and blacks the negotiating team of Reese, Brown, and Moss. These three men rose naturally to leadership positions within the black community, but whites were amazingly unaware of the dynamics within black Selma. Other blacks had legitimate claims to leadership status, but Smeltzer, with his knowledge of both black and white Selma, knew which individuals would be most conducive to productive conversations. The moderate business leaders' group accepted Smeltzer's suggestion of Reese, Brown, and Moss as the black representatives, and Smitherman honored that precedent for the fall 1964 informal conversations. These talks were the first interracial negotiations in Selma's history, and Smeltzer was one of the key figures in their creation. Blacks are the members of the community who recall Smeltzer with the greatest fondness, and although black leaders best remember their specific contributions to the movement, several of them, notably Reese and Foster, generously praised Smeltzer. Although Smeltzer successfully maintained strict neutrality throughout the crisis, he secretly sympathized very much with the civil rights movement. He believed in the inevitability of its success, and he hoped that the campaign would remain nonviolent and that victory would be won without retaliation by whites. By helping blacks unite, by accelerating their appearance at the bargaining table, and by enhancing the articulation of their agenda, Smeltzer believed he was simultaneously advancing the cause of civil rights and easing community tensions. The best example of Smeltzer's contribution to black unity was the meeting of black leaders he arranged at Selma University in the summer of 1964. Although some black leaders deny the divisions within black leadership, there seems little doubt of their existence. In his notes, Smeltzer writes that he had worked hard at achieving black unity, but his diary is unfortunately devoid of specifics.

The group with whom Smeltzer was least successful were the die-hard segregationists. A precondition for successful mediation is a desire for agreement by all parties, but the die-hards were interested in domination, not conciliation. They wanted racial peace only on their terms, and the process of negotiation itself implied at least partial recognition of black grievances and rights. Segregationists knew what they wanted: race relations to remain as they had been since the last century. Their unwillingness to talk with anyone who "had not dug the river" not only indicated the ideological provincialism of Dallas County die-hards but also put Smeltzer at a severe disadvantage. Smeltzer was unsuccessful with this unreceptive group, but it is doubtful that any strategy or approach that contained conciliation would have been accepted by the die-hards.

Smeltzer could boast of limited success with moderate segregationists because they listened to him and accepted some of his suggestions and analyses. What held them back was their well-founded fear of retaliation and community pressures, and their lack of confidence in Selma's ability to accept moderation. Race was such an untouchable topic of conversation in some settings that many moderates felt isolated on this issue, but Smeltzer put several moderates in contact with each other (e.g., Arthur Lewis and Art Capell). He helped begin the process of building a collective backbone among the moderates.

Smeltzer advised the moderates, many listened to him, and some implemented his suggestions. Ego and its effects on memory dissuade individuals from recalling that Smeltzer, or anyone else, assisted them, and the situation's complexity prevents a qualitative gauging of Smeltzer's specific impact. Nevertheless, he directly influenced several issues and often had an indirect impact. Specific examples of his work are his direct mediation in the threatened walkout at Hudson High, negotiations regarding the parade regulations preceding the first King march, and Frank Wilson's conversation with Harry Boyte. Smeltzer's presence and position in Selma were respected by many; that he was able to overcome the "outsider" rap with many whites (albeit not the segregationists) was an achievement in itself.

A good indicator of Smeltzer's success was the respect that others had for his work. People at CRS kept coming to him for advice and information, and they offered to put him on their payroll. The government asked Smeltzer to work in other cities, and several Selma preachers suggested that others be assigned a similar role elsewhere. Secrest had Smeltzer hang on the phone while he tried to convince his boss to put a man in Chicago to do the things Smeltzer had done in Selma.[11]

Assessment of Smeltzer's effectiveness requires caution.

Smeltzer had almost no impact on the national voting rights campaign; his mission and chief labors were devoted to local affairs in Selma. It would be wrong to claim that Smeltzer controlled or profoundly altered events, and it would be wrong to argue that he was as important to the Selma story as were Martin Luther King, George Wallace, Joe Smitherman, F. D. Reese, Jim Clark, Wilson Baker, and so on. It would be just as wrong to say that Smeltzer failed in Selma.

The multilayered nature of the Selma campaign also influenced Smeltzer's role. Actors in the drama included Selmians, with whom Smeltzer experienced general but not complete success, and national and even international personages, whom Smeltzer could hope to influence only indirectly. Smeltzer never met Martin Luther King, but Smeltzer enjoyed cordial relations with SCLC aides Andy Young, Harry Boyte, and others. Smeltzer collaborated closely with Mac Secrest of CRS, but conversed only once with the agency's head, LeRoy Collins. Smeltzer's contact in the Justice Department was John Doar, who was Burke Marshall's assistant in the Civil Rights Division. Smeltzer had no contact with Governor Wallace's office. Locally, Jim Clark remembers Smeltzer unfavorably, and Smitherman claims not to remember him at all. In contrast, Smeltzer talked frequently during the crisis with Wilson Baker, and during the most critical periods of early 1965, Smeltzer conversed almost daily with F. D. Reese, the local black leader.

Would Selma have been different without Smeltzer? The interracial communication fostered by Smeltzer and his contributions to the lessening of tension must have lowered the probability of violence. Selma's streets would have been more dangerous without him. It was in the nature of his work that some of his greatest successes involved relatively minor events—the Selma University meeting and the Reese–Moss–Brown talks with Grist–Morthland–Wilson are two examples—but these events were important steps in Smeltzer's plans to build communication channels. Smeltzer's ministry was not without setbacks; he failed to move the moderate whites at the bank meeting—in fact, they do not even remember the meeting—and the appearance-book proposal caused ill feelings before its eventual adoption. Smeltzer met his initial goal of establishing interracial communication; there was none when he arrived, but the channels were opened and utilized by the time he left. Considering the conditions under which Smeltzer labored—the local dread of outsiders and his total strangeness to the town—his accomplishments are remarkable.

Although always a humble person, Smeltzer was quietly pleased with his performance in Selma and believed that it was a model for further Brethren activity. Smeltzer evaluated his Selma efforts, realistically, I believe, as follows:

> Although we were not able to establish sufficient dialogue and negotiations between white and Negro leaders to avoid Martin Luther King's campaign from January through March, we were able to moderate the conflict, initiate and keep open several lines of communication, serve as mediator in a few situations, and on three occasions negotiate a settlement of issues at the last moment before planned demonstrations took place.[12]

Because Smeltzer believed that in Selma both he and the CRS were effective, he concluded that private mediators as well as government officials could contribute to justice and peace in a wide variety of domestic and international situations. Neutral third parties could help victims become more aware of their victimization, assist victims in the organization and articulation of their grievances, and lead oppressors to correct injustices. He dreamed that his denomination would create a Brethren Reconciliation Service—the name obviously modeled after the denomination's popular Brethren Volunteer Service—that would train others to repeat his Selma effort in other troublespots. He wrote: "This could become a distinctive Brethren contribution to peace in our time."[13]

Smeltzer's Ministry as a Role Model

What lessons can be learned from Ralph Smeltzer's work in Selma? Is mediation a realistic response for churches to a crisis? Can mediation advance the cause of social justice? Again, let us caution that Smeltzer's achievements were subtle and limited, although significant. He was Selma's peacemaker, not its saviour.

Smeltzer's Selma experiences convinced him that mediation was a major peacemaking opportunity available to his denomination. Churches, unlike the government, lack political self-interest in the outcome of a situation. Small denominations such as the Brethren, because of their obscurity, are especially unencumbered with identity with one side or another; that almost no one in Selma had heard of Smeltzer's denomination was a distinct advantage, while partisanship caused by the federal role in integration tainted the federal mediators. Smeltzer anticipated that the Brethren corps of mediators would "be building upon the church's past peace heritage and projecting that heritage into a needed peace ministry of the future." Certainly the role of mediator, of peacemaker, is consistent with the nonviolent tradition of the Brethren and offers the historic peace churches an opportunity to participate constructively in tense situations.[14]

The same biblical text that extolls peacemaking—"Blessed are the peacemakers"—also suggests the personality traits used so effectively by Smeltzer in Selma: empathy, humility, and righteousness. ("Blessed are those who mourn. . . . Blessed are the meek. . . . Blessed are those who hunger and thirst for righteousness."[15]) Churches should be skilled at training mediators with these talents, which are essential for successful mediation.

Critical to Smeltzer's effectiveness was his empathy, his apparent concern (amounting at times to "mourning") for people, which aided immeasurably his acceptance by many Selmians. He was a good listener, and he respected everyone's situation in Selma; he convinced his contacts that he cared about people as individuals and as a community. Meekness was another significant ingredient in Smeltzer's ministry. He kept his promise that he would not become involved for personal honor or reward: in fact, his reticence about his achievements impeded research on this book. Not only did he maintain confidentiality within Selma, but his close friends know only generally about his Selma activities; he never divulged details. And Smeltzer's righteousness—his commitment to social justice and personal integrity—were instrumental in winning the confidence of many locals. Blacks recognized his belief in civil rights and his concern for those who suffered from oppression, and Selmians of both races saw him as fundamentally honest.

If Smeltzer's Selma ministry shows the value of church-sponsored mediation, why has his ministry not been replicated to a greater extent? If churches are well suited to producing empathetic, righteous, and humble mediators, why is mediation a neglected area of church outreach?

Part of the answer lies in the fact that Smeltzer's achievements point to the difficulties of establishing mediation ministries; the story of his overcoming so many obstacles shows just how difficult mediation is. Mediation strains institutional resources of money and staff time. Effective mediators need to be present in the early stages of a crisis because winning the confidence of all parties involved is a painstaking process. Once the situation reaches a climax, it is much more difficult for a newly arrived mediator to gain the trust of all concerned. Smeltzer was in Selma for over a year before the SCLC campaign began, and he estimated that Selma consumed one-fourth of his time for the duration of the project.

Smeltzer's performance also demonstrates the extraordinary skills required of a mediator. Tact, articulateness, and an understanding of social psychology are relatively rare, making the recruitment and training of mediators time-consuming and expensive.

Smeltzer's achievements in Selma were indirect; mediation probably advances the cause of social justice more subtly than directly. Mediation contributes to social justice most by lessening tensions, by transforming shouts across a street into a handshake across a bargaining table. Mediation reverses the process of polarization, thereby enabling a rational consideration of social issues, and it reduces fear and distrust, which are major causes of prejudice and oppression. Also, mediation tends to win consensus much more quickly than more direct forms of advocacy do. Mediation is a potentially rewarding option for churches seeking to influence scenes of social crisis.

At this writing, the Church of the Brethren has a fledgling program under way to train mediators for use within the denomination, chiefly for strife-torn congregations. Because of its peace heritage, the Church of the Brethren from time to time receives requests to mediate but is unable to act on them because of limited resources. The use of mediators for national or international crises remains a vision.

Selma Today

Contemporary Selma has undergone much change. Black activists have hopes of one day electing a black mayor, and many of the social wounds of the 1960s have healed. Nevertheless, racial divisions are still endemic to Selma.

Blacks took a strong step toward political parity in 1984 when Federal District Judge W. B. Hand ordered Selma to redraw City Council ward lines and reduce City Council seats from ten to five. The new boundaries cut through white and black residential areas, creating racially balanced districts. Blacks, who are a majority of the city's population, had a chance to win in each district and thus achieve a majority on the City Council.

The 1984 mayoral campaign, on the twentieth anniversary of the Civil Rights Act, was a landmark election, pitting challenger F. D. Reese against incumbent Joe Smitherman, who had won five consecutive elections. Each of the men was fifty-four years old and had been both antagonists and allies over the years. Smitherman campaigned as a populist who grew up in poverty; he knew "what it's like to be poor," enabling him to recognize black needs. Smitherman anticipated black support because of the progress blacks had experienced during his terms as mayor. Smitherman boasted of his contributions: "The personnel board has three blacks and two whites, the library board four and four and the school board five blacks to four whites." Forty percent of the police force was black, including the assistant chief and several captains and lieutenants. Several municipal department heads were black. Yet Selma's poverty exceeded the national average, and black income was about the same fraction of white income that it had been in 1964. Rumors spread that Reese would fire all whites from city jobs if he won.[16]

Despite the campaign's intensity, Reese and Smitherman remained civil toward one another and were publicly gracious after the election. Although Reese managed to call Smitherman a "segregationist," and the mayor hinted that a Reese victory would presage a race problem, both candidates otherwise skirted the issue of race. They debated such issues as garbage collection: Smitherman wanted to continue the back-door system, and Reese favored switching to front yards. But even garbage collection had racial overtones because all the trash collectors were black, and Reese complained that they should not have to carry heavy garbage cans from back yards to a truck waiting out front. Presumably, whites still liked to have their black servants come to the back door.

Voter registration reemerged as a controversial issue in this "anniversary" campaign. An aggressive and successful black registration campaign prompted Cecil Williamson, a white preacher and city councilman, to warn that "if the blacks get political control here, I imagine many whites will leave town." After a white state senator from Dallas County, Earl Goodwin, complained of "problems and irregularities" in registration, Selma's white politicians called a strategy meeting that included all members of the Board of Voter Registration except Edwin Moss, who was not notified. All deputy registrars were dismissed pending an investigation; later, all were reinstated except Marie Foster and one other black. Foster, who pursued registration with evangelistic fervor, believed that she was dismissed because of her effectiveness.[17]

Although voting generally followed racial lines, Smitherman's pork barrel paid dividends and gave him enough black votes to win an impressive victory, 5,952 to 3,948. Significant numbers of blacks voted for a white man, but whites refused to support a black candidate. Smitherman's hard-line conservative enemies, who for years had castigated him for appeasing blacks, supported him against Reese. Once again, whites united and blacks divided. Whites remained in control, with three whites and two blacks on the City Council. Carl Morgan, Jr., a former Selma mayor, defeated a black man, Raymond Major, for president of the council. Major led four white opponents in the first election, but Morgan defeated him handily in a runoff.[18]

Electoral achievement for blacks in Dallas County has been difficult. Although blacks constitute a majority in Dallas County, they had never won a countywide elective office until Jackie Walker was elected tax collector in 1984. Tragically, she died in an auto accident before taking office. Blacks pleaded with county officials to follow tradition and appoint the deceased official's spouse, an attorney, to the post, but the white candidate who lost the election received the position instead. Blacks were bitterly disappointed and angered.[19]

In the twenty years since the march to Montgomery, much in Selma has changed, however. The score or more of restaurants that resisted integration so steadfastly in 1964 have been replaced with a row of golden arches, fried-chicken outlets, and Taco Bells. Blacks and whites interact freely, whether in businesses or restaurants. Downtown Selma is undergoing a restoration that will re-create its antebellum heyday as an early Victorian river town. A new brick City Hall sits on the site of the Hotel Albert, a money-loser that was torn down a few years after King integrated it.

According to a 1985 interview, Smitherman has told his story so often "that he rushes through it pell-mell, in an off-hand way full of humor but lacking in emotion, as if he were playing a cassette." The mayor relaxes with interviewers, putting his feet up on his desk and flicking cigarette ashes on the floor. Some of the quotes in my interview with the mayor appeared in a Philadelphia *Inquirer* story a year later.[20]

What of the others in the Selma story? Jim Clark, after losing a bid for reelection, worked at several jobs and was sent to prison for marijuana smuggling. He now sells mobile homes in Scottsboro, Alabama. Art Capell handles public relations for a mental hospital near Mobile, and Roswell Falkenberry sold the *Times-Journal* and retired. Chris Heinz sells insurance; L. L. Anderson still fills the Tabernacle Baptist pulpit. F. D. Reese, as principal of East Side Junior High, greets visitors in a carpeted, paneled office with a built-in television set. Amelia Boynton has remarried and now lives in Tuskegee. Marie Foster and Ed Moss are both still active in voter registration in Selma. Wilson Baker, C. C. Brown, and Art Lewis have died. Frank Wilson, now retired, reflects on the traditional racism in Selma's society and confesses that he "would like to think that I've purged myself of this narrowness." In June 1965, Father Ouellet was ordered out of Selma by his archbishop. Ouellet said the archbishop told him that he was "too wild on this racial question."[21]

In spite of significant progress, color is still a barrier in Selma. But as the high point of the civil rights campaign, which was the greatest reform movement in American history, Selma to many is a victorious battleground where second-class citizens nonviolently captured their rightful place in the temple of American democracy. It was a struggle whose victory spread beyond the Black Belt, beyond the South, beyond the nation; the Selma campaign and the Voting Rights Act inspire disenfranchised minorities everywhere.

Selma has reacted to its fame with diffidence. Many Selmians claim not to understand the interest of historians in their city. Although many civil rights disagreements have been forgiven and heated emotions have cooled, old animosities are still visible. Muriel Lewis, whose outspoken courage caused her to face the storm of segregationist anger as much as any Selmian, lists numerous examples of her gradual forgetting of the civil rights days; for example, she no longer exchanges Christmas cards with journalists befriended in the 1960s, but she bitterly condemns three local segregationists whom she considers responsible for the stress that produced her husband's fatal heart disease. On the other side, Sol Tepper, who sees Jim Clark as Selma's saviour, has little sympathy for local people who witnessed the facts but drew the wrong conclusions.[22]

The Selma of the 1960s defied stereotyping, and so does contemporary Selma. While animosities from the civil rights era linger, there are hopeful signs. In March 1985, nearly two thousand people came to Brown's Chapel to reenact the march to Montgomery. In dramatic contrast to events twenty years earlier, Mayor Smitherman presented keys to the city to Jesse Jackson, Rainbow Coalition candidate for the Democratic presidential nomination in 1984, and to Joseph Lowery, president of the SCLC, and shared a hymnal with Jackson during the singing of "The Battle Hymn of the Republic." In his remarks, the mayor said that it would take the combined efforts of blacks and whites to produce what Selma really needed—more jobs—and he asserted that every American had the right to vote. "For the last twenty years," he said, "they have been telling us, 'The niggers are coming ... the niggers are coming.' Well, you all have arrived."[23]

Smeltzer After Selma

After Selma, Ralph Smeltzer continued his efforts in behalf of minorities and the disadvantaged. He served on the Church of the Brethren denominational staff in Elgin until 1971, with activities aimed at helping Hispanic Americans, migrant workers, and Indian Americans, among others. His commitment to biblical pacifism found outlets in organizations such as the National Committee for the World Peace Tax Fund and the Historic Peace Church Seminar, and he engaged in such peace-related activities as hosting religious leaders from Eastern Europe for a committee of the Christian Peace Conference. In 1970, the church transferred him to Washington, D.C., to head the Washington Office because he was more familiar with the nation's capital than anyone else on the staff and because much of his portfolio could be carried out from Washington just as well as Elgin. Smeltzer's enthusiasm and workaholic ethics gave the office new visibility within the church.

In 1971, Smeltzer suffered a heart attack and was placed in an intensive-care unit in a hospital. There, he learned to know his fellow patients by name and their medical histories, and he had his bed placed so that he could observe the monitors of everyone else in the room. He died of a second heart attack in 1976.[24]

During the summer of 1985 influential blacks and whites in Selma received anonymous invitations to attend monthly dinners at a local restaurant. Each person was to bring a friend of the opposite race, making the evenings especially significant by defying the old taboo against interracial eating. The invitations were signed *Salt and Pepper*. Forty people showed up for the June dinner, sixty in July, and almost one hundred in August. Ralph Smeltzer would have been pleased. At the August meeting, the major topic of discussion was the disappointing local economy; another issue was also considered, however: the placement of a marker at the foot of the Pettus Bridge. It was an indication that after twenty years, Selma had begun to accept its recent history as well as its older heritage.[25]

A rainbow is the division of light into colors, and it is a symbol of hope. Selma is both.

Notes

Abbreviations Used in the Notes

Brethren Archives	Church of the Brethren Archives, Elgin, Illinois
MLK Papers	Martin Luther King Papers, King Library and Archives, The Martin Luther King, Jr., Center for Nonviolent Social Change, Atlanta, Georgia
NYT	New York Times
SCLC Papers	Southern Christian Leadership Conference Papers, King Center, Atlanta, Georgia
Smeltzer Papers	Ralph E. Smeltzer Papers, Brethren Historical Library and Archives, Elgin, Illinois
SNCC Papers	Student Non-Violent Coordinating Committee Papers, King Center, Atlanta, Georgia
STJ	Selma Times-Journal

Chapter 1

1. Traditional beliefs of the Church of the Brethren include simple living, aversion to violence and war, refusal to take oaths, a literal observance of the Last Supper that includes the washing of one another's feet, adult baptism featuring trine immersion, and the absence of any professed creed except the New Testament. The denomination began in Germany in 1708 but by the 1740s had fully transplanted itself to colonial Pennsylvania. When Smeltzer went to Selma, there were approximately two hundred thousand Brethren nationally, but almost none in Alabama.

2. Samuel Klaus to Kramer, December 8, 1942, FBI documents, 100-165892-1; John Edgar Hoover to SAC, Los Angeles, "Ralph Emerson Smeltzer, Mary Smeltzer, Internal Security, Custodial Detention," FBI documents, 100-165892-1; and two reports prepared by the Los Angeles office, "Ralph Emerson Smeltzer, Mary Smeltzer," dated March 18, 1943, and May 5, 1943, FBI documents, 100-165892-2 and 100-165892-4.

3. Michi Weglyn, *Years of Infamy: The Untold Story of America's Concentration Camps* (New York: Morrow, 1976), p. 77.

4. Ibid., p. 84.

5. The guard claimed that the Japanese ran away when ordered to halt, but the man was shot in the front making the guard's story suspect. See ibid., 79. See also Edward H. Spicer, Asael T. Hansen, Katherine Luomala, and Marvin K. Opler, *Impounded People: Japanese-Americans in the Relocation Centers* (Tucson: University of Arizona Press, 1969), pp. 65-71.

6. Spicer et al., *Impounded People*, pp. 53-54; and Weglyn, *Years of Infamy*, p. 42.

7. Dillon S. Myer, *Uprooted Americans: The Japanese Americans and the War Relocation Authority during World War II* (Tucson: University of Arizona Press, 1971), p. 64; and Spicer et al., *Impounded People*, pp. 136-137.

8. Myer, *Uprooted Americans*, p. 141.

9. "Ralph Emerson Smeltzer, Mary Smeltzer," July 6, 1943, August 24, 1943, and September 2, 1943, FBI documents, 100-165892-5, 100-165892-9, and 100-165892-7; and Phoenix FBI File 100-2465.

10. The passages on the Smeltzer activities with the Japanese

Americans are based on Mary Blocher Smeltzer, "Japanese-American Re-settlement Work," in *To Serve the Present Age: The Brethren Service Story,* ed. Donald F. Durnbaugh (Elgin, Ill.: Brethren Press, 1975).

11. Ralph E. Smeltzer, "Brethren Service in Austria," in Durnbaugh, ed., *To Serve the Present Age.*

12. "Ralph E. Smeltzer Biographical Data," March 20, 1973, Brethren Archives.

13. Lee Whipple and Leland Wilson, interviews.

14. After Smeltzer's heart attack in 1971 walking replaced running in place as an exercise. He walked his route in Washington, D.C., every day with a small transistor radio pressed to his ear so that he could use his time efficiently by listening to the news while walking. When I began working in Smeltzer's Church of the Brethren Washington Office in 1974, Smeltzer knew where I would live and suggested that we walk to work rather than ride the bus; he told me how far the walk was and how long it would take. He knew because he had paced it off!

15. "The Christian Faith and Politics," Smeltzer's notes for a sermon he delivered, no doubt with great conviction, throughout the 1950s. See also Smeltzer to Jerry Flory, Chairman, Personnel Nominating Committee, Highland Avenue Church of the Brethren, Elgin, Illinois, March 13, 1963.

16. Smeltzer articles not mentioned elsewhere include "Summer Race Relations Institutes," *Gospel Messenger,* June 2, 1956; "We Held a School of Race Relations," *Gospel Messenger,* February 1958; and "A Race Relations Emphasis," *Leader,* December 1958.

17. Ralph E. Smeltzer, "Toward Open-Occupancy Housing," *Gospel Messenger,* July 5, 1958, pp. 22–23.

18. "My Developing Strategy," October 28, 1963, Smeltzer note to himself on interview strategy for meeting with civil rights leaders in Atlanta, Smeltzer Papers.

19. Smeltzer's "Report on Peace and Social Education" for the years 1962–1964, prepared for Brethren Service Commission meetings in November 1963, and November 1964, Brethren Archives.

20. There are reports that claims of flooding at Cahaba were exaggerated by rival politicians interested in moving the capital and that yellow fever was a more serious problem. William H. Brantley, *Three Capitals: A Book about the First Three Capitals of Alabama: St. Stephens, Huntsville and Cahawba* (University: University of Alabama Press, 1976; originally published, 1947), pp. 167–171. See also Walter M. Jackson, *The Story of Selma* (Birmingham: Birmingham Printing, 1954), pp. 1–3, 21–25; John Hardy, *Selma: Her Institutions and Her*

Men (Spartanburg, S.C.: Reprint Company, 1978; originally published, 1879), pp. 6–8; and two anonymous, undated pamphlets, *Selma and Dallas County Chamber of Commerce* and *Old Cahawba: Alabama's First Permanent State Capital*, published by the Selma/Dallas County Chamber of Commerce.

21. Charles Fager, *Selma, 1965* (New York: Scribner's, 1974), pp. 12–13; and Hardy, *Selma*, pp. 14–15.

22. One of Selma's newspapers backed John C. Breckenridge, the other supported Stephen Douglas, and former Whigs held a statewide convention in Selma to support John Bell's Constitutional Union ticket. See Jackson, *Story of Selma*, pp. 191–192.

23. The unusual request for "chamber lye" produced a series of verse. Following are several excerpts from ibid., pp. 199–201.

> We thought the women did enough
> At sewing skirts and kissing;
> But you have put the lovely dears
> To patriotic p-----g.

> Indeed, the thing is so very odd,
> Gunpowder like and cranky,
> That when a lady lifts her skirt
> She shoots a horrid Yankee!

> And . . . what could make
> A Yankee soldier sadder,
> Than dodging bullets fired from
> A pretty woman's bladder.

24. Shelby Foote, *The Civil War: A Narrative* (New York: Random House, 1963), 2:819, and 3:104, 736–738, 850, 904, 905; Hardy, *Selma*, pp. 46–53; Jackson, *Story of Selma*, pp. 215–219, 242–243; and James Russell Soley, "The Union and Confederate Navies," *Battles and Leaders of the Civil War* (New York: Thomas Yoseloff, 1956; originally published 1887), 1:628, and 4:759–760.

25. Fager, *Selma, 1965*, pp. 14–15.

26. Amelia Platts Boynton, *Bridge Across Jordan: The Story of the Struggle for Civil Rights in Selma, Alabama* (New York: Carlton Press, 1979), pp. 20, 21, 23–28, 46–50, 66–69. Another infamous southern town, Philadelphia, Mississippi, has a history of oppression very similar to Selma's; see Florence Mars, *Witness in Philadelphia* (Baton Rouge and

London: Louisiana State University Press, 1977), pp. 1–41 and passim.

27. "Dallas County, Alabama," *SNCC Research*, September 8, 1965, SNCC Papers; and "Special Report: Alabama Project," SNCC Press Release, September 26, 1963.

28. After successfully registering, Foster signed Bill Boynton's "honor roll," a list he kept of blacks who had successfully navigated the maze of obstacles to the ballot box. Marie Foster, interview. See also, J. A. Pickard, interview; and Howard Zinn, *SNCC: The New Abolitionists* (Boston: Beacon Press, 1965), p. 153.

29. David J. Garrow, *Protest at Selma: Martin Luther King, Jr., and the Voting Rights Act of 1965* (New Haven: Yale University Press, 1978), pp. 11, 31.

30. Fager, *Selma, 1965*, p. 17.

31. Garrow, *Protest at Selma*, p. 31.

32. Quote is from Edwin Moss, interview. See also Boynton, *Bridge Across Jordan*, p. 145; Fry, "The Voter-Registration Drive in Selma, Alabama," *Presbyterian Life*, January 15, 1964, p. 17; and Bernard Lafayette, interview.

33. Lafayette, interview. A similar version of this song is found in Boynton, *Bridge Across Jordan*, p. 150, and is attributed to Sharon and Germaine Platts and Arlene Ezell.

34. Marie Foster, interview.

35. L. L. Anderson, interview.

36. Ibid.

37. Untitled, undated report, SCLC Papers, Box 148, File 10; SNCC, "Special Report: Alabama Project"; Boynton, *Bridge Across Jordan*, p. 140; Garrow, *Protest at Selma*, pp. 31–32; and Zinn, *SNCC*, pp. 147, 149. Lafayette, who confesses to vague memory and secondhand information on this point, is under the impression that the football coach at Selma High School was responsible for turning back the table-leg-wielding whites; Lafayette, interview.

38. Lafayette admits to blurred vision at the time because of the running blood and says that the object in the white man's hand appeared to be a gun. Lafayette, interview.

39. Ibid.

40. Smeltzer interview with Father Ouellet, November 27, 1963; Dallas County Improvement Association letters to all businesses, August 29, 1963, and to Police Chief Ed Mullen, August 8, 1963; all in Smeltzer Papers.

41. Fry, "Voter-Registration Drive," p. 14; Garrow, *Protest at Selma*, p. 32; and John M. Pratt, "Report on Factfinding Trip to Selma,

Alabama," October 1, 1963, Smeltzer Papers. Pratt served on the National Council of Churches Commission on Religion and Race.

42. The estimate of attendance is Moss's.

43. See the following articles, all *NYT:* "Selma, Ala., Jails 165 in 2 Marches," September 24, 1963, p. 32; "Selma, Ala., Jails 28 More Negroes," September 26, 1963, p. 29; John Herbers, "Selma, Ala., Balks Negro Marchers," September 27, 1963, p. 30; and untitled articles of September 18, 1963, p. 24, and September 24, 1963, p. 29. See also SNCC, "Special Report: Alabama Project"; affidavits in SNCC Papers; and Pratt, "Report."

44. Quoted in Zinn, *SNCC,* pp. 150–151. The emphasis is Zinn's.

45. John Herbers, "Alabama Police Rough Up 4 As Selma Negroes Seek Vote," *NYT,* October 8, 1963, p. 37; Zinn, *SNCC,* pp. 152–166; and Carver Nesbitt statement, SNCC papers. Zinn also wrote about his observations in "Registration in Selma," *New Republic,* October 26, 1963, pp. 11–12.

46. Arthur Capell, "Troop Plan Disclosure May Provide New Grand Jury Lead," *STJ,* March 9, 1964.

47. Mrs. Amelia Boynton to Martin Luther King, Jr., November 30, 1963, SCLC Papers, Box 21, File 10.

48. Smeltzer, "My Developing Strategy."

Chapter 2

1. John Newton, interview.

2. Smeltzer, conversations with Ray Kyle and W. Harold Rowe; and Smeltzer to James Foreman, November 18, 1963, Smeltzer Papers.

3. Ralph E. Smeltzer, "Racial Revolution in the South," *Gospel Messenger,* May 26, 1956, p. 6.

4. Smeltzer, "My Developing Strategy Plans," November 28, 1963, and January 19, 1964, Smeltzer Papers.

5. Interviews with Fager, Lewis, Newton, Reese, Wilson, and Windham.

6. Patricia Blalock, the head librarian, remembers the chairs being removed for only a few days, maybe a weekend. Smeltzer's diary records that a librarian told him that a rush of black patrons when the library was integrated stimulated the removal of the chairs, and the *STJ* reported that the chairs were out in May. *STJ,* September 22, 1963.

7. John Fry, who visited Selma in October 1963, agreed with Smeltzer that Selma was really two communities, one black and one white. See Fry's "The Voter-Registration Drive in Selma, Alabama,"

Presbyterian Life, January 15, 1964, p. 15.

8. Charles Fager, *Selma, 1965* (New York: Scribner's, 1974), pp. 19–20; and John Herbers, "Whites in Selma, Ala., Disturbed over Determined Negro Drive," *NYT,* October 13, 1963.

9. I found Clark to be affable and hospitable in a 1985 interview. The story of the white-gloved woman comes from the Kathryn Windham interview. See also Louise Clark, interview.

10. The quotes are from an interview with a business person who wishes to remain anonymous. See also Fager, *Selma, 1965,* pp. 5, 18, 37; "Sheriff Speaks on Race Views," *STJ,* February 28, 1964; and Thomas R. Wagy, "Governor LeRoy Collins of Florida and the Selma Crisis of 1965," *Florida Historical Quarterly,* April 1979, p. 404.

11. Ouellet supervised St. Elizabeth's Mission, a ministry to blacks that included a grade school, boys' and girls' clubs, a hospital, and a nursing school. Two priests from the Society of St. Edmund began the mission in 1937, and according to tradition they picked Selma because the bishop of Alabama said it would be the most difficult place in which to work. See Smeltzer interview with Ouellet, November 27, 1963, Smeltzer Papers; and Herbers, "Whites Disturbed over Negro Drive."

12. From this description, it may be reasonably questioned whether this person was a moderate. Nevertheless, in other ways she disassociated herself from the Citizens Council philosophy and demonstrated sufficient concern for blacks to earn a label as a moderate—by Selma's standards.

13. John Fry reported that every white person with whom he talked leveled the charge of outside agitation. See Fry, "Voter-Registration Drive," pp. 19–20.

14. George Dugan, "Fact-Finders Get Selma 'Brush-off,'" *NYT,* October 6, 1963, p. 79. Although Smeltzer's notes indicate that the women complained to him that the article caused them trouble, the two women no longer remember the article, and neither Smeltzer's notes nor subsequent interviews disclose the nature of the problem.

15. Conversation with Brown, January 15, 1964, Smeltzer Papers; and Amelia Boynton, *Bridge Across Jordan: The Story of the Struggle for Civil Rights in Selma, Alabama* (New York: Carlton Press, 1979), pp. 95–111. In 1958, Boynton's son, Bruce, was arrested in a Trailways bus station in Richmond, Virginia, when he asked to be served on the white side of the restaurant. His case went to the U.S. Supreme Court, which overturned his trespassing conviction. See Boynton, *Bridge Across Jordan,* p. 112.

16. This summary of Brown's position is based on Smeltzer's interview with him, Smeltzer Papers.

17. Edwin Moss, interview.

18. Frederick Reese, interview; and the Reese interview in the Moorland–Spingarn Research Center at Howard University, 1968.

19. Smeltzer's notes contain a surprising number of scurrilous rumors that blacks spread about one another. I have not included specific accusations about individuals in this text in order to protect the reputations of people still living. Other than the circulating gossip, there is little evidence that any of the charges is true.

20. The quote comes from notes, Smeltzer Papers, and is based on Brown's recollection of Anderson's statement. Anderson confirmed the statement in our interview.

21. Arthur Capell, "Voter Registration Rally Concluded Quietly Here," *STJ*, May 15, 1963.

22. The use of the word *radical* should not be interpreted as a black power or Black Muslim position. Reese was dedicated to Martin Luther King's strategy of nonviolence, but his enthusiasm for the movement sometimes struck Brown and Moss as radical or extreme.

23. Joyce was under the impression that many whites would not talk with Smeltzer, and so she did. Sommers does not remember any of these events. Rosa Miller Joyce and Carol Sommers, interviews. Hazel Peters provided the insight on Smeltzer's ability to generate enthusiasm.

24. The Negro Airmen of Craig A.F.B. to the United States Senate, Armed Services Committee, and the United States Justice Department, Civil Rights Division, January 7, 1964, Smeltzer Papers.

25. Smeltzer talked several times with Fitt.

26. "Justice Department Denies Chauffering Dr. King," *Chicago Sun Times*, October 19, 1963; and "Justice Department Admits King Used Auto," *Chicago Sun Times*, November 11, 1963.

27. "'Civil Rights Smog' Hangs over Solons," *Courier*, November 21, 1963; "Grand Jury Privacy Held Inviolate by Judge Here," *STJ*, December 6, 1963; and David J. Garrow, *Protest at Selma: Martin Luther King, Jr., and the Voting Rights Act of 1965* (New Haven: Yale University Press, 1978), p. 33.

28. "Notes on Selma Arrests (from Dinky)," SNCC Papers.

29. Marie Foster, interview. Amelia Boynton writes that Smeltzer was responsible for sending two of the Dunn women to Maryland for training. See Boynton, *Bridge Across Jordan*, p. 152.

30. Smeltzer to W. Ray Kyle, February 17, 1964, Smeltzer Papers.

31. Clark does not remember the statement but maintains that he did not consider Smeltzer to be an NCC spy. He also says that Smeltzer

had no reason to fear for his safety. Jim Clark, interview. See also "Sheriff Speaks on Race Views," *STJ*, February 28, 1964.

32. Interviews with Fager, Foster, Lewis, Newton, Reese, Wilson, and Windham.

Chapter 3

1. This incident occurred in the early 1960s. In comparison, the last major league baseball team to be integrated, the Boston Red Sox, broke the color line in 1962 with the addition of the immortal Pumpsie Green to their roster.

2. Quoted in Alan L. Gropman, *The Air Force Integrates: 1945 – 1964* (Washington, D.C.: Office of Air Force History, 1978), p. 206.

3. Ault maintains that black servicemen never complained to him about the biracial committee or about base conditions in general. Richard L. Ault, interview.

4. This may have been inaccurate because a Selma citizen later told Smeltzer that the contract would have been canceled if necessary to avoid integration.

5. The account of this meeting comes from Smeltzer notes, "Negro Airmen Meeting," March 24, 1964, Smeltzer Papers.

6. Smeltzer telephone conversation with Ault, March 25, 1964, Smeltzer Papers.

7. It is unclear if this single meeting was the one that occurred the day after the Elks meeting or if there was an additional meeting. Nevertheless, it is clear that committee meetings were rare.

8. Ault does not remember this particular investigation but states that his base was absolved of all forms of discrimination by numerous inquiries; Ault, interview. See also Smeltzer letter to E. Vincent Suitt, HQ ATCMD, AFSC, Atlanta, June 6, 1964, Smeltzer Papers.

9. Smeltzer interview with Ault, May 15, 1964, Smeltzer Papers.

10. Unfortunately, Ault remembers very little from his discussions with Smeltzer. For example, incidents concerning Sergeant Black, the city bus line, the Elks raid, and the biracial committee's meeting schedule all escape his memory twenty years later; Ault, interview. See also Smeltzer's notes for a talk to the District Executive Secretaries Field Staff Conference, May 5, 1964, and "Report to Staff," May 25, 1964, both in Smeltzer Papers.

11. This paragraph is based on Smeltzer's "Chart of Many Deep

South Communities," March 22, 1964, Smeltzer Papers.

12. Clark remembers that Smeltzer did most of the talking; Jim Clark, interview.

13. R. W. Head, memo to Major W. R. Jones, Commander, Investigation and Identification Division, Department of Public Safety (June 11, 1964), Box 26, Burke Marshall Papers, the John F. Kennedy Presidential Library, Boston.

14. The discussion of white segregationist politicians is based on Smeltzer's notes, Smeltzer Papers, and my interview with Clark.

15. "Crew Shoots Film at Boynton Home," STJ, March 23, 1964.

16. Letter from James G. Clark, Jr., March 11, 1964.

17. Deliveries were also segregated. One former newspaper boy recounted to Smeltzer that white newsboys went in and picked up their papers first; blacks waited outside, coming in later to get the "colored" edition. Smeltzer interview with David Ellwanger, March 22, 1964, Smeltzer Papers.

18. Smeltzer interview with Amelia Boynton, April 16, 1964, Smeltzer Papers.

19. The alleged misquote was a *Times-Journal* article claiming James Bevel had told the audience that "there are three bastards in Alabama—George Wallace, Al Lingo and Jim Clark," and that he had counseled young black men to refuse to enter the army because they were needed at home to fight for their freedom in this country. See "Negroes Told to Decline Draft" and "Officers' Entry at Negro Church Draws Statement," STJ, May 10, 1964, and May 15, 1964.

20. R. W. Head, memorandum to Major W. R. Jones, Box 26, Burke Marshall Papers. Investigator Head's memo is generously sprinkled with "police talk"; for example, we "began to get a line on him" and "subject must have stayed in Hotel."

21. "King Aligns Selma for Rights Testing" and "Cross Burned Near Brown Chapel," STJ, June 22, 1964, and June 23, 1964.

Chapter 4

1. Smeltzer's diary and miscellaneous notes, July 11, 1964, Smeltzer Papers.

2. An SCLC report claims that Clark chased the blacks out of the theater, that whites in the line argued and blocked blacks from buying tickets, and that blacks were beaten and struck with cattle prods. If the

SCLC version is correct, the shouting man who entered the theater could have been Clark. See an undated, untitled report of the event, SCLC Papers.

3. *STJ*, July 11, 1964; and "Violence Threat Quelled at Movie," *STJ*, July 5, 1964.

4. See the following articles from *STJ*: "Testimony Starts in Second Case Before U.S. Court," December 8, 1964; "Violence Threat Quelled at Movie"; and "Defendants Take Stand in Federal Court Case," December 22, 1964. See also Jerry DeMuth, "Black Belt, Alabama: Total Segregation," *Commonweal*, August 6, 1964.

5. Boone Aiken, "Several Are Injured in Selma Race Melee," *Birmingham News*, July 7, 1964; and "Officers Deny Brutality at Parley Here," *STJ*, December 13, 1964.

6. *NYT*, July 6, 1964; and *STJ*, July 6, 1964. The two journalists were Jerry DeMuth and David Price. DeMuth was working for the Black Star Agency of New York, and both DeMuth and Price had been previously employed by SNCC. Selma officials were especially upset with DeMuth because they understood that he had written an unfavorable article about Selma without ever being in the city. See DeMuth, "Black Belt, Alabama"; and "Out of State Newsman Rights Case Witness," *STJ*, December 9, 1964. See also William G. Bryant, "Two Say They Were Beaten at Selma," *Birmingham Post-American*, December 10, 1964; "Mullen Called to Testify in Rights Hearing," *STJ*, December 10, 1964; Boone Aiken, "Witnesses Tell of Mistreatment," *Birmingham News*, December 10, 1964; and "Defendants Take Stand in Federal Court Case."

7. Smeltzer conversation with John Doar, "Phone from Atlanta," July 6, 1964, Smeltzer Papers.

8. Smeltzer, "Report to General Board Staff," September 22, 1964, Smeltzer Papers.

9. "49 Negroes Seized in Selma Protest," *NYT*, July 7, 1964, p. 20; and "Mullen Called to Testify in Rights Hearing."

10. "Report to General Board Staff."

11. *STJ*, July 9 and 10, 1964.

12. Reese received his copy of the injunction while in jail; F. D. Reese, interview. See also David J. Garrow, *Protest at Selma: Martin Luther King, Jr., and the Voting Rights Act of 1965* (New Haven: Yale University Press, 1978), p. 34.

13. Smeltzer conversation with Hohenburg, July 15, 1964, Smeltzer Papers.

14. This paragraph is based on Smeltzer's notes of conversations

with several whites in Selma in July 1964, Smeltzer Papers.

15. Smeltzer interview with James Hare, July 8, 1964, Smeltzer Papers.

16. Smeltzer's notes, July 9, 1964, Smeltzer Papers.

17. Did the injunction in fact cover a Voters League committee meeting in a private home? According to what Hare told Smeltzer, probably not, but Voters League people met in secret under the assumption that their committees were a violation. Also, Clark justified his raid of the black Elks club in late July because Smeltzer met there with a group of Craig airmen, a civil rights activity that violated the injunction.

18. The porter was too afraid of Smeltzer to approach him directly but evidently understood something of his work. See also Smeltzer interview with Bill Speed, July 14, 1964, Smeltzer Papers.

19. Smeltzer's notes credit Judge Thomas with the formation of the group when he lost confidence in the ability of Selma's elected officials to deal with the situation. Neither Stewart nor Wilson confirmed this in my interviews with them.

20. Smeltzer had several conversations with Stewart, most of them very short, but one, on July 25, 1964, lasted twenty-five minutes.

21. The quotes are from Smeltzer's notes, Smeltzer Papers.

22. Art Lewis, interview, July 7, 1964, Smeltzer Papers; and "49 Negroes Seized in Selma Protest," p. 20.

23. The use of the word *informant* refers to a provider of information rather than a spy. See "Report to General Board Staff."

24. Smeltzer interview with Ouellet, July 20, 1964, Smeltzer Papers.

25. See Smeltzer's notes, Smeltzer Papers.

26. Manchester was not able to accept Brown's daughter. Also, Brown cautioned Smeltzer never to mention that "nighttime" integration had united his family with one of white Selma's finest. Brown said he was related to one of the leading white moderates. He named the white, whose name I have omitted because discretion seems appropriate.

27. Marie Foster, interview.

28. Smeltzer conversation with Fitt, July 17, 1964, Smeltzer Papers.

29. See Smeltzer's notes on the meeting, Smeltzer Papers; and "Report to General Board Staff."

30. A report that Pickard would put the classes back in Selma without board approval was given to Smeltzer by Major Ely, June 24, 1964, Smeltzer Papers.

31. That law enforcement people monitored Smeltzer's phone calls is undeniable considering that the state police investigation of Smeltzer

produced a list of his phone calls, but Clark firmly denies tapping Smeltzer's phone conversations. Jim Clark, interview.

32. On the same day that Smeltzer spent hours on the phone between Washington and Selma on the Elks raid, Art Lewis heard that there may have been a meeting at the Elks, which would have violated the injunction. Among the sources on the Elks raid are "Report to General Board Staff"; Smeltzer telephone conversations with Enoch Fears on July 28, 1964, and with Ault on July 29; and Smeltzer letter to Ault, July 30, 1964, Smeltzer Papers. See also my interview with Ed Moss.

33. Smeltzer interview with Art Lewis, July 22, 1964, Smeltzer Papers.

Chapter 5

1. Frank Wilson, interview.

2. The Heinz quote comes from Frank Wilson, who implied that he played an important role in organizing the group.

3. School desegregation was delayed a year, but the business leaders never learned whether Israel had persuaded local blacks to delay, whether he had bribed key blacks, or whether coincidence had been kind to them. Wilson and Edgar Stewart, interviews.

4. Smeltzer telephone conversation with Reese, August 27, 1964, Smeltzer Papers.

5. Falkenberry explains the black news section as an old custom ended when the time seemed right; Roswell Falkenberry, interview.

6. Stewart and Wilson, interviews. See also Smeltzer's "Report to General Board Staff," September 22, 1964, Smeltzer Papers.

7. Smeltzer telephone conversation with Doar, September 24, 1964, Smeltzer Papers.

8. STJ, December 8 and 9, 1964; and Smeltzer telephone conversation with Jansen, December 9, 1964, Smeltzer Papers.

9. "The first thing Rex said to me was, 'Ed, If I'm the first to get out there and do this thing, this bank will go bankrupt. What you all need to do is go and talk to the rest of the bankers and see if we can't do it together.'" Later, Morthland approved a $300,000 loan to Moss's Elks Lodge at a time when banks were extremely reluctant to loan to blacks. Ed Moss, interview.

10. "Report to General Board Staff."

11. Moss, interview.

12. Smeltzer telephone conversations with Lewis, November 25,

1964, and with Brown, December 6, 1964, Smeltzer Papers.

13. Smeltzer telephone conversation with Brown, September 10, 1964, Smeltzer Papers. Brown was so complimentary to Smeltzer in this conversation that it raises suspicion of exaggeration.

14. Annalee Stewart, legislative and branch liaison, WILPF, letter to Smeltzer, August 21, 1964, Smeltzer Papers.

15. The quote "looks like the Congo" was relayed by Art Lewis in a phone call to Smeltzer, September 24, 1964, Smeltzer Papers.

16. Smeltzer telephone conversations with Jansen, September 24, 1964, with Reese, October 22, 1964, and with Lewis, November 11, 1964, Smeltzer Papers.

17. Smitherman explained to Art Lewis his opposition to a biracial committee. Smitherman confides that at this time he considered himself "very politically naive." Joseph Smitherman, interview.

18. Smeltzer telephone conversations with Jansen, October 24, 1964, and with Lewis, October 30, 1964, Smeltzer Papers.

19. The "even better project" quote is from Smeltzer's agenda for his conversation with Reese, Smeltzer Papers; see also Smeltzer telephone conversations with Brown, November 10, 1964, with Reese, November 10, 1964, and with Capell, November 11, 1964, Smeltzer Papers.

20. The incident was kept out of the paper. See undated, untitled SCLC report, SCLC Papers; and Smeltzer telephone conversations with Lewis, October 16, 1964, and with Capell, October 17, 1964, Smeltzer Papers.

21. Marie Foster, interview; and Smeltzer telephone conversations with Moss and Reese, December 9, 1964, Smeltzer Papers.

22. The quotes are John Newton's recounting of the speech and therefore are secondhand, although Newton was probably as accurate an observer in Selma as could be found. December 12, 1964, Smeltzer Papers.

23. The quote comes from Smeltzer's telephone conversation with Jansen, December 8, 1964, Smeltzer Papers. Art Capell heard about Clark's confrontation with Smeltzer and confirmed that Clark was drunk; Smeltzer's notes on telephone conversation with Capell, December 23, 1964, Smeltzer Papers. Clark does not remember the incident; Jim Clark, interview.

24. See the following articles from *STJ*: "Three Men Are Held in Connection with Beating of Soldier," December 20, 1964; "Robbery Charge Added in Local Case to Murder Intent," December 21, 1964; and "Defendants Take Stand in Federal Court Case," December 22, 1964.

25. Mrs. P. L. Tippett wrote that "our city is guilty of tolerating an

attitude which makes such outrages inevitable." At the Catholic church, "a fairly sizeable group of people stood by and quietly watched a particularly degrading spectacle. Of the onlookers, only the sergeant, a newcomer to our town, made any overt protest." Letter to the Editor, *STJ*, December 28, 1964. Mrs. M. B. Tidwell commented, "All peoples' rights and freedoms should be respected, or else our rights are endangered." Letter to the Editor, *STJ*, December 31, 1964.

26. "Assault Charges Filed Against Two," *STJ*, December 22, 1964; and "Hearing Slated on Assault Case," *STJ*, December 24, 1964.

27. Baker told Smeltzer about the incident and the way it was handled during their conversation on December 30, 1964, Smeltzer Papers.

28. Coretta Scott King states matter-of-factly in her book that her husband chose Selma. See King, *My Life with Martin Luther King, Jr.* (New York: Holt, Rinehart & Winston, 1969), p. 253. Stephen B. Oates writes that the locals contacted Atlanta through James Bevel; see Oates, *Let the Trumpet Sound: The Life of Martin Luther King, Jr.* (New York: Harper & Row, 1982), pp. 326–328. Ed Moss believes that the SCLC members "invited themselves," but his memory struck me as uncertain on the matter; Moss, interview. When asked whether the Voters League lost any control over local developments, Marie Foster exclaimed that she was "just so glad to have 'em [SCLC]!"; Foster, interview. Reese, during my interview with him, said, "I invited Dr. King and the SCLC resources here"; also see Reese interview, Moorland-Spingarn Center, pp. 3, 20–21. John Love of SNCC expressed the concern of an SCLC bailout at a black strategy meeting; see Smeltzer's notes of the December 14, 1964, meeting, Smeltzer Papers. SCLC knew that local blacks feared a quick pullout; see Harry G. Boyte memorandum to R. T. Blackwell, December 11, 1964, Box 146, File 8, SCLC Papers. See also Smeltzer notes on telephone conversation with Harry Boyte, December 14, 1964, Smeltzer Papers.

29. A comparative reading of Smeltzer's notes of his telephone conversation with Boyte, December 14, 1964, and Boyte's memo, December 14, Smeltzer Papers, reveals striking similarity. Boyte made no contact with black leaders in Selma, and it seems a reasonable assumption that his information on Selma's blacks came from Smeltzer.

30. Leaders of SNCC understood that the Montgomery strategy meeting with SCLC in mid-December produced an agreement that there would be no action in Selma before January 4, when the Mississippi delegation to Congress would be challenged. The long-term work of SNCC in dangerous Mississippi had brought death to three young volun-

teers in Philadelphia, Mississippi, and SNCC wanted nothing to divert attention from the climax of that drive. Leaders of SNCC also thought that there would be no further steps taken in Selma without SCLC–SNCC consultations. See Clayborne Carson, *In Struggle: SNCC and the Black Awakening of the 1960s* (Cambridge and London: Harvard University Press, 1981), pp. 157–158; Smeltzer interviews with Andy Young and C. T. Vivian at SCLC headquarters and with Julian Bond and John Love of SNCC in Atlanta, December 29, 1964, and his interviews with Reese and Frank Soracco (SNCC staff in Selma), December 30, 1964, Smeltzer Papers.

31. Smeltzer asked Reese at 7:00 A.M. to arrange a meeting for that evening, a Friday. Smeltzer notes on telephone conversation with Vivian, December 10, 1964, Smeltzer Papers.

32. Sol Tepper and Jim Clark, both evidently with contacts in the local Klan, state that Selma Ku Kluxers did not possess the rabid violence of Klan members in other areas; Clark and Tepper, interviews.

33. "Selma Rally to Hear King in Vote Drive," *Birmingham News*, January 3, 1964. Smeltzer interview with Brown, December 29, 1964, and Smeltzer telephone conversations with Jansen, December 30, 1964, and Reese, January 1, 1965, Smeltzer Papers.

34. Smeltzer's notes on the Baker–Capell meeting, December 30, 1964, Smeltzer Papers.

35. Smeltzer interview with Reese, December 30, 1964, and telephone conversations with Baker and Reese, December 31, 1964, Smeltzer Papers.

Chapter 6

1. L. L. Anderson, interview.

2. Smeltzer phone conversation with Reese, January 1, 1965, Smeltzer Papers. See also "A Visitation to Be Ignored," *STJ*, December 30, 1964.

3. The *Times-Journal's* coverage of Baker's speech all but ignored his comments about moderation, reporting only that Baker wanted to have "the most courteous department anywhere." See "Baker Calls for Higher Payroll in City Ranks," *STJ*, January 1, 1965.

4. John Herbers, "Alabama Vote Drive Opened by Dr. King," *NYT*, January 3, 1965, p. 1; "Negro Vote Drive Focuses on Selma," *NYT*, January 4, 1965, p. 58; "King Calls for Drive in County on Regis-

tration," *STJ*, January 3, 1965; and "Tear Gas Charge Draws 180 Days," *STJ*, January 6, 1965.

5. Smeltzer telephone conversation with Baker, January 6, 1965, Smeltzer Papers.

6. Quotes "just let him" and "to hell with anyone" from Smeltzer telephone conversation with Baker, January 2, 1965, Smeltzer Papers.

7. Several days later, Baker took his few days off and asked Smeltzer to tell the blacks not to do anything until he returned. Smeltzer telephoned Diane Bevel and Amelia Boynton with the message; Smeltzer telephone conversation with Baker, January 6, 1965, Smeltzer Papers. The "making a fool" quote is from the same telephone conversation. See also Smeltzer telephone conversation with Reese and interview with Baker, January 4, 1965, and with Boyte, January 5, 1965, Smeltzer Papers. See also Chalres Fager, *Selma, 1965* (New York: Scribner's, 1974), pp. 24–25.

8. Mayor Smitherman does not remember the conversation or even Smeltzer. This material is based on Smeltzer's interview with Smitherman, January 4, 1965, Smeltzer Papers, and on my interview with Smitherman.

9. Smeltzer telephone conversation with Reese, January 5, 1965, Smeltzer Papers; "Registrars of Voters, Dallas Co., Ala., Voting Discrimination, Civil Rights–Elections," FBI Document 44-12831-235, January 8, 1965.

10. "Registrars of Voters," January 8, 1965.

11. Robert Frye, director of the Selma FBI office, denies that he gave white leaders any information about black plans. Frye also is unaware of King's briefcase being stolen; Frye, interview. Clark says he learned about black plans through the raid on the SNCC office, but that occurred in late 1963, over a year before the Alabama Project began; undoubtedly Clark's memory is faulty. Incredibly, Smeltzer did not make notes of this important meeting, and there is not even an attendance record. However, he did produce a three-page "Strategy/Presentation at City Officials Strategy Session," January 6, 1965, Smeltzer Papers, an agenda or talking paper that he likely followed closely. The fact that the length of the meeting, 10:30 A.M. to 12:30 P.M., appears at the top indicates that this is Smeltzer's only record, and therefore no account of the discussion and dynamics exists other than his reports to others on what transpired. His phone call to Boyte immediately after the meeting is particularly useful in this regard. Frank Wilson does not remember the meeting; Wilson, interview. See David J. Garrow, *Protest at Selma: Martin*

Luther King, Jr., and the Voting Rights Act of 1965 (New Haven: Yale University Press, 1978), p. 35, for the King briefcase incident.

12. Smeltzer and Boyte took the same airplane out of Montgomery and talked on the way to the airport and on the plane, January 7, 1965, Smeltzer Papers.

13. Smeltzer interview with Bob Gay, manager of the Hotel Albert, January 7, 1965, Smeltzer Papers.

14. "Facing-Up to Reality," *STJ*, January 7, 1965; and Smeltzer telephone conversation with Capell, January 7, 1965, Smeltzer Papers.

15. Smeltzer telephone conversation with Newton, January 10, 1965, Smeltzer Papers.

16. Smeltzer telephone conversation with Newton, January 14, 1965, Smeltzer Papers.

17. From the *Frederick Douglass Free Press* 2, no. 1 (January 15, 1965); and Fager, *Selma, 1965*, pp. 22–25.

18. "King Sets Plan of Registering Voters Monday," *STJ*, January 15, 1965; and Fager, *Selma, 1965*, pp. 25–26.

19. Smeltzer notes on conversations with Baker, January 14, 1965, and with Reese, January 15, 1965, Smeltzer Papers.

20. "The Bill That Became a Law!" *STJ*, January 17, 1965.

21. Smeltzer telephone conversations with Capell, January 15, 1965, and with Reese, January 16, 1965, Smeltzer Papers.

22. Smeltzer telephone conversation with Baker, January 18, 1965, Smeltzer Papers.

23. Smitherman says that the group of white early arrivals was organized by Clark and his people. Clark says that they were merely people who wanted to vote and denies any organized action; Smitherman and Clark, interviews. See also, "Group Arrives at Courthouse for Registration," *STJ*, January 18, 1965; and Fager, *Selma, 1965*, pp. 26–28. Another work of interest is Sheyann Webb and Rachel West Nelson, *Selma, Lord, Selma: Girlhood Memories of the Civil-Rights Days*, ed. Frank Sikora (New York: Morrow, 1980), pp. 26–28. Webb and Nelson were eight and nine years old, respectively, and participated in many of the mass meetings and marches. They also sat on Dr. King's lap while he waited to preach at mass meetings. Although the book was written fifteen years after the events, and Webb and Nelson were only children at the time, their story agrees with other accounts.

24. Fager, *Selma, 1965*, pp. 28–29; "Man Arrested Here, Disorderly Charge," *STJ*, January 19, 1965; and Smeltzer telephone conversation with Reese, January 19, 1965, Smeltzer Papers.

25. Rockwell never made it to Brown's Chapel that night because

Baker arrested him and two supporters as they approached the building. See Fager, *Selma, 1965*, pp. 29–31; John Herbers, "Dr. King Punched and Kicked in an Alabama Hotel," *NYT*, January 19, 1965, p. 1; and Coretta Scott King, *My Life with Martin Luther King, Jr.* (New York: Holt, Rinehart & Winston, 1969), p. 254.

26. Fager, no doubt relying on his interviews with Baker, calls the informer an "unwilling double agent." See *Selma, 1965*, pp. 31, 226n. Smitherman confirms the story, but Ed Moss denies vigorously the existence of a spy; Smitherman and Moss, interviews.

27. Smeltzer's notes on conversation with Reese, January 19, 1965, Smeltzer Papers; and Fager, *Selma, 1965*, pp. 31–32.

28. Fager, *Selma, 1965*, pp. 33–34; and John Herbers, "67 Negroes Jailed in Alabama Vote Drive," *NYT*, January 20, 1965 p. 1.

29. The FBI reported that King said he would have taken the movement to Montgomery if Clark had not made the arrests; "Registrars of Voters," FBI Document 44-12831-324, February 5, 1965. Also, Amelia Platts Boynton, *Bridge Across Jordan: The Story of the Struggle for Civil Rights in Selma, Alabama* (New York: Carlton Press, 1979), pp. 161–162; Fager, *Selma, 1965*, p. 34; and Garrow, *Protest at Selma*, p. 43.

30. The "cut my heart out" quote appears in "Robinson Appeals Fine, Hard Labor Sentence," *STJ*, January 20, 1965; and Herbers, "67 Negroes Jailed."

31. Fager, *Selma, 1965*, pp. 35–36; and John Herbers, "Two Alabama Officials Clash over Arrests in Negro Vote Drive," *NYT*, January 21, 1965, p. 1.

32. "Some of you think" and "forbearing" quotes from John Herbers, "Negro Teachers Protest in Selma," *NYT*, January 23, 1965, p. 18; "my courthouse" quote from my interview with Reese. See also Stewart and Pickard, interviews; Smeltzer telephone conversation with Reese, January 23, 1965, Smeltzer Papers; Fager, *Selma, 1965*, pp. 36–40; Reese interview, Moorland–Spingarn Center; and Webb and Nelson, *Selma, Lord, Selma*, pp. 34–37. "Registrars of Voters," FBI Document 44-12531-267, January 25, 1965.

33. Smeltzer telephone conversations with Capell, January 21 and 22, 1965, and with Frank Wilson, January 22, 1965, Smeltzer Papers; and Muriel Lewis and Edgar Stewart, interviews.

34. When asked how Cooper got her hands on the billy club in the first place, Clark suggests that perhaps she pulled it off the snap on his belt. In all likelihood, he had the club out and her grasp deflected a blow. The King quote and "I wish you would" are from John Herbers,

"Woman Punches Alabama Sheriff," *NYT,* January 26, 1965, p. 1; the "she's a nigger woman" is quoted from "Registration of Voters Attended by Violence; Woman Hits Sheriff," *STJ,* January 25, 1965. See also Clark, Windham, and Tepper, interviews; Fager, *Selma, 1965,* pp. 44–45; and Garrow, *Protest at Selma,* pp. 45–46.

35. *STJ,* January 25, 1965.

36. Wilson, interview.

37. Fager, *Selma, 1965,* pp. 45–46. Fager witnessed the speech.

38. Moss, interview.

39. The "residual hostility" quote is from Smeltzer telephone conversation with Harry Boyte, January 26, 1965, Smeltzer Papers. See also Smeltzer telephone conversations with F. D. Reese, C. C. Brown, and Art Lewis, January 27, 1965, and with Frank Wilson, January 26, 1965, Smeltzer Papers.

40. Smeltzer's prediction of the political consequences of the conflict turned out to be remarkably accurate because in 1966 Wilson Baker defeated Jim Clark's bid for reelection. Baker's margin of victory was the black vote.

41. "The Path of the 'Judas Goat,'" *STJ,* January 31, 1965.

42. Smeltzer telephone conversations with Reese, January 30 and February 1, 1965, Smeltzer Papers.

43. Smeltzer telephone conversation with A. M. Secrest, February 1, 1965, Smeltzer Papers.

Chapter 7

1. Kathryn Windham, interview.

2. Martin Luther King, Jr., *Where Do We Go from Here: Chaos or Community?* (Boston: Beacon Press, 1967), p. 56; and John J. Ansbro, *Martin Luther King, Jr.: The Making of a Mind* (Maryknoll, N.Y.: Orbis Books, 1982), pp. 243–248.

3. John Herbers, "Negro Goals in Selma," *NYT,* February 6, 1965, p. 1.

4. According to one source, before arresting them, Baker gave the marchers two chances to depart by saying that anybody who did not know why they were being arrested could leave. Had large numbers of blacks left the line, it would have confirmed white charges of SCLC manipulation and agitation of the generally satisfied local black population. Many southern whites, with their assumptions of black ignorance and complacency, may have genuinely believed that marchers had no idea

why they were there. See Sheyann Webb and Rachel West Nelson, *Selma, Lord, Selma: Girlhood Memories of the Civil-Rights Days,* ed. Frank Sikora (New York: Morrow, 1980), pp. 60–61.

5. Windham, interview.

6. Fager spent five days incarcerated at Camp Selma; see Charles Fager, *Selma, 1965* (New York: Scribner's, 1974), pp. 48–55. Another first-person account is "The Stench of Freedom" by Ralph Featherstone, field secretary, SNCC, February 20, 1965, SNCC Papers. See also, "270, Including King, Arrested Here for Parade Violation," *STJ,* February 1, 1965; and "Orderly Group Departs After Instructions," *STJ,* February 3, 1965; David J. Garrow, *Protest at Selma: Martin Luther King, Jr., and the Voting Rights Act of 1965* (New Haven: Yale University Press, 1978), pp. 47–48; John Herbers, "Dr. King and 770 Others Seized in Alabama Protest," *NYT,* February 2, 1965, p. 1; idem, "520 More Seized in Alabama Drive," *NYT,* February 3, 1965, p. 1; idem, "Negroes Step Up Drive in Alabama; 1,000 More Seized," *NYT,* February 4, 1965, p. 1.

7. Quoted in Garrow, *Protest at Selma,* p. 51.

8. *NYT,* February 5, 1965, p. 15.

9. Thomas ordered the registrars to process at least a hundred applicants per day and to review all applications received before June 1 by the end of that month. If the board did not comply, Thomas would send in a referee, and rejected applicants could appeal directly to his federal court. Thomas also told the registrars to stop using the difficult knowledge-of-government test and not to reject applicants for minor mistakes. Because there were only eight more registration days before June 1, the injunction meant that only eight hundred more could apply, and undoubtedly many of them would be rejected. Even if rejections could be appealed directly to Thomas, it would be a costly and sluggish process at best. The next day, L. L. Anderson led a six-member black delegation around town probing futilely for any change in the white position. See "70 Negroes Arrested After Violation of Judge Hare Order, *STJ,* February 5, 1965; Fager, *Selma, 1965,* pp. 58–59; Garrow, *Protest at Selma,* p. 49; and Herbers, "Negro Goals in Selma."

10. Our attempts to receive clarification from Young regarding King's notes and instructions were unsuccessful. Letters to Ralph Abernathy were unanswered, and Hosea Williams returned a brief response indicating that Smeltzer's mediation made it more difficult for SCLC to expose the evils of segregation. Local blacks seemed unaware of King's directive and viewed the night march more as a bargaining chip with local authorities than a device to draw out white extremist violence;

Reese and Moss interviews. Martin Luther King, Jr., to Andrew Young, February 1–5, 1965, Box 22, File 6, MLK Papers; and "Registrars of Voters," FBI Document 44-12831-324, February 5, 1965.

11. "Mayor Endorses Request for Investigation Here," *STJ*, February 4, 1965.

12. Roy Reed, "Negroes Suspend Selma Protests," *NYT*, February 7, 1965, p. 45.

13. "A Time for Decision" and "Student Rights March Expected," *STJ*, February 11, 1965; Roy Reed, "165 Selma Negro Youths Taken on Forced March," *NYT*, February 11, 1965, p. 1; Fager, *Selma, 1965*, pp. 66–67; Garrow, *Protest at Selma*, pp. 57–58; and Webb and Nelson, *Selma, Lord, Selma*, pp. 66–68. Segregationists claim that the story is false and that Clark never left his car during the movement of the students; Sol Tepper, interview.

14. "Clark Admitted to Hospital for 'Chest Pains,'" *STJ*, February 12, 1965; and Fager, *Selma, 1965*, pp. 68–69.

15. Smeltzer telephone conversation with Reese, February 17, 1965, Smeltzer Papers; Fager, *Selma, 1965*, pp. 69–70; Garrow, *Protest at Selma*, pp. 60–61; "Wednesday Seen as Calm After Two Incidents," *STJ*, February 17, 1965; John Herbers, "Taunted Sheriff Hits Rights Aide," *NYT*, February 17, 1965, p. 35; and "The Sheriff Is Uncertain," *NYT*, February 17, 1965, p. 35; David J. Garrow, *Bearing the Cross: Martin Luther King, Jr., and the Southern Christian Leadership Conference* (New York: Morrow, 1986), p. 391.

16. Editorial, *STJ*, February 18, 1965.

17. Smeltzer's conversations with Reese and mine with Fager. See also Dr. King to Seek New Voting Law, *NYT*, February 6, 1965, p. 1.

18. The *Times-Journal* did not report the Clark–Bevel altercation; "Voter Referees Being Considered for County," *STJ*, February 9, 1965. See also "Negroes May Boycott Appearance List Made Available by Board," *STJ*, February 8, 1965; Roy Reed, "Negroes in Selma Bar Voting Offer," *NYT*, February 9, 1965, p. 17; Fager, *Selma, 1965*, p. 65; and Garrow, *Protest at Selma*, pp. 55–56.

19. "Registration Group Largest Ever Here," *STJ*, February 15, 1965.

20. Smeltzer telephone conversation with Reese, February 17, 1965, Smeltzer Papers.

21. Fager, *Selma, 1965*, pp. 72–75; John Herbers, "Negroes Beaten in Alabama Riot," *NYT*, February 19, 1965, p. 1; and Roy Reed, "Wounded Negro Dies in Alabama," *NYT*, February 27, 1965, p. 1.

22. "Notes Taken at a Meeting of Dallas County WCC," February

22, 1965, SNCC Papers; "Barnett Warns Council Group," *STJ*, February 23, 1965; and Fager, *Selma, 1965*, pp. 78–79.

23. Smeltzer conversation with Reese, February 21, 1965, Smeltzer Papers; "Smitherman Backs Trooper Presence," *STJ*, February 21, 1965; "Twilight March on Courthouse Planned Today," *STJ*, February 23, 1965; Fager, *Selma, 1965*, pp. 76–78; John Herbers, "Two Inquiries Open on Racial Clash in Alabama Town," *NYT*, February 20, 1965, p. 1; "Dr. King, Back in Alabama, Calls for March on Capitol to Push Voting Drive," *NYT*, February 23, 1965, p. 16; and Moss and Reese, interviews.

24. "Barnett Warns Council Group."

25. Garrow, *Protest at Selma*, p. 64; "Lull Likely for Demonstration Activity Here," *STJ*, February 24, 1965; and Smeltzer telephone conversations with Reese, February 20 and 23, 1965, Smeltzer Papers.

26. "Hundreds Attend Memorial for Marion Youth," *STJ*, March 3, 1965; and Reed, "Wounded Negro Dies in Alabama."

27. Rongstad read a statement, which was also signed by two local black clergy, acknowledging that "demonstrations in Selma have been fruitful, peaceful and constructive," but told Ellwanger's group that "we do not need your interference in our problems" and that Selma needed time to heal itself.

28. Kathryn Windham witnessed this event and saw no lawmen. Neither did Fager, but although he was in Selma, he apparently was not downtown during this incident. The *New York Times* reported that twenty of Clark's men were present. See "Registrars of Voters," FBI Documents 44-12831-463, March 3, 1965; 44-12831-464, March 3, 1965; and 44-12831-490, March 5, 1965; Windham, interview; Fager, *Selma, 1965*, pp. 87–89; "Lutheran Leader Voices Protest of March Here," *STJ*, March 7, 1965; "Massive Disorder Averted Here When Officers Intervene," *STJ*, March 7, 1965; and Roy Reed, "Alabama Whites Support Negroes," *NYT*, March 7, 1965, p. 1.

29. "Civil Rights Leader Will Seek Sanction of Court for March," *STJ*, March 8, 1965; Wayne Greenhaw, *Watch Out for George Wallace* (Englewood Cliffs, N.J.: Prentice-Hall, 1976), pp. 168–169; George C. Wallace, *Stand Up for America* (Garden City, N.Y.: Doubleday, 1976), pp. 98–99; Garrow, *Protest at Selma*, pp. 68–73, 272–273; Fager, *Selma, 1965*, pp. 86–90; and Smitherman, interview. Garrow and Greenhaw quote substantially from Bill Jones's biography, *The Wallace Story* (Northport, Ala.: American Southern Publishing, 1966). Jones was Wallace's press secretary.

30. Amelia Platts Boynton, *Bridge Across Jordan: The Story of the*

Struggle for Civil Rights in Selma, Alabama (New York: Carlton Press, 1979), pp. 169–171; "Civil Rights Leader Will Seek Sanction of Court for March," *STJ*, March 8, 1965; Fager, *Selma, 1965*, pp. 91–97; James Foreman, "Report from Selma," SNCC Papers; Garrow, *Protest at Selma*, pp. 73–82; Roy Reed, "Alabama Police Use Gas and Clubs to Rout Negroes," *NYT*, March 8, 1965, p. 1; Gay Talese, "New York Doctors Barred at Scene," *NYT*, March 8, 1965, p. 20; Reese interview, Moorland–Spingarn Center, pp. 6–8, 21; Smeltzer telephone conversation with Reese, March 8, 1965, Smeltzer Papers; and Webb and Nelson, *Selma, Lord, Selma*, pp. 87–102. See also my interviews with Reese and Wilson. The right-wing version of what happened on the bridge denies that any police brutality or attack took place; officers enforced the law and the governor's ban on marches by pushing the marchers back, but the troopers did not hit marchers, who fell down for the cameras. Clark emphasizes that there were no broken bones that Sunday; Jim Clark, Louise Clark, and Sol Tepper, interviews.

31. After "Bloody Sunday," congressional speeches expressing "shock" over the behavior of Alabama authorities began to describe more often the law officers' weapons—the clubs, whips, and gas—and to emphasize that the protestors were "nonviolent" and "innocent" people including men, women, and children. See Garrow, *Protest at Selma*, pp. 88, 146–148.

32. Smitherman, interview; John Herbers, "Selma's Moderate Police Give Way to Troopers," *NYT*, March 9, 1965, p. 23; and Wallace, *Stand Up for America*, p. 99.

33. Smeltzer, "Report to General Board Staff," March 9, 1965, Smeltzer Papers; Smeltzer telephone conversations with Lewis and Secrest, March 8, 1965, Smeltzer Papers; and "Our Considered Opinion," *STJ*, March 9, 1965.

34. "Federal Judge's Order Banning March Defied," *STJ*, March 9, 1965; Carson, *In Struggle*, 159; Coretta Scott King, *My Life with Martin Luther King, Jr.* (New York: Holt, Rinehart & Winston, 1969), p. 261; Paul L. Montgomery, "Hundreds on Way to Join in March," *NYT*, March 9, 1965, p. 23; Harvard Sitkopf, *The Struggle for Black Equity, 1954–1980* (New York: Hill & Wang, 1981), p. 191; and Alan F. Westin and Barry Mahoney, *The Trial of Martin Luther King* (New York: Crowell, 1974), pp. 170–171.

35. Seven hundred troops were ready in case the Collins mission failed; Tom Wicker, "Johnson Reveals Alert to Troops in Selma Crisis," *NYT*, March 13, 1965, p. 1. According to Secrest, in a conversation with Smeltzer, Wallace ordered Lingo to permit the march, March 9, 1965,

Smeltzer Papers. See also "Federal Judge's Order Banning March Defied"; Fager, *Selma, 1965*, pp. 97–106; Roy Reed, "Dr. King Leads March at Selma; State Police End It Peaceably under a U.S.-Arranged Accord," *NYT*, March 10, 1965, p. 1.; Reese telephone conversation with Smeltzer, March 10, 1965, Smeltzer Papers; Wagy, "Governor Leroy Collins of Florida and the Selma Crisis of 1965," pp. 409–415; and Harris Wofford, *Of Kennedys and Kings: Making Sense of the Sixties* (New York: Farrar, Straus & Giroux, 1980, pp. 183–185.

36. Within forty-eight hours, four men were arrested by the police and charged with the attack; three of them had police records and one had been arrested twenty-five times, including seventeen charges of assault and battery. "Four Make Bond Here in Assault on Ministers," *STJ*, March 11, 1965; "Civil Rights Demonstrations Banned Here," *STJ*, March 10, 1965; *Selma, 1965*, pp. 107–111.

37. *STJ*, March 14, 1965. See also, my interview with Newton and Smeltzer telephone conversation with Newton, March 11, 1965, Smeltzer Papers.

38. "Civil Rights Demonstrations Banned Here"; and Fager, *Selma, 1965*, pp. 112–113.

39. Fager, *Selma, 1965*, p. 116.

40. "Sylvan Street Demonstration Continues," *STJ*, March 11, 1965; "City Authorities Cancel March Plans Here, *STJ*, March 12, 1965; and John Herbers, "Clergyman Dies of Selma Beating," *NYT*, March 10, 1965, p. 1. Segregationists told lurid tales of interracial sex in the ranks of civil rights demonstrators, and typical were detailed descriptions of orgylike public displays of affection and even intercourse between blacks and whites in the street. See Robert Mikell, *Selma* (Charlotte, N.C.: Citadel Press, 1965), pp. 13–18.

41. The CRS and Wilson Baker were also part of the negotiations that resulted in the courthouse march. See "Selma Civil Rights Leaders Want Shift into Montgomery," *STJ*, March 16, 1965; John Herbers, "Selma Stiffens Ban on Marches," *NYT*, March 14, 1965, p. 1; and "Selma March Held After U.S. Court Arranges Accord," *NYT*, March 16, 1965, p. 1.

42. Following the speech, the *Times-Journal* attacked President Johnson in one of its most vitriolic editorials of the campaign. See "A Modern Mussolini Speaks 'We Shall Overcome,'" *STJ*, March 21, 1965.

43. Fager, *Selma, 1965*, pp. 142–143.

44. Smitherman and Windham, interviews.

45. During my interview with him, Smitherman remarked three times that the reactions from his old friends hurt, and he emphasized that

the episode "aged me considerably."

46. Clark, Smitherman, Tepper, and Wilson, interviews.

47. Smeltzer telephone conversation with Art Lewis, March 12, 1965, Smeltzer Papers.

48. Ault, interview; Fager, *Selma, 1965*, pp. 148–149; John Herbers, "Selma Arrests Ministers Picketing Home of Mayor," *NYT*, March 17, 1965, p. 1; Cabell Philips, "Johnson Offers to Call up Guard in Ala.; Wallace Won't," *NYT*, March 19, 1965, p. 1; Ben A. Franklin, "Wallace Pleads Poverty and Bids U.S. Call up Guard," *NYT*, March 20, 1965, p. 1; and Fendall W. Yerxa, "LBJ Calls up Guard, Deplores Wallace's Acts; Alabama March on Today," *NYT*, March 21, 1965, p. 1. See also "Hootenanny and Revival Flavor at Local Siege," *STJ*, March 17, 1965; "Reese Requests Stadium Start for March Here," *STJ*, March 18, 1965; "Marchers Given City Hall Okay," *STJ*, March 20, 1965.

49. Windham and Tepper, interviews.

50. Gay Talese, "Selma: Bitter City in the Eye of a Storm," *NYT*, March 14, 1965, p. 1.

51. John Newton, interview.

52. Muriel Lewis, Windham, and Wilson, interviews.

53. Roswell Falkenberry, interview.

54. Newton, interview.

55. Clark, interview.

56. Windham and Falkenberry, interviews. See also Talese, "Selma," p. 1.

57. "Marchers Given City Hall Okay."

58. Renata Adler, "Letter from Selma," *New Yorker*, April 10, 1965, pp. 121–157; "King Allots 14 Miles Today for Marchers," *STJ*, March 22, 1965; "Selma Citizens Praised Here," *STJ*, March 22, 1965; Roy Reed, "Freedom March Begins at Selma; Troops on Guard," *NYT*, March 22, 1965, p. 1; Paul L. Montgomery, "The Marchers on Highway 80 Are of All Sorts and One Belief," *NYT*, March 22, 1965, p. 27; Roy and Gwendolyn Stone, "We Drove Five Thousand Miles to Walk in Alabama," Box 21, File 12, MLK Papers.

59. Fager, *Selma, 1965*, pp. 150–159; and Roy Reed, "Rights Marchers Push into Region Called Hostile," *NYT*, March 23, 1965, p. 1.

60. Fager, *Selma, 1965*, pp. 160, 163; and Roy Reed, "Twenty-five Thousand Go to Alabama's Capitol; Wallace Rebuffs Petitioners; White Rights Worker Is Slain," *NYT*, March 26, 1965, p. 1.

61. Fager, *Selma, 1965*, pp. 163–164; Jack Mendelsohn, *The Martyrs: Sixteen Who Gave Their Lives for Racial Justice* (New York: Harper & Row, 1966), chap. 9; and Paul L. Montgomery, "Woman Is Shot to Death on Lowndes County Road," *NYT*, March 26, 1965, p. 1.

62. Smeltzer conversation with Reese, March 1, 1965, Smeltzer Papers.

63. The "war on" quote is from Smeltzer conference with W. Harold Rowe, chairman of the World Ministries Commission, and Norman J. Baugher, executive director, March 10, 1965, Smeltzer Papers.

Chapter 8

1. Charles Fager, *Selma, 1965*, (New York: Scribner's, 1974), pp. 170–171.

2. "Mayor Reflects on Misadventure during Trip to Washington," *STJ*, April 6, 1965. See also Thomas Buckley, "Mayor of Selma Urged to Resign," *NYT*, April 11, 1965, p. 51; and Hosea Williams, Tape 50, April 25, 1965, MLK Papers. See also Smeltzer telephone conversation with Secrest, April 5, 1965, Smeltzer Papers; and Joseph Smitherman, interview.

3. On Clark's activities with far-right groups, see Roy Reed, "Birch Society Is Growing in the South," *NYT*, November 18, 1965, p. 1; and Benjamin R. Epstein and Arnold Forster, *The Radical Right: Report on the John Birch Society and Its Allies* (New York: Random House, 1967), pp. 58, 213.

4. "That's Your Cue to Leave, Dr. King," *STJ*, April 8, 1965.

5. Her letter was about Wilson Baker but *Time* excerpted it. Muriel N. Lewis, Letter to the Editor, *Time*, April 2, 1965.

6. The Lewises suspected an extra copy of the letter was made at the copier's office and disseminated about town. For years thereafter, the Lewises opened their envelopes from the bottom, as a security measure. Smeltzer telephone conversation with Art Lewis, April 4, 1965, Smeltzer Papers; and my interview with Muriel Lewis.

7. Muriel Lewis, interview.

8. Smeltzer conversations with Art Lewis, April 12 and 13, 1965, Smeltzer Papers; and Muriel Lewis, interview.

9. Smeltzer telephone conversation with Frank Wilson, April 7, 1965, Smeltzer Papers.

10. Smeltzer conversations with John Newton, April 7 and 13, 1965, Smeltzer Papers.

11. Smeltzer telephone conversation with Wilson.

12. Falkenberry is certain that Hammermill had little to do with the chamber's ultimate decision to publish a statement. He was acquainted with Hammermill's president and believes that Hammermill would have built its mill "come hell or high water." According to Fal-

kenberry, Hammermill was invulnerable to civil rights pressure; Roswell Falkenberry, interview. Elizabeth Jacoway, "An Introduction: Civil Rights and the Changing South," in *Southern Businessmen and Desegregation,* ed. Jacoway and David R. Colburn (Baton Rouge and London: Louisiana State University Press, 1982), pp. 6–9, argues that by placing profit above traditional southern racial relations, southern business people experienced a "change of the first magnitude" and that by holding profit above other values, somehow had begun to behave like business communities in other parts of the nation. According to Jacoway, southern businessmen abandoned the traditional southern attitude of resistance to social change at whatever cost. Regretfully, Jacoway and Colburn do not include Selma in their book, but Selma's experience is consistent with many of the patterns they discuss. See also Fager, *Selma, 1965,* pp. 185–187; *STJ,* April 15, 18, and 19. 1965; Smitherman and Wilson, interviews; Smeltzer telephone conversations with Art Lewis, April 12, 13, and 15, 1965, Smeltzer Papers; and Smeltzer conversation with Mac Secrest, April 13, 1965, Smeltzer Papers. The chamber statement appeared in the paper on about the ninth day of the Lewises' moratorium on involvement.

13. Smeltzer telephone conversation with Secrest, April 5, 1965, Smeltzer Papers; and Smeltzer conversations with Baker, Falkenberry, Jansen, and Reese, April 6, 1965, Smeltzer Papers.

14. Smeltzer telephone conversations with Baker, Brown, and Reese, April 7, 1965, Smeltzer Papers.

15. Smeltzer telephone conversations with Reese, Moss, and Brown, April 14, 1965, Smeltzer Papers.

16. Pickard remembers that the students were failed because they had not made up their work and not because of absenteeism. According to him, a deal was struck allowing students individually to arrange with their teachers to make up their work; Superintendent Pickard, interview. See also Smeltzer interview with John Masterson, April 14, 1965, Smeltzer Papers; and Smeltzer telephone conversations with Reese and Secrest, April 14, 1965, Smeltzer Papers.

17. Smeltzer interview with Comer Sims, April 16, 1965, Smeltzer Papers; and Smeltzer telephone conversation with Reese, April 30, 1965, Smeltzer Papers.

18. "If Selma Loses Bus Service, It Could Well Lose Craig Air Force Base, Too." Letter from M. L. Miles, general manager, Selma and Dallas County Chamber of Commerce, Smeltzer Papers. The letter is undated, but Smeltzer received a copy on April 15, 1965.

19. Dave Smith letter to Smeltzer, April 23, 1965, Smeltzer Papers;

Smeltzer conversation with Reese, April 16 and 22, 1965, Smeltzer Papers.

20. Smeltzer telephone conversations with Reese, May 4, and with Fred Miller, CRS, April 26, May 3 and 4, 1965, Smeltzer Papers.

21. "What the Negroes of Selma and Dallas County Want," *STJ,* May 2, 1965.

22. Smeltzer telephone conversation with Reese, May 7, 1965, Smeltzer Papers.

23. Smeltzer telephone conversation with Reese, May 13, 1965, Smeltzer Papers; and Dave Smith letter to Smeltzer, May 19, 1965, Smeltzer Papers.

24. Smith letter to Smeltzer, May 25, 1965, Smeltzer Papers; and Lewis telephone conversation, May 26, 1965, Smeltzer Papers.

25. Smith letter to Smeltzer, June 28, 1965, Smeltzer Papers.

26. Smeltzer telephone conversation with Lewis, June 3, 1965, Smeltzer Papers; and Smith letter to Smeltzer, June 4, 1965, Smeltzer Papers.

27. Fager, *Selma, 1965,* p. 172.

28. According to one board member, Reese missed twenty-five school days during the 1964–1965 school year, which averages out to two days for every three weeks. The tally includes eight sick days, ten and one-half unexcused absences, and the remainder probably for court appearances. Reese asserts that he never took a day off to rest or sleep in, but he told Smeltzer on several occasions that he did take a day off to rest. Reese interview, Moorland–Spingarn Center, p. 37. See also Smeltzer telephone conversation with Windham, June 10, 1965, and Smith letters to Smeltzer, June 3 and 4, 1965, Smeltzer Papers. And Pickard, Reese, and Windham, interviews.

29. A typical example is "Jesuit Describes Fear in Alabama," *NYT,* April 15, 1965, p. 62.

30. Fager, *Selma, 1965,* pp. 202–203; "Rights Worker Jailed by Police," *STJ,* June 24, 1965; and "Rights Worker Jailed Again," *STJ,* June 25, 1965.

31. Clark and Reese, interviews. Smith wrote a letter and also telephoned Smeltzer on July 7, 1965, Smeltzer Papers. See also Fager, *Selma, 1965,* pp. 172–178, 190–200; "Reese Held for Embezzlement," *STJ,* June 6, 1965; "Negro Minister Claims Expense Was Authorized," *STJ,* June 8, 1965; "Theft of Rights Fund Laid to Selma Cleric," *NYT,* July 7, 1965, p. 1; and "Reese Released from Selma Jail on $5,000 Bond," *NYT,* July 8, 1965, p. 21. The Reese and Abernathy quotes are found in both Fager and the *Times* article.

32. Smeltzer interview with Steven Shulman and Phillip Timpone, May 12, 1965, Smeltzer Papers.

33. Selma Future Program Proposals, April 21, 1965, Smeltzer Papers.

34. Smeltzer to A. M. Secrest, May 18, 1965, Smeltzer Papers.

35. Smith letter to Smeltzer, July 21, 1965, Smeltzer Papers. Fager to Randolph Blackwell, July 31, 1965, Box 146, File 10, SCLC Papers. Reese to King, October 10, 1965, Box 21, File 14, MLK Papers.

36. Fred Powledge, "Negroes in Selma Flock to Register," NYT, August 11, 1965, p. 20.

Chapter 9

1. Roy Reed, "Five Years After, Selma Cannot Forget Historic Rights March," NYT, March 22, 1970, p. 44.

2. Clark maintains that witnesses were threatened and refused to testify. The best guess is that Clark's camp dropped the charges in order to paint Baker as a persecutor of an innocent man. Jim Clark, interview.

3. Charles Fager, Selma, 1965 (New York: Scribner's, 1974), pp. 207–211; David R. Garrow, Protest at Selma: Martin Luther King, Jr., and the Voting Rights Act of 1965 (New Haven: Yale University Press, 1978), pp. 187–188; Reed, "'Bloody Sunday' Was Year Ago; Now Selma Negroes Are Hopeful," NYT, March 6, 1965, p. 76; F. D. Reese interview, Moorland–Spingarn Center, p. 10; and "Selma Rejects Bid by Sheriff Clark," NYT, November 9, 1966, p. 30.

4. Reese interview, Moorland–Spingarn Center, pp. 32–33, 35; my interview with Reese; and Box 21, Folder 15, MLK Papers.

5. L. L. Anderson, interview; Reese interview, Moorland–Spingarn Center, pp. 11–12; "3 Negroes Gain a Run-off for City Council in Selma," NYT, March 6, 1968, p. 16; "Negroes in Selma Lose Council Race," NYT, April 3, 1968, p. 34; and "Mayor Receives Grievance List," STJ, November 11, 1965.

6. "Blacks Elected in Selma," NYT, August 9, 1972, p. 16; and Garrow, Protest at Selma, p. 205.

7. In 1971 Carmichael's conviction was overturned by a U.S. Supreme Court ruling that Alabama's antiriot law was too vague to be constitutional. "Carmichael Held by Selma Police," NYT, November 6, 1966, p. 28; "Carmichael Gets 60-Day Sentence," NYT, November 11, 1966, p. 23; and "U.S. Court Rejects Alabama Riot Law as Unconstitutional," NYT, April 10, 1971, p. 30.

8. "Negro Poor Enter Selma on March," *NYT*, May 7, 1965, p. 37; and "Poor March into Montgomery, 2,000 Following Rights Leader," *NYT*, May 8, 1965, p. 31.

9. "Selma Police Aide Indicted," *NYT*, January 28, 1970, p. 41; and Roy Reed, "Five Years After, Selma Cannot Forget Historic Rights March," *NYT*, March 22, 1970, p. 44.

10. Charles Fager, "Marching in Selma While Reading Ellul," *Sojourners*, June 1977.

11. Smeltzer notes, July 21, 1965, Smeltzer Papers.

12. "Report on Peace and Social Education, 1964–65," Brethren Service Commission Agenda, November 1965, Smeltzer Papers.

13. Smeltzer, "The Church as Change Agent" (October 30, 1975), p. 10, and "Our Future Social Witness" (November 25, 1975), pp. 16–23, chapters in an incomplete manuscript, Smeltzer Papers.

14. Smeltzer, "Our Future Social Witness," pp. 17–23.

15. Matthew 5:4–6, 9. I have interpreted "Blessed are those who mourn" as a call for compassion and empathy; Pastor Emeritus Murray Wagner assisted with this interpretation. I use this Beatitude paradigm with some caution and hope that readers will not see this as an unwarranted exaggeration of Smeltzer's attributes.

16. Smitherman, interview; John Herbers, "More Blacks Are Turning to the Politics of Frustration," *NYT*, July 15, 1984, p. E3; and John Herbers, "Blacks Press for Control in Selma Election Today," *NYT*, July 10, 1984, p. 12.

17. Julia Cass, "Selma: The Struggle Continues," *Inquirer*, August 11, 1985, pp. 20–22; and Marie Foster, interview.

18. Peter J. Boyer, "In Selma Mayoral Election, Issue Is Garbage, Not Race," *Los Angeles Times*, July 8, 1984, p. 1; John Herbers, "White Mayor of Selma Is Returned to Office," *NYT*, July 11, 1984, p. 16; and "Black Loses Bid in Selma, Ala.," *NYT*, August 1, 1984, p. 16.

19. Charles Fager, "The March Back," *City Paper*, January 11–17, 1985, p. 1; and Foster, interview.

20. Cass, "Selma," *Inquirer*, p. 20.

21. Frank Wilson, interview; John Cogley, "Archbishop Ousts Selma Priest Who Aided Voter Registration Drive," *NYT*, June 26, 1965; and "Ouellet Transfer to Vermont Is Announced," *STJ*, June 27, 1965.

22. The Lewises opened their home to out-of-town newspaper reporters during the crisis in order to give them a safe, quiet place to relax and to help the national press realize that there was another side to Selma besides the rednecks. Muriel Lewis remembers her husband staying up into the early morning hours waiting for reporters, especially Gay

Talese, to finish their work and come in for drinks and conversation. An angle to the Selma story that I anticipated was personal stress, but little evidence surfaced to support my hypothesis regarding a significant amount of stress. Muriel Lewis and Joe Smitherman acknowledged personal tension, but many others denied that the late-night phone calls and inflammatory atmosphere had bothered them. Perhaps to admit that the harassment got to them would be to grant opponents an effective weapon. Blacks were caught up in the excitement, and although they experienced fatigue, they felt little stress. Muriel Lewis, Smitherman, and Sol Tepper, interviews.

23. "Long Way Yet to Go: Lowery," *STJ*, March 4, 1985, p. 1.

24. The reasons for his transfer are from an interview with Mary Blocher Smeltzer. The story of his hospitalization is from "Better a Nettle Than an Echo," *Messenger*, July 1976, p. 40.

25. William E. Schmidt, "On Dining, Traveling and Eggs," *NYT*, August 24, 1985, p. 18.

Index